Bloom's Shakespeare Through the Ages

Antony and Cleopatra

As You Like It

Hamlet

Henry IV (Part I)

Julius Caesar

King Lear

Macbeth

The Merchant of Venice

A Midsummer Night's Dream

Othello

Romeo and Juliet

The Sonnets

The Taming of the Shrew

The Tempest

Twelfth Night

Bloom's Shakespeare Through the Ages

A MIDSUMMER NIGHT'S DREAM

Edited and with an introduction by
Harold Bloom
Sterling Professor of the Humanities
Yale University

Volume Editor
Janyce Marson

BLOOM'S
LITERARY CRITICISM
An imprint of Infobase Publishing

Bloom's Shakespeare Through the Ages: A Midsummer Night's Dream

Copyright © 2008 by Infobase Publishing

Introduction © 2008 by Harold Bloom

Bloom's Literary Criticism
An imprint of Infobase Publishing
132 West 31st Street
New York NY 10001

Library of Congress Cataloging-in-Publication Data
A midsummer night's dream / edited and with an introduction by Harold Bloom ; volume editor, Janyce Marson.
    p. cm. — (Bloom's Shakespeare through the ages)
  Includes bibliographical references and index.
  ISBN-13: 978-0-7910-9595-9 (acid-free paper) 1. Shakespeare, William, 1564–1616. Midsummer night's dream. I. Bloom, Harold. II. Marson, Janyce.
  PR2827.M527 2008
  822.3'3—dc22   2008005230

Bloom's Literary Criticism books are available at special discounts when purchased in bulk quantities for businesses, associations, institutions, or sales promotions. Please call our Special Sales Department in New York at (212) 967-8800 or (800) 322-8755.

You can find Bloom's Literary Criticism on the World Wide Web at
http://www.chelseahouse.com

Series design by Erika K. Arroyo
Cover design by Ben Peterson
Cover photo © The Granger Collection, New York

Printed in the United States of America

Bang EJB 10 9 8 7 6 5 4 3 2 1

This book is printed on acid-free paper.

CONTENTS
❧

SERIES INTRODUCTION

Shakespeare Through the Ages presents not the most current of Shakespeare criticism, but the best of Shakespeare criticism, from the seventeenth century to today. In the process, each volume also charts the flow over time of critical discussion of a particular play. Other useful and fascinating collections of historical Shakespearean criticism exist, but no collection that we know of contains such a range of commentary on each of Shakespeare's greatest plays and at the same time emphasizes the greatest critics in our literary tradition: from John Dryden in the seventeenth century, to Samuel Johnson in the eighteenth century, to William Hazlitt and Samuel Coleridge in the nineteenth century, to A.C. Bradley and William Empson in the twentieth century, to the most perceptive critics of our own day. This canon of Shakespearean criticism emphasizes aesthetic rather than political or social analysis.

Some of the pieces included here are full-length essays; others are excerpts designed to present a key point. Much (but not all) of the earliest criticism consists only of brief mentions of specific plays. In addition to the classics of criticism, some pieces of mainly historical importance have been included, often to provide background for important reactions from future critics.

These volumes are intended for students, particularly those just beginning their explorations of Shakespeare. We have therefore also included basic materials designed to provide a solid grounding in each play: a biography of Shakespeare, a synopsis of the play, a list of characters, and an explication of key passages. In addition, each selection of the criticism of a particular century begins with an introductory essay discussing the general nature of that century's commentary and the particular issues and controversies addressed by critics presented in the volume.

Shakespeare was "not of an age, but for all time," but much Shakespeare criticism is decidedly for its own age, of lasting importance only to the scholar who wrote it. Students today read the criticism most readily available to them, which means essays printed in recent books and journals, especially those journals made available on the Internet. Older criticism is too often buried in out-of-print books on forgotten shelves of libraries or in defunct periodicals. Therefore, many students, particularly younger students, have no way of knowing that some of the most profound criticism of Shakespeare's plays was written decades or centuries ago. We hope this series remedies that problem, and, more importantly, we hope it infuses students with the enthusiasm of the critics in these volumes for the beauty and power of Shakespeare's plays.

INTRODUCTION BY
HAROLD BLOOM

For me, it is "bully Bottom's" play, though its four realms of being—fairies, ancient Athenians, contemporary rustics, and erotically confused young women and men—all afford extraordinary vistas upon colliding dreams and realities. I cannot reread or teach the *Dream* without being amazed by it. This comedy is a labyrinth, in which we are delighted to be lost.

Bottom is the only rustic who can see, hear, and speak to the fairy folk, perhaps because he is a weaver and worldwide tradition credits that craft with occult aspects. Or is there not something in Bottom's rollicking personality that attracts the night-world? If he is a clown, and a malaprop, he also is wise, charming, courageous, and so much himself that his transformation by Puck scarcely affects his consciousness. His good humor and high spirits carry him through his startling adventures with Titania (who does not move him to lust) and with the little folk, towards whom he shows humane dignity.

After four centuries the *Dream* remains an unique work of literary art, with a highly individual place within the Shakespeare canon. That place is obscured by *all* contemporary productions, which are prurient and obsessed with bestiality, which is their concept and not Shakespeare's (or Bottom's!). For the sweetly mild weaver, the charming elves—Peaseblossom, Cobweb, Moth, and Mustardseed—are far more interesting than the lovesick Titania.

Whose dream is it? Partly Bottom's, partly ours. Bottom is one of the "mechanicals" or artisans, and yet his dream is beyond us. We do not encounter fairies, so far as we ever know. Bottom, at home in all spheres, parodies a striking passage of St. Paul's 1 Corinthians (2: 9-10), in a mode that suggests William Blake or James Joyce. The most famous interchange in the *Dream* is between Theseus and the Amazon queen, Hippolyta which debates the relation between dream and "imagination," a word meaning mere fantasy in Shakespeare's day, but subtly transformed by him into what will become its High Romantic sense. For Theseus, "strong imagination" is a trickster, "shaping fantasies." Hippolyta, surely speaking for Shakespeare, hints at a more poetic apprehension:

But all the story of the night told over,
And all their minds transfigur'd so together,

More witnesseth than fancy's images,
And grows to something of great constancy;
But howsoever, strange and admirable.

Transfiguration is the method and the glory of *A Midsummer Night's Dream*. Knowing what he has wrought in this wonderful comedy, Shakespeare asks us both to apprehend and comprehend the play as our own dream-vision. Nothing in literature is so exquisitely sustained as this is. Had Shakespeare written only this superb marriage-song, his greatness would have been established forever after. "It shall be called 'Bottom's Dream', because it hath no bottom." Our own dream, as we experience the play, also touches an uncanny depth.

BIOGRAPHY OF
WILLIAM SHAKESPEARE

WILLIAM SHAKESPEARE was born in Stratford-on-Avon in April 1564 into a family of some prominence. His father, John Shakespeare, was a glover and merchant of leather goods who earned enough to marry Mary Arden, the daughter of his father's landlord, in 1557. John Shakespeare was a prominent citizen in Stratford, and at one point, he served as an alderman and bailiff.

Shakespeare presumably attended the Stratford grammar school, where he would have received an education in Latin, but he did not go on to either Oxford or Cambridge universities. Little is recorded about Shakespeare's early life; indeed, the first record of his life after his christening is of his marriage to Anne Hathaway in 1582 in the church at Temple Grafton, near Stratford. He would have been required to obtain a special license from the bishop as security that there was no impediment to the marriage. Peter Alexander states in his book *Shakespeare's Life and Art* that marriage at this time in England required neither a church nor a priest or, for that matter, even a document—only a declaration of the contracting parties in the presence of witnesses. Thus, it was customary, though not mandatory, to follow the marriage with a church ceremony.

Little is known about William and Anne Shakespeare's marriage. Their first child, Susanna, was born in May 1583 and twins, Hamnet and Judith, in 1585. Later on, Susanna married Dr. John Hall, but the younger daughter, Judith, remained unmarried. When Hamnet died in Stratford in 1596, the boy was only 11 years old.

We have no record of Shakespeare's activities for the seven years after the birth of his twins, but by 1592 he was in London working as an actor. He was also apparently well known as a playwright, for reference is made of him by his contemporary Robert Greene in *A Groatsworth of Wit*, as "an upstart crow."

Several companies of actors were in London at this time. Shakespeare may have had connection with one or more of them before 1592, but we have no record that tells us definitely. However, we do know of his long association with the most famous and successful troupe, the Lord Chamberlain's Men. (When James I came to the throne in 1603, after Elizabeth's death, the troupe's name changed to the King's Men.) In 1599 the Lord Chamberlain's Men provided the financial backing for the construction of their own theater, the Globe.

The Globe was begun by a carpenter named James Burbage and finished by his two sons, Cuthbert and Robert. To escape the jurisdiction of the Corporation of London, which was composed of conservative Puritans who opposed the theater's "licentiousness," James Burbage built the Globe just outside London, in the Liberty of Holywell, beside Finsbury Fields. This also meant that the Globe was safer from the threats that lurked in London's crowded streets, like plague and other diseases, as well as rioting mobs. When James Burbage died in 1597, his sons completed the Globe's construction. Shakespeare played a vital role, financially and otherwise, in the construction of the theater, which was finally occupied sometime before May 16, 1599.

Shakespeare not only acted with the Globe's company of actors; he was also a shareholder and eventually became the troupe's most important playwright. The company included London's most famous actors, who inspired the creation of some of Shakespeare's best-known characters, such as Hamlet and Lear, as well as his clowns and fools.

In his early years, however, Shakespeare did not confine himself to the theater. He also composed some mythological-erotic poetry, such as *Venus and Adonis* and *The Rape of Lucrece*, both of which were dedicated to the earl of Southampton. Shakespeare was successful enough that in 1597 he was able to purchase his own home in Stratford, which he called New Place. He could even call himself a gentleman, for his father had been granted a coat of arms.

By 1598 Shakespeare had written some of his most famous works, *Romeo and Juliet*, *The Comedy of Errors*, *A Midsummer Night's Dream*, *The Merchant of Venice*, *Two Gentlemen of Verona*, and *Love's Labour's Lost*, as well as his historical plays *Richard II*, *Richard III*, *Henry IV*, and *King John*. Somewhere around the turn of the century, Shakespeare wrote his romantic comedies *As You Like It*, *Twelfth Night*, and *Much Ado About Nothing*, as well as *Henry V*, the last of his history plays in the Prince Hal series. During the next 10 years he wrote his great tragedies, *Hamlet*, *Macbeth*, *Othello*, *King Lear*, and *Antony and Cleopatra*.

At this time, the theater was burgeoning in London; the public took an avid interest in drama, the audiences were large, the plays demonstrated an enormous range of subjects, and playwrights competed for approval. By 1613, however, the rising tide of Puritanism had changed the theater. With the desertion of the theaters by the middle classes, the acting companies were compelled to depend more on the aristocracy, which also meant that they now had to cater to a more sophisticated audience.

Perhaps this change in London's artistic atmosphere contributed to Shakespeare's reasons for leaving London after 1612. His retirement from the theater is sometimes thought to be evidence that his artistic skills were waning. During this time, however, he wrote *The Tempest* and *Henry VIII*. He also wrote the "tragicomedies," *Pericles, Cymbeline,* and *The Winter's Tale.* These were thought to be inspired by Shakespeare's personal problems and have sometimes been considered proof of his greatly diminished abilities.

However, so far as biographical facts indicate, the circumstances of his life at this time do not imply any personal problems. He was in good health and financially secure, and he enjoyed an excellent reputation. Indeed, although he was settled in Stratford at this time, he made frequent visits to London, enjoying and participating in events at the royal court, directing rehearsals, and attending to other business matters.

In addition to his brilliant and enormous contributions to the theater, Shakespeare remained a poetic genius throughout the years, publishing a renowned and critically acclaimed sonnet cycle in 1609 (most of the sonnets were written many years earlier). Shakespeare's contribution to this popular poetic genre are all the more amazing in his break with contemporary notions of subject matter. Shakespeare idealized the beauty of man as an object of praise and devotion (rather than the Petrarchan tradition of the idealized, unattainable woman). In the same spirit of breaking with tradition, Shakespeare also treated themes previously considered off limits—the dark, sexual side of a woman as opposed to the Petrarchan ideal of a chaste and remote love object. He also expanded the sonnet's emotional range, including such emotions as delight, pride, shame, disgust, sadness, and fear.

When Shakespeare died in 1616, no collected edition of his works had ever been published, although some of his plays had been printed in separate unauthorized editions. (Some of these were taken from his manuscripts, some from the actors' prompt books, and others were reconstructed from memory by actors or spectators.) In 1623 two members of the King's Men, John Hemings and Henry Condell, published a collection of all the plays they considered to be authentic, the First Folio.

Included in the First Folio is a poem by Shakespeare's contemporary Ben Jonson, an outstanding playwright and critic in his own right. Jonson paid tribute to Shakespeare's genius, proclaiming his superiority to what previously had been held as the models for literary excellence—the Greek and Latin writers. "Triumph, my Britain, thou hast one to show / To whom all scenes of Europe homage owe. / He was not of an age, but for all time!"

Jonson was the first to state what has been said so many times since. Having captured what is permanent and universal to all human beings at all times, Shakespeare's genius continues to inspire us—and the critical debate about his works never ceases.

SUMMARY OF
A MIDSUMMER NIGHT'S DREAM

%

Act I

In Act I of *A Midsummer Night's Dream*, Shakespeare introduces the main characters of his comedy and his play's central themes, one of which is best expressed by this act's well-known line: "The course of true love never did run smooth." In some ways Lysander's declaration becomes the play's structural and thematic point of departure, as the comedy interlocks the misadventures of five pairs of lovers—six if one counts Pyramus and Thisby, who appear in Act V's play within the play—and uses their tribulations to explore its theme of love's difficulties. Central to the play is the tension between desire and social mores. Characters are repeatedly required to quell their passion for the sake of law and propriety. Another important conflict is between love and reason, with the heart almost always overruling the mind. The comedy of the play results from the powerful, and often blinding, effects that love has on the characters' thoughts and actions.

The play opens in Athens, ruled by Theseus, who is to wed Hippolyta, queen of the Amazons, in four days. At the start of the play, Theseus voices his impatience for his marriage, immediately establishing the disjunction between desire and social dictates. The introduction of Egeus and his daughter Hermia reinforces this conflict, for the pair has come to Theseus to resolve a dispute over Hermia's future husband. Although Egeus has promised Hermia in marriage to Demetrius, Hermia wants to marry Lysander, who, Egeus complains, "[w]ith cunning hast . . . filched my daughter's heart." Egeus asserts his paternal right to determine Hermia's husband, and Theseus supports this, saying "[b]e advised, fair maid / To you your father should be a god." Hermia quickly shows that she is not cowed by her father's decision or Theseus's decree, wishing instead that the men consider her feelings. The strength of her spirit and willpower is clear as she says to Theseus, "I would that my father looked with my eyes," to which the duke replies, "[r]ather your eyes with his judgment look." Shakespeare employs images of eyes and eyesight throughout the play. Making continual reference to different characters' vision—that they see things differently and that they are often not

5

sure what they see—he suggests, among other things, that love deprives a person of clear sight and clear thought.

Hermia inquires what her choices are if she refuses to marry Demetrius, and Theseus proposes two options: to die or to become a nun. Theseus, newly in love himself, gently tries to persuade her to reconsider and gives her until the morning of his marriage day to make her final decision. The two suitors, Demetrius and Lysander, also assert themselves in this scene: Demetrius urges Hermia to obey the law and her father's will, while Lysander scornfully suggests that as Demetrius has Egeus's love, the two should marry and leave Hermia and himself alone. Lysander also suggests that Demetrius has been inconstant as a lover; he has already "made love to Nedar's daughter, Helena / And won her soul." Theseus admits that he had heard about Demetrius's involvement with Helena but had forgotten about it.

After Demetrius, Theseus, Egeus, and Hippolyta depart, Lysander and Hermia are left alone and swear their devotion to each other. Hermia's defiance is reasserted as she laments to Lysander, "O cross! . . . O spite! . . . O hell! to choose love by another's eyes." In order to escape the fate that awaits Hermia, Lysander suggests that they flee Athens to the home of his widowed aunt, where, beyond the constraints of Athenian law, they can be married. They agree to meet the next night in the woods outside Athens, and as the play progresses, it becomes clear that the woods—a place of magic and possibility—serve as a foil to the rational order of the Athenian court. Helena, Hermia's close friend who is in love with Demetrius, now comes upon the two, and Lysander reveals their plan to her:

> To-morrow night, when Phoebe doth behold
> Her silver visage in the wat'ry glass,
> Decking with liquid pearl the bladed grass
> A time that lovers' flights doth still conceal
> Through Athens' gates have we devis'd to steal.

The moon, in this scene and throughout the play, is a silent but crucial character. On a literal level, the moon is necessary to illuminate the characters' nocturnal activities and so is a beneficent force, rendering love possible. Yet the moon is also negative, as when Theseus tells Hermia that as a "barren sister" (a nun), she will spend her life "[c]hanting hymns to the cold fruitless moon." The title of the play alludes to Midsummer Night—traditionally a time of revelry, magic and transition; the woodland setting, the presence of the fairy world, the cover of darkness, and the presence of the moon evoke the mystery and enchantments of this time.

In the scene's final speech, Helena decides to tell Demetrius of Hermia and Lysander's elopement in hopes of gaining his confidence and love, although it means betraying her best friend: "and for this intelligence / If I have thanks, it is a dear expense. / But herein mean I to enrich my pain, / To have his sight thither and back again."

Act I, scene 2 opens with an assembly of local craftsmen—Bottom the weaver, Flute the bellows-mender, Snout the tinker, Starveling the tailor, Quince the carpenter, and Snug the joiner—who hope to present a play at the wedding of Theseus and Hippolyta and to be financially rewarded for their efforts. What the craftsmen lack in professional experience they make up for in enthusiasm. Quince immediately takes charge of the group, giving out parts and direction. Their choice of play, "The most lamentable comedy and most cruel death of Pyramus and Thisby," builds on the theme of star-crossed lovers who must decide their fate. It also demonstrates how Shakespeare juxtaposes divergent elements to create comedy. It is unusual that a tragic love story would be performed at a nuptial celebration, yet in their eagerness the men overlook this. The text of *A Midsummer Night's Dream* itself also reflects Shakespeare's use of opposition. Employing a device he uses in many of his plays, he has the characters at the Athenian court speak in verse and the craftsmen speak in prose, emphasizing the contrast between the "high" and "low" elements of the play's comedy.

As they plan their performance, each of the men begins to assert his personality: Bottom volunteers for every part; Snug confesses he is "slow of study" and wants only to play the role of the lion, for it requires nothing except that he roar. The craftsmen's only acknowledgment of the impropriety of their dramatic selection comes when, remembering that they will be at court, they mention that the "lion" must not "fright the ladies out of their wits." In his eagerness to play the part, Bottom, who is eventually cast as Pyramus, promises to roar like a dove or a nightingale. Quince asks the group to meet in the woods the next night for a rehearsal. Their bumbling earnestness is expressed by Bottom's exhortation that there the troupe can "rehearse most obscenely and courageously."

Act II

In Act II, scene 1, Shakespeare introduces the fairy world, whose presence is central to the play's aura of enchantment and mystery. As the act opens, a fairy is speaking with Robin Goodfellow, better known as Puck, a household spirit who is chief attendant to Oberon, king of the fairies. The fairy, a servant to the fairy queen, Titania, details her duties: "I must go seek some dewdrops here, / And hang a pearl in every cowslip's ear." Likewise, Puck reveals his purposes: "I am that merry wanderer of the night, / I jest to Oberon and make him smile." He also confesses to playing household tricks: "The wisest aunt, telling the saddest tale, / Sometimes for a three-foot stool mistaketh me; / Then slip I from her bum, down topples she."

Puck reveals that there has been a quarrel between Titania and Oberon, who shortly enter with their trains. While Titania and Oberon are ethereal, spiritual creatures with magical powers, they clearly possess some very human emotions and are not above jealousy or revenge. At the moment they are accusing each other of infidelity. Titania mentions that she has seen Oberon "versing love / To amorous Phillida" and accuses him of having loved Hippolyta. Oberon counters that she should not reprimand him when he knows of her love for Theseus. Titania then describes how their conflict has led to the neglect of the earth, instigating "[c]ontagious fogs," floods, poor harvests, and sickness. She tells Oberon, "And this same progeny of evils comes / From our debate, from our dissension, / We are their parents and original." Their lovers' quarrel reintroduces the theme of love's difficulties and foreshadows the jealousy, dissension, and confusion that the human characters will soon suffer as well.

Oberon proposes ending their argument if Titania will give him "a little changeling boy / To be [his] henchman," but Titania refuses. The boy in question is the child of a devotee of Titania's who has died in childbirth, and Titania has vowed to raise the child herself. Turning to metaphor, she recalls how she and the child's mother sat talking as they watched traders' ships come in: "we have laugh'd to see the sails conceiv'd / and grow big-bellied with the wanton wind / Which she, with pretty and with swimming gait / Following—her womb then rich with my young squire— / Would imitate." Titania's fidelity to her former companion is touching and will be mirrored in an exchange between Helena and Hermia that likewise recalls their girlhood friendship. Titania then proposes a truce, which Oberon will not accept, because the queen still refuses to relinquish the child. The two part in anger.

Oberon, furious, calls upon Puck to help devise his revenge. The fairy king describes how he once watched Cupid shoot an arrow that missed its intended target—a young virgin's heart—and instead hit a white flower, which turned purple "with love's wound." The juice of the flower, when squeezed on the eyelids of a sleeping person, will make the sleeper fall in love with the first creature he or she sees upon awakening. Oberon orders Puck to find the flower, and Puck departs, resolving to "put a girdle round the earth" in his rapid quest for it.

Hearing others approach, Oberon renders himself invisible and watches an exchange between Demetrius and Helena, who has chased Demetrius through the woods as he searches for Lysander and Hermia. Demetrius, intending to kill Lysander and win Hermia, is hardhearted toward Helena, who declares that, despite his harsh words, she still loves him: "Use me but as your spaniel, spurn me, strike me / Neglect me, lose me; only give me leave / Unworthy as I am, to follow you." Demetrius claims that he becomes sick when he looks at her, while Helena becomes sick when she does not look at him—again, Shakespeare's joining of opposites. Demetrius threatens to run from Helena and leave her to the wild beasts. She implores him to reconsider, scolding him for his cruelty: "Fie, Demetrius! / Your wrongs do set a scandal on my sex. / We cannot fight for love as men may do; / We should be woo'd, and were not made to woo."

Demetrius at last leaves, and Helena vows again to follow him. Thus, although Helena is initially represented as more docile than Hermia, she shows herself to be quite as determined.

When Puck returns with the magic flower, Oberon instructs him to anoint the eyes of a "disdainful youth," whom Puck will recognize "by the Athenian garments he hath on." Having observed the scene between Demetrius and Helena, Oberon seeks to reverse the situation so Demetrius will pursue Helena and "prove / More fond on her than she upon her love."

Act II, scene 3 opens with Titania being sung to sleep by her fairies, who wish her safe rest and chant spells to ward off evil spirits. Upon finishing, they leave to attend to their duties: "Some to kill cankers in the musk-rose buds / Some to war with rere-mice [bats] for their leathern wings." In spite of the fairies' protective charms, as soon as Titania is asleep, Oberon steals in and squeezes the love potion on her eyelids, chanting,

> What thou seest when thou dost wake,
> Do it for thy true-love take;
> Be it ounce [lynx] or cat, or bear,
> Part [panther], or boar with bristled hair,
> In thy eye that shall appear
> When thou wak'st, it is thy dear.
> Wake when some vile thing is near.

Hermia and Lysander next enter, having lost their way in the woods. They agree to rest and begin a playful argument over how near to each other they should sleep. Because they are to be married, Lysander declares, "One turf shall serve as pillow for us both, / One heart, one bed, two bosoms, and one troth." Yet Hermia protests, "Lie further off; in human modesty, / Such separation as may well be said / Becomes a virtuous bachelor and a maid." Hermia then wishes Lysander good night, saying, "With half that wish the wisher's eyes be press'd," words that take on further significance with Puck's arrival. Seeing that they are not sleeping side by side and observing Lysander's Athenian garb, Puck takes Lysander for the youth about whom Oberon spoke and anoints his eyes: "Churl, upon thy eyes I throw / All the power this charm doth owe."

After Puck departs, Demetrius enters with Helena in hot pursuit. As she pauses to catch her breath, Demetrius runs off. In yet another allusion to eyes and eyesight, Helena speaks enviously of how attractive Hermia is, while she, Helena, feels too unwanted and forlorn: "Happy is Hermia, wheresoe'er she lies, / For she hath blessed and attractive eyes." Helena does not know that Hermia is nearby or that their situations will shortly be reversed. She soon sees Lysander and, not knowing if he is asleep or dead, wakes him. Lysander starts up and, true to the love potion's power, he falls instantly in love with Helena.

Lysander repudiates his former love, swearing it is "not Hermia, but Helena I love: / Who will not change a raven for a dove?" Now the very sight of Hermia "[t]he deepest loathing to the stomach brings." Lysander's language becomes florid as he ironically attributes his change of affections to clear thinking: "And touching now the point of human skill, / Reason becomes marshall to my will, / And leads me to your eyes, where I o'erlook / Love's stories, written in Love's richest book." Helena, bewildered by his behavior and certain that she is being mocked, chastises Lysander and laments, "O, that a lady, of one man refus'd, / Should of another therefore be abus'd!" The two exit, and Hermia awakes, upset from a prophetic nightmare that a serpent was crawling on her breast and eating at her heart while Lysander "sat smiling at his cruel prey." She is terrified by Lysander's absence and leaves in search of him.

Act III

Act III begins with another installment of the night's activities in the woods, as the craftsmen assemble to rehearse their play. They discuss details of the plot, such as whether Pyramus should draw a sword to kill himself and whether this will upset the ladies of the court. In an even more absurd twist, Bottom suggests that the play's prologue should explain that the actors are not really being killed and that Pyramus is actually Bottom the weaver. Snout proposes also mentioning that the lion is really an actor and advises that the actor's face remain visible to reassure the ladies of their safety. As one of the scenes requires that two characters meet by moonlight, they consult the almanac to find out if the moon will shine on the night of their performance.

As they begin to rehearse, Puck enters unseen and starts to make trouble. Spooked, the actors all flee except for Bottom, upon whom Puck places an ass's head. Snout reenters and cries, "O Bottom, thou art chang'd." Bottom, unaware of his transformation, believes he is being mocked, and there is much subsequent punning on the phrase "to make an ass of me."

Puck then leads Bottom to Titania, who wakes and falls instantly in love with him. In response to her declaration of love, the confused Bottom speaks a line that captures one of the play's key themes: "[T]o say the truth, reason and / love keep little company together nowadays." For this sagacity, Titania tells Bottom, "Thou art as wise as thou art beautiful." She wills him to stay and summons four fairies—Peaseblossom, Cobweb, Moth, and Mustardseed—to serve Bottom, who greatly enjoys his changed status without understanding its source.

In Act III, scene 2, Puck reports this turn of events to Oberon, who is delighted. Puck also tells his king that he has "latch'd" the eyes of the Athenian youth. Demetrius and Hermia soon come into view, Hermia frantic with concern for Lysander's well-being and fearful that Demetrius has done him harm. She scolds Demetrius ("Out, dog! Out, cur!") and says she has lost patience with his wooing. When Hermia leaves angry and disgusted, Demetrius decides to rest and lies down to sleep. Oberon quickly realizes Puck's mistake: There is "[s]ome true love turn'd and not a false turn'd true." Oberon, upset by this error, commands Puck to fly through the woods until he finds Helena and to lead her to the sleeping Demetrius, whose eyes Oberon will "charm . . . against she do appear." Oberon then anoints Demetrius's eyes and chants his charm. Puck returns with Helena and Lysander and, anticipating the coming events, speaks another of the play's most-famed lines: "Lord, what fools these mortals be!"

Lysander is pleading with Helena, who still believes that he is mocking her. Demetrius then wakes and sees Helena, with whom he falls instantly in love. His speech becomes overblown: "O Helen, goddess, nymph, perfect, divine!" In a neat reversal of the plot, both men now love Helena when once they both loved Hermia. Helena, who subsequently takes on the vibrancy and vigor previously ascribed to Hermia, exclaims, "O spite! Oh hell! I see you all are bent / To set against me for your merriment / . . . If you were men, as men you are in show, / You would not use a gentle lady so." Lysander and Demetrius have begun to quarrel over who loves Helena more when Hermia enters the scene. After Lysander refuses her affections, she joins Helena in her bewilderment. Helena, however, thinks that Hermia is involved in a conspiracy to mock her and believes herself further betrayed. In a touching speech, Helena appeals to Hermia, reminding her of their childhood friendship: "So we grew togeth'r / Like to a double cherry, seeming parted, / But yet an union in partition; / Two lovely berries moulded on one stem; / So, with two seeming bodies, but one heart." This speech, reminiscent of Lysander's earlier words to Hermia ("[o]ne heart, one bed, two bosoms, and one troth"), reflects Shakespeare's theme of twinning: the girls were once practically indistinguishable, and their situation has now turned them into mirror opposites.

Hermia is amazed and insulted by Helena's accusation that she, as a joke, is making Lysander woo Helena and having Demetrius pretend to love her again. The two men continue to vie for Helena's affection and begin to speak more harshly to Hermia, now mocking her dark complexion and short stature. Anger grows between the two women. Helena appeals again to Hermia, saying she was always a loyal friend and only revealed the elopement of Lysander and Hermia to Demetrius so she could follow him. Setting up more comedy through the positioning of opposites, Hermia is ruthlessly mocked for her short stature as she argues with Helena, who exits with the line, "Your hands than mine are quicker for a fray, / My legs are longer though, to run away."

Oberon and Puck, who have witnessed the scene, seek a way to set things right. Oberon tells Puck to lead the men astray and to shroud the forest in fog so they cannot fight. When Lysander lies down to sleep, Puck is to anoint his eyes with the antidote to love-in-idleness, "[w]hose liquor hath this virtuous property,

/ To take from thence all error with his might / And make his eyeballs roll with wonted sight." Oberon will also ask Titania for the child and, when she acquiesces, he will release "her charmed eye . . . from monster's view," remarking that then "all things shall be peace."

Puck, making haste because "Aurora's harbinger," the dawn, is approaching, departs to lead Lysander and Demetrius through the woods. He keeps them from each other's sight by mimicking in turn the voice and movements of each man in yet another instance of doubling. Exhausted by their chase, the men finally lie down to sleep, and Puck applies the antidote to Lysander's eyes. Helena, weary with wandering and distress, lies down, hoping that sleep "that sometimes shuts up sorrow's eye," will "[s]teal [her] awhile from [her] own company." Hermia, equally spent and miserable, also soon lies down, remarking, "[M]y legs can keep no pace with my desires." Puck admits, "Cupid is a knavish lad, / Thus to make poor females mad."

Act IV

Act IV, scene 1 finds Titania lovingly placing roses in Bottom's mane and her fairies still doting on his every whim. When she falls asleep with Bottom cradled in her arms, Oberon and Puck enter. Oberon begins to feel some remorse for his actions and tells Puck that Titania has yielded to his demand and sent him the child. Having gotten what he wanted, Oberon releases Titania from the spell. She awakens, bewildered: "My Oberon, what visions have I seen! / Methought I was enamored of an ass." After Titania recoils at the sight of Bottom, Oberon tells Puck to remove the ass's head from the weaver. The king and queen appear reconciled, and Oberon says, "Come, my queen, take hands with me, / . . . Now thou and I are new in amity." The pair exit with the amazed Titania asking, "Tell me how it came this night / That I sleeping here was found / With these mortals on the ground."

After the fairies leave, Theseus enters with his train, which includes Hippolyta and Egeus. They are hunting but soon come upon the four Athenians mysteriously sleeping in the woods. Theseus recognizes Hermia and remembers that it is her day to respond to his edict. The four waken and become confused when asked how they came to be in the woods. Lysander replies, "Half sleep, half waking: but as yet, I swear, / I cannot truly say how I came here." He confesses that he and Hermia were planning to elope, angering Egeus. Demetrius can remember that Helena had revealed their plan and that he "in fury" had followed the lovers, but he now claims to love only Helena: "To her, my lord / Was I betroth'd ere I saw Hermia / But, like in sickness, did I loathe this food; / But, as in health, come to my natural taste, / Now I do wish it, love it, long for it. / And will for evermore be true to it."

Upon hearing about Demetrius's change of heart, Theseus makes a decision: "Egeus, I will overbear your will; / For in the temple by and by with us / These couples shall eternally be knit." The hunting trip is suspended, and the group departs for Athens, resolved to hear the tales of the night, though the four lovers agree that they are unsure of the events. "Methinks I see these things with parted eye / When everything seems double," says Hermia. And Demetrius wonders, "Are you sure / That we are awake? It seems to me / That yet we sleep, we dream."

The group departs, and the last of the night's dreamers awakens. Bottom, who is now alone in the woods, thinks he is still in rehearsal and speaks of having a strange dream. "Man is but an ass if he go about to expound this dream," he comments, again expressing the idea of accepting misunderstanding and uncertainty: "The eye of man hath not heard, the ear of man hath not seen, man's hand is not able to taste, his tongue to conceive, nor his heart to report, what my dream was." The mixing up of body parts and their functions both literally and figuratively reflects the night's confusions, inversions of relationships, and blurred distinctions between dreams and reality. He speaks of getting Quince to write a ballet humorously called "'Bottom's Dream,' because it has no bottom."

Act IV, scene 2 opens on the rest of the craftsmen frantically preparing their play. They are alarmed that there has been no sign of Bottom and wonder how their play might go on without him, for Bottom "hath simply the best wit of any handicraft / man in Athens." Snug reports that the duke is approaching the temple with "two or three lords and ladies more married," and Flute complains that Bottom has cost them their financial reward. Bottom suddenly appears, instantly takes charge, and says that he will recount his adventures later, promising (in a further pun on his name), "I will tell you everything, right as it fell out."

Act V

The single scene of Act V begins with Hippolyta and Theseus speaking about the oddness of the lovers' tales of the night. "The lunatic, the lover, and the poet / Are of imagination all compact," says Theseus. Each is unique in his perception of reality, with the poet so steeped in his imagination that he can almost create his own world from his fantasies:

The poet's eye, in a fine frenzy rolling,
Doth glance from heaven to earth, from earth to heaven;
And as imagination bodies forth
The forms of things unknown, the poet's pen
Turns them to shapes and gives to airy nothing
A local habitation and a name.
Such tricks hath strong imagination
That, if it would but apprehend some joy,
It comprehends some bringer of joy;

Or in the night, imagining some fear,
How easy is a bush supposed a bear?

The lovers enter and discuss the entertainments that will occupy them until they can retire to bed and consummate their marriages. Theseus asks Philostrate, his master of revels, what "abridgment" he has for the evening, and Philostrate presents a list of possible plays. Theseus is intrigued by the mention of "[a] tedious brief scene of young Pyramus / And his love Thisby; very tragical mirth" and, upon hearing that it is presented by Athenian craftsmen, orders it performed. He respects the actors' earnestness, saying, "For never anything can be amiss / When simpleness and duty tender it." Although Hippolyta protests that she does not like poor theater, Theseus insists that they view the production.

The play begins with Quince giving the prologue. In his nervous desire to please, he declares, "If we offend, it is with our good will," saying the opposite of what he intends and leading Theseus to comment that "[h]is speech was like a tangled chain; nothing / impaired, but all disordered." In an interesting reversal, the craftsmen now speak in verse and the members of the court in prose. The prologue continues, giving a synopsis of the tragic fate of Pyramus and Thisby. Separated by a wall through which they can only whisper, the lovers plan to meet secretly at Ninus's tomb. Thisby arrives first but is scared by a lion and flees, dropping her mantle, which the lion bloodies. Pyramus arrives, sees the bloody cloak, and, believing Thisby dead, stabs himself. Thisby, distraught, then stabs herself with Pyramus's dagger.

When Wall (Snout) presents his speech, Theseus asks, "Would you desire lime and hair to speak better?" Hippolyta, however, is not impressed, muttering, "This is the silliest stuff that ever I heard." Theseus replies, "The best in this kind are but shadows; and the worst / are no worse, if imagination amend them." Snug, who plays the lion, includes a disclaimer that assures the ladies of his true identity as Snug the joiner. Theseus reflects, "A very gentle beast, and of good conscience." The play continues with the appearance of Starveling as Moonshine and with Demetrius and Theseus commenting generally on the action as Hippolyta complains. Finally, all catch the play's ridiculous spirit and begin to respond to the actors: Demetrius, "Well roared, Lion"; Theseus, "Well run, Thisby"; Hippolyta, "Well shone, Moon. Truly, the moon shines with a / good grace"; and Theseus, "Well moused, Lion."

At the end of the play, Theseus reassures the actors that there is no need of an epilogue, "for [their] play needs no excuse." There is a dance instead, and finally Theseus proclaims, "The iron tongue of midnight hath told twelve. / Loves, to bed; 'tis almost fairy time."

The lovers exit, and Puck, the spirit in charge of housekeeping, enters with a broom. He tells the audience that, during this enchanted time of night, "[N]ot a mouse / Shall disturb this hallow'd house. / I am sent with broom before, /

To sweep the dust behind the door." Oberon, Titania, and their trains enter, and Oberon tells his fairies, "And each several chambers bless, / Through this palace, with sweet peace; / And the owner of it blest / Ever shall in safety rest. / Trip away; make no stay; meet me all by break of day." Once again, the night is described as the domain of the fairy world, which interacts with and shapes the fate of the human world. Yet, in this closing scene, the benevolence of the world of spirits is established.

Puck ends the drama with a speech that further toys with the comedy's play between illusion and reality:

> If we shadows have offended,
> Think but this, and all is mended
> That you have but slumb'red here
> While these visions did appear
> And this weak and idle theme,
> No more yielding but a dream

Calling himself "an honest Puck" who has meant no harm, Puck utters the play's closing lines, "So, good night unto you all. / Give me your hands, if we be friends / And Robin shall restore amends."

Key Passages in
A Midsummer Night's Dream
🪷

Act I, i, 1-19

Theseus: Now, fair Hippolyta, our nuptial hour
Draws on apace; four happy days bring in
Another moon: but, O, methinks, how slow
This old moon wanes! she lingers my desires,
Like to a step-dame or a dowager
Long withering out a young man revenue.

Hippolyta: Four days will quickly steep themselves in night;
Four nights will quickly dream away the time;
And then the moon, like to a silver bow
New-bent in heaven, shall behold the night
Of our solemnities.

Theseus: Go, Philostrate,
Stir up the Athenian youth to merriments;
Awake the pert and nimble spirit of mirth;
Turn melancholy forth to funerals;
The pale companion is not for our pomp.

Exit PHILOSTRATE

Hippolyta, I woo'd thee with my sword,
And won thy love, doing thee injuries;
But I will wed thee in another key,
With pomp, with triumph and with revelling.

As a rule, the first lines in Shakespeare reveal a great deal about the plays they begin. In *A Midsummer Night's Dream*, the very first word of the text, "Now," reveals the dynamic that governs both the action of the drama and the psychology of the characters. Duke Theseus, the ruler of Athens; the four confounded

17

lovers in the forest: Hermia, Helena, Lysander and Demetrius; Hermia's father, Egeus; Oberon and Titania, the warring king and queen of the fairies; and Pyramus and Thisby, the comically tragic lovers as they are presented by the "rude mechanicals," are all impatient that their desires be gratified "now." "Now . . . our nuptial hour / Draws on apace," Theseus tells Hippolyta, the warrior queen he conquered and whose love he won in his battle against the Amazons. He is impatient and eager for the time to pass. "Four happy days," he says, "bring in / another moon." He wishes that later were now: "but, O, methinks, how slow / This old moon wanes! She lingers [delays] my desires." The moon becomes in his succeeding image like an old and near relation who lives on, depleting a young man's wealth because he must support her.

Only Hippolyta is not impatient. She responds to Theseus's complaint, echoing the form of his utterance and inverting his phrase "Four days." While she appears to be in rhetorical accord with Theseus because her rhetoric mirrors his, she actually shows herself to be somewhat at odds with him emotionally. While his rhetorical figure was intended to indicate the slowness of time between "now" and their wedding day and the impatience that must signify the force of his desire, her use of the "Four days" figure and her variation of it as "Four nights" shows that she is not impatient, that the event will be soon enough for her. Subtly, through the disparity in desire expressed by their rhetoric, Shakespeare distinguishes between apparent surface agreement and stifled conflict. That conflict between two characters' needs and desires repeatedly shapes the action of the play. Theseus's next speech reveals that Hippolyta is more than just his fiancée; she is a spoil of war. "I wooed thee with my sword, / And won thy love, doing thee injuries." In all its manifestations in *A Midsummer Night's Dream*, love exists inside conflict and struggle as a desire to command, as well as within a context of mutual attraction, accord, and affection.

———— ———— ————

Act I, i, 22–64

Egeus: Full of vexation come I, with complaint
Against my child, my daughter Hermia.
Stand forth, Demetrius. My noble lord,
This man hath my consent to marry her.
Stand forth, Lysander: and my gracious duke,
This man hath bewitch'd the bosom of my child;
Thou, thou, Lysander, thou hast given her rhymes,
And interchanged love-tokens with my child:
Thou hast by moonlight at her window sung,
With feigning voice verses of feigning love,
And stolen the impression of her fantasy

With bracelets of thy hair, rings, gawds, conceits,
Knacks, trifles, nosegays, sweetmeats, messengers
Of strong prevailment in unharden'd youth:
With cunning hast thou filch'd my daughter's heart,
Turn'd her obedience, which is due to me,
To stubborn harshness: and, my gracious duke,
Be it so she will not here before your grace
Consent to marry with Demetrius,
I beg the ancient privilege of Athens,
As she is mine, I may dispose of her:
Which shall be either to this gentleman
Or to her death, according to our law
Immediately provided in that case.

Theseus: What say you, Hermia? be advised fair maid:
To you your father should be as a god;
One that composed your beauties, yea, and one
To whom you are but as a form in wax
By him imprinted and within his power
To leave the figure or disfigure it.
Demetrius is a worthy gentleman.

Hermia: So is Lysander.

Theseus: In himself he is;
But in this kind, wanting your father's voice,
The other must be held the worthier.

Hermia: I would my father look'd but with my eyes.

Theseus: Rather your eyes must with his judgment look.

Hermia: I do entreat your grace to pardon me.
I know not by what power I am made bold,
Nor how it may concern my modesty,
In such a presence here to plead my thoughts;
But I beseech your grace that I may know
The worst that may befall me in this case,
If I refuse to wed Demetrius.

Theseus has no sooner spoken of "pomp . . . triumph, and . . . reveling"
than Egeus enters and, bringing a conflict for Theseus to adjudicate, seems to

shift the tone and direction of the play radically. Egeus introduces one of the recurring dramatic patterns that runs through all of Shakespeare's plays: the conflict between a father and his daughter regarding whom she will marry. Egeus wants his daughter, Hermia, to marry Demetrius. As her father, he has that right, he asserts, and Theseus corroborates it. "To you," Theseus tells Hermia, "your father should be as a god . . . To whom you are but as a form in wax." Although Hermia eventually outwits her father, defeating his will by her own willfulness, the action of *A Midsummer Night's Dream* nevertheless shows that she and everyone else, including the nonmortal fairies, are "but as a form of wax," whose temperaments, physical shape, desires, and dispositions are not exclusively of their own making.

Hermia loves Lysander and refuses to obey her father despite the awful punishments of either immediate death or lifetime confinement in a convent. Although such a father/daughter power struggle can have tragic consequences, as it does in *Romeo and Juliet, King Lear,* and *Othello,* for example, in *A Midsummer Night's Dream* it is the spur for a comic plot.

Rhetorically, Egeus's speech reveals the extent of his desire to exercise the power of possession by the repeated use of the words "my," "mine," "me," and "I." He speaks of "my child," "my daughter," "my consent." His conclusion is that "As she is mine, I may dispose of her." In Act I, scene 1, line 96, Egeus reasserts his right of possession after Hermia has assured him and Theseus of her defiance. She declares she will die before surrendering herself to her father's wish to marry Demetrius, but Egeus insists that "what is mine my love shall render him / And she is mine, and all my right of her / I do estate unto Demetrius."

The tangles of the forest plot reveal that such confidence in one's own power of possession and determination is misplaced, as does the story of Pyramus and Thisby and the struggle between Oberon and Titania for the orphan boy. There are invisible, often capricious, forces at the heart of human affection and behavior. Theseus seems to have some sense of this, for even after he sees the apparent irreconcilability of father and daughter, he forestalls uttering judgment, advising Hermia to "Take time to pause," to think about her decision, and give her answer again on his wedding day. He is also, as his first words have shown, aware of his own need to wait for the satisfaction of his wish to possess Hippolyta.

Act II, i, 42–57

Puck: Thou speak'st aright;
I am that merry wanderer of the night.
I jest to Oberon and make him smile
When I a fat and bean-fed horse beguile,
Neighing in likeness of a filly foal:

And sometime lurk I in a gossip's bowl,
In very likeness of a roasted crab,
And when she drinks, against her lips I bob
And on her wither'd dewlap pour the ale.
The wisest aunt, telling the saddest tale,
Sometime for three-foot stool mistaketh me;
Then slip I from her bum, down topples she,
And 'tailor' cries, and falls into a cough;
And then the whole quire hold their hips and laugh,
And waxen in their mirth and neeze and swear
A merrier hour was never wasted there.

Puck's description of himself to the fairy and to the audience introduces a vivid set of sketches of peasant life and of folk beliefs. It is narrated in rhymed couplets which give it a playful comic and folkloric aspect. In addition, his speech returns to the theme of the dialectic of control. It shows the impotence of willfulness, such as that which Egeus reveals in his assertion of parental control or that which is shown through Hermia's stubborn determination to follow her heart rather than submit to her father's will. Their wills are rendered ineffective by more powerful, capricious forces, which are embodied by Puck. Those forces are independent of them, yet they nevertheless influence them.

In a series of tableaux, Puck describes his power to subvert human (and animal) desire, will, and intention. Narrating his tricks, he also produces vivid scenes of peasant life, the old woman's clumsiness while drinking her ale, the woman who misses her chair and finds the ground when she sought to sit, and even the horse snorting with excitement, deceived by Puck's phantom neighing. Not just accidents, these slips and eruptions are indications of a hidden world with clandestine forces. They illustrate the theory of poetry that Theseus postulates in Act V when he explains that the imagination assigns causes to otherwise inexplicable events. Puck is not only an agent of mischief but an imaginative contrivance invented in folklore to account for inexplicable events.

Act II, i, 81–117

Titania: These are the forgeries of jealousy:
And never, since the middle summer's spring,
Met we on hill, in dale, forest or mead,
By paved fountain or by rushy brook,
Or in the beached margent of the sea,
To dance our ringlets to the whistling wind,
But with thy brawls thou hast disturb'd our sport.

Therefore the winds, piping to us in vain,
As in revenge, have suck'd up from the sea
Contagious fogs; which falling in the land
Have every pelting river made so proud
That they have overborne their continents:
The ox hath therefore stretch'd his yoke in vain,
The ploughman lost his sweat, and the green corn
Hath rotted ere his youth attain'd a beard;
The fold stands empty in the drowned field,
And crows are fatted with the murrion flock;
The nine men's morris is fill'd up with mud,
And the quaint mazes in the wanton green
For lack of tread are undistinguishable:
The human mortals want their winter here;
No night is now with hymn or carol blest:
Therefore the moon, the governess of floods,
Pale in her anger, washes all the air,
That rheumatic diseases do abound:
And thorough this distemperature we see
The seasons alter: hoary-headed frosts
Far in the fresh lap of the crimson rose,
And on old Hiems' thin and icy crown
An odorous chaplet of sweet summer buds
Is, as in mockery, set: the spring, the summer,
The childing autumn, angry winter, change
Their wonted liveries, and the mazed world,
By their increase, now knows not which is which:
And this same progeny of evils comes
From our debate, from our dissension;
We are their parents and original.

Amid the near doggerel of rhymed couplets—Puck's, for example, or the dialogue between Lysander and Hermia in Act II, scene 2, lines 35-65—Titania's aria is remarkable for the beauty of its poetry. When the lovers speak to each other, they make a deliberate effort to construct their discourse in a way that reflects their courtlike ability to present a language of wit and sensuality. Their conversation shows the passion of youthful inexperience and impatience. Pyramus and Thisby, in their ridiculous attempts at a tragic and melodramatic sublime, are actually the lovers' caricatures. Titania, however, does not attempt to shape her rhetoric. Her speech is delivered in a varied iambic pentameter, unrhymed, a mature verse that flows effortlessly from her and represents her as a natural force of the imagination.

In this speech, Titania presents the metaphysical structure of the play, the interconnection and interdependency of the larger forces at work. The discord between Titania and Oberon, for example, resonates throughout the world and makes living grim and dangerous. "The winds . . . have suck'd up from the sea / Contagious fogs." These fogs, "falling in the land," have turned to rain and caused rivers to flood. Shakespeare's image of the rivers swollen with pride shows the intimate connection between pride and disaster that is a comic theme threading through *A Midsummer Night's Dream*. Titania continues to enumerate a catalogue of ecological disasters, including the seasons no longer bringing their proper weather. "And this same progeny of evils," she concludes, "comes / From our debate, from our dissension; / We are their parents and original." The events of the world, disparate as they may appear, are seamlessly connected and interdependent in *A Midsummer Night's Dream*.

Shakespeare does not give space beyond this speech to develop the dramatic consequences of Titania's vision. She is quickly turned into a pastoral figure and then into a figure of fun who is bested by her husband, more truly made an ass of than even Bottom. And yet the beauty of her verse and its sincerity protect her from ever losing her fairy dignity, despite Oberon's tricks and manipulations.

⌐᳝ᠬ᳝— —᳝ᠬ᳝— —᳝ᠬ᳝—

II, i, 146 - 194

Oberon: Well, go thy way: thou shalt not from this grove
Till I torment thee for this injury.
My gentle Puck, come hither. Thou rememberest
Since once I sat upon a promontory,
And heard a mermaid on a dolphin's back
Uttering such dulcet and harmonious breath
That the rude sea grew civil at her song
And certain stars shot madly from their spheres,
To hear the sea-maid's music.

Puck: I remember.

Oberon: That very time I saw, but thou couldst not,
Flying between the cold moon and the earth,
Cupid all arm'd: a certain aim he took
At a fair vestal throned by the west,
And loosed his love-shaft smartly from his bow,
As it should pierce a hundred thousand hearts;
But I might see young Cupid's fiery shaft

Quench'd in the chaste beams of the watery moon,
And the imperial votaress passed on,
In maiden meditation, fancy-free.
Yet mark'd I where the bolt of Cupid fell:
It fell upon a little western flower,
Before milk-white, now purple with love's wound,
And maidens call it love-in-idleness.
Fetch me that flower; the herb I shew'd thee once:
The juice of it on sleeping eye-lids laid
Will make or man or woman madly dote
Upon the next live creature that it sees.
Fetch me this herb; and be thou here again
Ere the leviathan can swim a league.

Puck: I'll put a girdle round about the earth
In forty minutes.

Exit

Oberon: Having once this juice,
I'll watch Titania when she is asleep,
And drop the liquor of it in her eyes.
The next thing then she waking looks upon,
Be it on lion, bear, or wolf, or bull,
On meddling monkey, or on busy ape,
She shall pursue it with the soul of love:
And ere I take this charm from off her sight,
As I can take it with another herb,
I'll make her render up her page to me.
But who comes here? I am invisible;
And I will overhear their conference.

Enter DEMETRIUS, HELENA, following him

Demetrius: I love thee not, therefore pursue me not.
Where is Lysander and fair Hermia?
The one I'll slay, the other slayeth me.
Thou told'st me they were stolen unto this wood;
And here am I, and wode within this wood,
Because I cannot meet my Hermia.
Hence, get thee gone, and follow me no more.

Helena: You draw me, you hard-hearted adamant;
But yet you draw not iron, for my heart
Is true as steel: leave you your power to draw,
And I shall have no power to follow you.

In this passage, Shakespeare moves with wonderful dramatic dexterity through several realms, weaving together disparate storylines and styles of speech. Oberon finishes his business with Titania in the first two lines, seemingly defeated by her but beginning now to make good on his threat to get revenge and assure his victory over her. As he turns to Puck, the dramatic landscape changes. This is no longer a scene representing discord and reflecting disaster, but now a fairy comedy. Oberon instructs Puck in the mischief he wishes him to perform that will render Titania compliant with Oberon's will. At the same time, although Oberon does not yet know it, he inaugurates the midsummer madness that the lovers will experience that night in the forest. The exchange between Oberon and Puck then gives way to a scene between Helena and Demetrius. Shakespeare links these yet unrelated actions by framing the encounter between Helena and Demetrius with Oberon's unseen gaze.

The rhetoric of the passage subsequently shifts from Oberon's poetry to the lovers' frenzy. Oberon's speech is marked by the richness of its imagery; it explodes with colors, sounds, and figures. In contrast, the speech of Demetrius and Helena glows with simple and straightforward human emotion, clearly and directly expressing the frenzy of their loves and hates.

Act III, i, 9–81

Bottom: There are things in this comedy of Pyramus and Thisby that will never please. First, Pyramus must draw a sword to kill himself; which the ladies cannot abide. How answer you that?

. . .

Starveling: I believe we must leave the killing out, when all is done.

Bottom: Not a whit: I have a device to make all well. Write me a prologue; and let the prologue seem to say, we will do no harm with our swords, and that Pyramus is not killed indeed; and, for the more better assurance, tell them that I, Pyramus, am not

Pyramus, but Bottom the weaver: this will put them
out of fear.

. . .

Snout: Will not the ladies be afeard of the lion?

. . .

Bottom: Masters, you ought to consider with yourselves: to
bring in—God shield us!—a lion among ladies, is a
most dreadful thing; for there is not a more fearful
wild-fowl than your lion living; and we ought to
look to 't

. . .

[Y]ou must name his name, and half his face must
be seen through the lion's neck: and he himself
must speak through, saying thus, or to the same
defect,—'Ladies,'—or 'Fair-ladies—I would wish
You,'—or 'I would request you,'—or 'I would
entreat you,—not to fear, not to tremble: my life
for yours. If you think I come hither as a lion, it
were pity of my life: no I am no such thing; I am a
man as other men are;' and there indeed let him name
his name, and tell them plainly he is Snug the joiner.

Quince: Well it shall be so. But there is two hard things;
that is, to bring the moonlight into a chamber; for,
you know, Pyramus and Thisby meet by moonlight.

Snout: Doth the moon shine that night we play our play?

Bottom: A calendar, a calendar! look in the almanac; find
out moonshine, find out moonshine.

Quince: Yes, it doth shine that night.

Bottom: Why, then may you leave a casement of the great
chamber window, where we play, open, and the moon
may shine in at the casement.

Quince: Ay; or else one must come in with a bush of thorns
and a lanthorn, and say he comes to disfigure, or to
present, the person of Moonshine. Then, there is

another thing: we must have a wall in the great
chamber; for Pyramus and Thisby says the story, did
talk through the chink of a wall.

Snout: You can never bring in a wall. What say you, Bottom?

Bottom: Some man or other must present Wall: and let him
have some plaster, or some loam, or some rough-cast
about him, to signify wall; and let him hold his
fingers thus, and through that cranny shall Pyramus
and Thisby whisper.

Quince: If that may be, then all is well. Come, sit down,
every mother's son, and rehearse your parts.
Pyramus, you begin: when you have spoken your
speech, enter into that brake: and so every one
according to his cue.

Enter PUCK behind

Puck: What hempen home-spuns have we swaggering here,
So near the cradle of the fairy queen?
What, a play toward! I'll be an auditor;
An actor too, perhaps, if I see cause.

Shakespeare shows the great diversion within *A Midsummer Night's Dream*, the play that craftsmen present in tribute to Theseus and Hippolyta on their wedding day, in all the stages of its development from the assigning of parts in Act I, scene II through a rehearsal in this scene to the actual production in Act V, scene 1. The problem confronting the actors in this passage is twofold: It concerns both the proper limits of dramatic imitation and representation and the manner in which dramatic representation can be convincingly accomplished. With what seems like naiveté, the actors worry about the fitness of several aspects of their play for presentation, especially before the "ladies." They worry about showing a drawn sword and a frightening lion. Bottom suggests that the solution is to diminish the force of illusion through a spoken prologue and by having the lion only half-masked, allowing Snug's human face to partially appear, and for Snug in the role of the lion to identify himself as Snug. The problem of how to represent things is the next challenge, particularly with regard to showing a wall and moonlight. Although the actors ascertain that the actual moon will be shining that night and that they need only to keep a window open in the chamber in which they present the play, Peter Quince, the director, decides instead to have an actor play moonlight, just as he suggests that "some man or other must present [play] wall." Thus the craftsmen decide that the illusion must be both convincing and simultaneously clearly presented as illusion.

Thus, within the context of illusion (the play *A Midsummer Night's Dream* itself) Shakespeare confronts the problem of illusion, thereby strengthening the power of the play. Illusion is, paradoxically, both challenged and confirmed when the play itself deals with the problem of illusion. Adding to the complexity of this construction is the presence of Puck watching the scene, for he is a master of illusion, even if a somewhat muddled practitioner. His manipulations—tainting the lovers' desires, bestowing an ass's head on Bottom's shoulders, and causing Titania to dote upon his monstrous creation—show that the actors were not really so naïve in their concern about the possibilities of deception through dramatic illusion.

Bottom intends to remind his audience of his play's unreal nature by showing Snug's face through the lion's mask, but, in a delightful irony, this plan will not work when he himself appears as an ass. He is completely transformed, and there is nothing to show Titania that the ass she adores is really a man. However, every member of Shakespeare's audience knows that the actor playing Bottom is actually a person in a costume. That recognition, along with the realization of how fitting it is for Bottom to be an ass, is at the crux of the comic delight. Moreover, even though Titania is hoodwinked and the object of her affection is an illusion, she experiences, like the audience or readers of the play, real emotions.

―――

Act III, i, 165-175

Titania : Be kind and courteous to this gentleman;
Hop in his walks and gambol in his eyes;
Feed him with apricocks and dewberries,
With purple grapes, green figs, and mulberries;
The honey-bags steal from the humble-bees,
And for night-tapers crop their waxen thighs
And light them at the fiery glow-worm's eyes,
To have my love to bed and to arise;
And pluck the wings from painted butterflies
To fan the moonbeams from his sleeping eyes:
Nod to him, elves, and do him courtesies.

Titania's richly visual lines are comic because they are spoken in devotion to an ass. The object of her language is far less glorious than her words make him out to be. The illusion and her blindness strip these words of their high romantic charge and make them comic. Their very elevation is the element that deflates them in the present context.

Additionally, the rhyme scheme of the lines, except for the first line, reveals her mental condition, that her field of perception has been significantly narrowed so that only Oberon's will governs her power of observation and response. For a contemporary speaker, the words "eyes," "dewberries," "bees," and "courtesies," are slant rhymes, not exact rhymes but very close in sound. In Elizabethan pronunciation, these words were more perfect rhymes. Whether using contemporary or Elizabethan pronunciations, Titania's verse shows a compulsive fixation, which, indeed, governs the present state of her mind. But as her thoughts are revealed, although their object may be unworthy, her own feelings are not to be condemned; they are sweet and gracious.

Act III, ii, 102-144

Oberon: Flower of this purple dye,
Hit with Cupid's archery,
Sink in apple of his eye.
When his love he doth espy,
Let her shine as gloriously
As the Venus of the sky.
When thou wakest, if she be by,
Beg of her for remedy.

Re-enter PUCK

Puck: Captain of our fairy band,
Helena is here at hand;
And the youth, mistook by me,
Pleading for a lover's fee.
Shall we their fond pageant see?
Lord, what fools these mortals be!

Oberon: Stand aside: the noise they make
Will cause Demetrius to awake.

Puck: Then will two at once woo one;
That must needs be sport alone;
And those things do best please me
That befal preposterously.

Enter LYSANDER and HELENA

Lysander: Why should you think that I should woo in scorn?
Scorn and derision never come in tears:
Look, when I vow, I weep; and vows so born,
In their nativity all truth appears.
How can these things in me seem scorn to you,
Bearing the badge of faith, to prove them true?

Helena: You do advance your cunning more and more.
When truth kills truth, O devilish-holy fray!
These vows are Hermia's: will you give her o'er?
Weigh oath with oath, and you will nothing weigh:
Your vows to her and me, put in two scales,
Will even weigh, and both as light as tales.

Lysander: I had no judgment when to her I swore.

Helena: Nor none, in my mind, now you give her o'er.

Lysander: Demetrius loves her, and he loves not you.

Demetrius: [Awaking] O Helen, goddess, nymph, perfect, divine!
To what, my love, shall I compare thine eyne?
Crystal is muddy. O, how ripe in show
Thy lips, those kissing cherries, tempting grow!
That pure congealed white, high Taurus snow,
Fann'd with the eastern wind, turns to a crow
When thou hold'st up thy hand: O, let me kiss
This princess of pure white, this seal of bliss!

Oberon's lovely address to the magical flower is as instrumental in provoking the spell under which Demetrius will fall as is the flower itself. His lines, like Titania's, each end in the same rhyme, giving his words the chantlike magic of a spell. Dramatically, his words serve for the audience as a kind of overture to the forthcoming action when Demetrius rises to speak boilerplate late-sixteenth-century romantic verse to Helena, overcome by his love for her. It is as if Oberon has cast a spell on the audience, too, charming their eyes with his words.

The impetuosity of Demetrius's verse contrasts with the grace of Oberon's. Oberon's verse directly follows Puck's hasty departure to find Helena so that Oberon can rectify Puck's error. Unlike Oberon, who is sympathetic to Helena's love-pain, Puck enjoys the confusion he has caused and fools he has made out of mortals. Their anguish is merely a spectacle for his amusement. The amusement itself is built into his verse, especially by the introduction of the four-line rhyme on the sound "ee." Indeed, the confusion about to occur is a play that Puck and Oberon have composed. Now they watch with enjoyment as Lysander and Helena play out their perplexity, just as later watching the suffering of Pyramus and Thisby will provide the courtiers with amusement. In both cases, the members of the audience are looking at the spectacle, too, over the shoulders of those inside the play who are watching. The spectators are watching both the observers and what they are seeing. Thus with a complex aesthetic awareness, the audience is drawn into each scene and yet kept at a distance because of the compound perspective engineered by the dramatic structure. As the characters in the play respond, the audience's responses are shaped by the characters' reactions.

In the chaos of the encounter between Helena and Lysander, Shakespeare subtly shows his control of their psychology through the narrative strategy of his verse. The fourteen lines that Lysander and Helena share, starting with "Why should you think that I should woo in scorn?"—the first six lines spoken by Lysander, the next six by Helena, the thirteenth by Lysander, and the fourteenth by Helena—constitute a kind of sonnet. Helena and Lysander each recite a sestet rhymed a,b,a,b,c,c, and their verse encounter ends with a rhymed couplet. The rhymed couplets completing each sestet serve to construct a short poem that indicates a division between its speakers.

Act IV, i, 1-48

Titania: Come, sit thee down upon this flowery bed,
While I thy amiable cheeks do coy,
And stick musk-roses in thy sleek smooth head,
And kiss thy fair large ears, my gentle joy.

Bottom: Where's Peaseblossom?

Peaseblossom: Ready.

Bottom: Scratch my head Peaseblossom. Where's Mounsieur Cobweb?

Cobweb: Ready.

Bottom: Mounsieur Cobweb, good mounsieur, get you your
weapons in your hand, and kill me a red-hipped
humble-bee on the top of a thistle; and, good
mounsieur, bring me the honey-bag. Do not fret

yourself too much in the action, mounsieur; and,
good mounsieur, have a care the honey-bag break not;
I would be loath to have you overflown with a
honey-bag, signior. Where's Mounsieur Mustardseed?

Mustardseed: Ready.

Bottom: Give me your neaf, Mounsieur Mustardseed. Pray you,
leave your courtesy, good mounsieur.

Mustardseed: What's your will?

Bottom: Nothing, good mounsieur, but to help Cavalery Cobweb
to scratch. I must to the barber's, monsieur; for
methinks I am marvellous hairy about the face; and I
am such a tender ass, if my hair do but tickle me,
I must scratch.

Titania: What, wilt thou hear some music,
my sweet love?

Bottom: I have a reasonable good ear in music. Let's have
the tongs and the bones.

Titania: Or say, sweet love, what thou desirest to eat.

Bottom: Truly, a peck of provender: I could munch your good
dry oats. Methinks I have a great desire to a bottle
of hay: good hay, sweet hay, hath no fellow.

Titania: I have a venturous fairy that shall seek
The squirrel's hoard, and fetch thee new nuts.

Bottom: I had rather have a handful or two of dried peas.
But, I pray you, let none of your people stir me: I
have an exposition of sleep come upon me.

Titania: Sleep thou, and I will wind thee in my arms.
Fairies, begone, and be all ways away.

Exeunt fairies

So doth the woodbine the sweet honeysuckle
Gently entwist; the female ivy so
Enrings the barky fingers of the elm.
O, how I love thee! how I dote on thee!

They sleep

Comic as this scene is, its tone is nevertheless infused with sweetness. Titania is gentle and even maternal in her devotion to her new beloved. She calls Bottom "my gentle joy." She brings him food and lulls him to sleep. This tenderness reflects her affection for the child who is, after all, at the heart of her conflict with Oberon.

Bottom, truly an ass now, shows himself to be less aggressive and self-centered or self-promoting than he had been when he inhabited an entirely mortal form. He responds to Titania's affection without surprise but also without egoism. He enjoys the creature comforts of being fed and scratched where he itches, but he is gentle with his ministers and thoughtful of them. He shakes hands in brotherly fashion with Mustardseed, and he is solicitous of Cobweb. When he asks him to "kill me a red-hipped humble-bee on the top of a thistle; and . . . bring me the honey-bag," he specifies, "Do not fret yourself too much in the action, mounsieur; and, good mounsieur, have a care the honey-bag break not." He adds, "I would be loath to have you overflown with a honey-bag, signior." Bottom is not concerned, in case of such an accident, that he will lose the honey but rather that Cobweb will get sticky. This is quite a contrast from the self-centered Bottom who, in the distribution of parts for the craftsmen's play in Act I, scene 2, wanted to play all of the roles in Pyramus and Thisby.

Act IV, i, 157-202

Egeus: Enough, enough, my lord; you have enough:
I beg the law, the law, upon his head.
They would have stolen away; they would, Demetrius,
Thereby to have defeated you and me,
You of your wife and me of my consent,
Of my consent that she should be your wife.

Demetrius: My lord, fair Helen told me of their stealth,
Of this their purpose hither to this wood;
And I in fury hither follow'd them,
Fair Helena in fancy following me.

But, my good lord, I wot not by what power,—
But by some power it is,—my love to Hermia,
Melted as the snow, seems to me now
As the remembrance of an idle gaud
Which in my childhood I did dote upon;
And all the faith, the virtue of my heart,
The object and the pleasure of mine eye,
Is only Helena. To her, my lord,
Was I betroth'd ere I saw Hermia:
But, like in sickness, did I loathe this food;
But, as in health, come to my natural taste,
Now I do wish it, love it, long for it,
And will for evermore be true to it.

Theseus: Fair lovers, you are fortunately met:
Of this discourse we more will hear anon.
Egeus, I will overbear your will;
For in the temple by and by with us
These couples shall eternally be knit:
And, for the morning now is something worn,
Our purposed hunting shall be set aside.
Away with us to Athens; three and three,
We'll hold a feast in great solemnity.
Come, Hippolyta.

Exeunt THESEUS, HIPPOLYTA, EGEUS, and train

Demetrius: These things seem small and undistinguishable,

Hermia: Methinks I see these things with parted eye,
When every thing seems double.

Helena: So methinks:
And I have found Demetrius like a jewel,
Mine own, and not mine own.

Demetrius: Are you sure
That we are awake? It seems to me
That yet we sleep, we dream. Do not you think
The duke was here, and bid us follow him?

Hermia: Yea; and my father.

Helena: And Hippolyta.

Lysander: And he did bid us follow to the temple.

Demetrius: Why, then, we are awake: let's follow him
And by the way let us recount our dreams.

In this passage, conflict resolutions follow one another in succession: Lysander once more loves Hermia, and Demetrius is again in love with Helena; the royal fairies Oberon and Titania are reconciled; Theseus and Hippolyta have their wedding day; and the actors are ready to present their play. When Theseus comes upon the lovers in the wood, Lysander, just waking from enchantment, tells him openheartedly how they came to be there. Egeus, as he did in the first act, interrupts the proceedings and stops Lysander's narrative and the pattern of resolution. He calls for "the law, upon his [Lysander's] head," because "[t]hey [Lysander and Hermia] would have stolen away." But when he seeks to enlist Demetrius's support, Demetrius confesses that he now loves Helena. Of all those who had been enchanted, Demetrius is the only one who remains so. Yet the fairy art applied to him can be seen as simply mending his nature instead of bending it, his inconstancy evidencing the faultiness that needed fixing.

In his sympathetic and levelheaded wisdom, Theseus overrides Egeus's will and announces that the wedding of the two couples will take place that day with his own. Thus the midsummer chaos is supplanted by social order and cannot be countered by the social rigidity demonstrated in Egeus's demands. Once Theseus speaks, Egeus is silent. It is up to the directors, actors, and audience to infer his unspoken response.

Now alone, the four young people review their memory of the previous night, which is quite vague by now. But they are all awake, they conclude, confirming this by comparing their individual memories of the scene that has just passed with the duke and Hermia's father. The irony is that the one who says "Why, then, we are awake" is Demetrius, the only one of them who has not been removed from his enchanted sleeplike state. This line thus supports the theory that the fairy's magic did not enchant Demetrius into a dream but rather woke him from a state of mind that did not reflect his true sentiments or desires.

Act IV, i, 203-222

Bottom: [Awaking] When my cue comes, call me, and I will
answer: my next is, 'Most fair Pyramus.' Heigh-ho!
Peter Quince! Flute, the bellows-mender! Snout,
the tinker! Starveling! God's my life, stolen

hence, and left me asleep! I have had a most rare
vision. I have had a dream, past the wit of man to
say what dream it was: man is but an ass, if he go
about to expound this dream. Methought I was—there
is no man can tell what. Methought I was,—and
methought I had,—but man is but a patched fool, if
he will offer to say what methought I had. The eye
of man hath not heard, the ear of man hath not
seen, man's hand is not able to taste, his tongue
to conceive, nor his heart to report, what my dream
was. I will get Peter Quince to write a ballad of
this dream: it shall be called Bottom's Dream,
because it hath no bottom; and I will sing it in the
latter end of a play, before the duke:
peradventure, to make it the more gracious, I shall
sing it at her death.

Alone in the woods after the fairies and the courtiers of Athens have departed,
Bottom wakes from his enchantment as if he has been frozen in time. He picks
up where he had left off before his transformation and begins to recite his part
as Pyramus before he realizes that his companions are not there. It is then when
he begins to recall in a sensuous way that is yet devoid of content the experiences
he had. His memories, however, are as vaporous as a dream—so ethereal that it
confounds the senses so that "man is but a patched fool, if he will offer to say
what methought I had. The eye of man hath not heard, the ear of man hath not
seen, man's hand is not able to taste, his tongue to conceive, nor his heart to
report." (The ungarbled original that informs Bottom's soliloquy can be found
in Chapter 2, verse 9 of *First Corinthians*.) The lovers have each other and the
court to tell of their mystifying experience, but Bottom has only himself, and the
uncanny quality of his experience resonates within him and becomes matter in
his mind for a "ballet . . . called 'Bottom's Dream.'"

Is Bottom still an ass in his self-absorption and pomposity? Perhaps not.
The play we are seeing is, in part, a dramatization of that ballad, being indeed
Bottom's dream. Additionally, the magnitude of his response is proportional to
his experience. It is reasonable that he is left with a sense that he has experienced
a moment of transcendence.

〜〜〜　〜〜〜　〜〜〜

Act V, i, 1-27

Hippolyta: 'Tis strange my Theseus, that these
lovers speak of.

Theseus: More strange than true: I never may believe
These antique fables, nor these fairy toys.
Lovers and madmen have such seething brains,
Such shaping fantasies, that apprehend
More than cool reason ever comprehends.
The lunatic, the lover and the poet
Are of imagination all compact:
One sees more devils than vast hell can hold,
That is, the madman: the lover, all as frantic,
Sees Helen's beauty in a brow of Egypt:
The poet's eye, in fine frenzy rolling,
Doth glance from heaven to earth, from earth to heaven;
And as imagination bodies forth
The forms of things unknown, the poet's pen
Turns them to shapes and gives to airy nothing
A local habitation and a name.
Such tricks hath strong imagination,
That if it would but apprehend some joy,
It comprehends some bringer of that joy;
Or in the night, imagining some fear,
How easy is a bush supposed a bear!

Hippolyta: But all the story of the night told over,
And all their minds transfigured so together,
More witnesseth than fancy's images
And grows to something of great constancy;
But, howsoever, strange and admirable.

The conversation between Theseus and Hippolyta is not just a dramatic discussion of the plot; it is also a discourse on poetry, one of the few such overt essays to be found in Shakespeare's works. It is in itself of interest because it may reflect some idea of how Shakespeare defined, or at least discussed, poetry. Theseus lumps together the poet, the madman, and the lover. They "[a]re of imagination all compact." The madman's imagination is overwrought with images of torment; the lover is betrayed by a distortion in sight; the poet is defined by his eye, which rolls in a "fine frenzy" and allows his imagination to embody and give shape to "the forms of things unknown." Theseus explains that when a sensation is experienced, the mind immediately imagines a cause for it. How easily, he concludes, are people deceived, believing in something that does not exist. Theseus's theory of imagined causes fits well with the power of agency that folklore has attributed to Puck, as Puck describes it in Act II, scene 1.

Hippolyta does not argue with Theseus's poetics or against his psychological assertions. Instead she ignores them, simply noting that the congruity of the lovers' four stories suggests to her that there is something more to them than delusion.

———

Act V, i, 425-440

Puck: If we shadows have offended,
Think but this, and all is mended,
That you have but slumber'd here
While these visions did appear.
And this weak and idle theme,
No more yielding but a dream,
Gentles, do not reprehend:
if you pardon, we will mend:
And, as I am an honest Puck,
If we have unearned luck
Now to 'scape the serpent's tongue,
We will make amends ere long;
Else the Puck a liar call;
So, good night unto you all.
Give me your hands, if we be friends,
And Robin shall restore amends.

It is fitting that in its call for applause, the epilogue for a play about mischief is delivered by the play's chief mischief-maker. Puck, in his role as the Epilogue, apologizes for the play but also taunts the audience by instructing them to consider the play a product of their own imagination: "you have but slumber'd here / While these visions did appear. / And this weak and idle theme, / No more yielding but a dream." Thus, Puck implies, if the audience is dissatisfied or offended by the play, they have no one to blame but themselves. Continuing the play's discourse on poetry, Puck defines the poetry of theater as an illusion that transports spectators into the same enchanted region that dreams inhabit. Thus the spectators have not only watched the dream of others but have, by that focus of attention, entered the dream state themselves.

———

LIST OF CHARACTERS IN
A MIDSUMMER NIGHT'S DREAM
❧

Theseus, duke of Athens, has the authority to determine the future of the play's human lovers. He is himself newly in love with Hippolyta, whose land he has won in a recent battle, and with whom he is engaged to be married. His wisdom is reflected in the respect that the other characters accord him.

Hippolyta, queen of the Amazons, has a relatively small role in the play. We learn that Theseus has conquered both her country and her heart. Her role reverses from one of (presumed) capability and authority to one of passivity, although her vehement criticism of the craftsmen's play suggests, ironically, a greater role than is ostensible. As Theseus' bride-to-be, she is half of one love relationship that has not suffered from confusion and mishap.

Hermia is a young Athenian woman who wishes to marry Lysander, although her father instead has arranged for her to marry Demetrius. Described as short, dark, spirited, and willful, Hermia expresses her choice of husband to Theseus, who decrees that she must obey her father's will, become a nun, or die. Again showing a fierce streak of determination, she agrees to Lysander's plan to elope, and when the two become lost in the woods, the play's "midsummer madness" begins.

Helena is Hermia's best friend and, serving as Hermia's mirror opposite, is described as tall and blond. In love with Demetrius, her suitor before his affections changed to favor Hermia, Helena tries to win him back, going so far as to betray to him Hermia's plans to elope. Although generally characterized as less spirited than Hermia, Helena reveals her determination when she follows Demetrius through the woods as he searches for the lovers, and she holds her own during the confusion that ensues.

Lysander is Hermia's beloved and suggests that they elope. However, his affections change when Puck mistakenly applies love-juice to his eyes, and he falls in love with Helena. Ultimately, the antidote is applied, and he marries Hermia.

Demetrius is Lysander's dramatic double, as Helena is Hermia's. He is also in love with Hermia, who does not love him, and is her father's choice of suitor. He wooed Helena, however, before transferring his affections to Hermia, and so earned a reputation for inconstancy. When he follows the lovers into the woods, he comes under the love-juice's power and falls in love with Helena again, marrying her at the end of the play.

Egeus is Hermia's father. His command that she marry Demetrius instead of Lysander sets the play's action in motion, causing Hermia and Lysander to flee from Athenian laws and escape into the woods—the magical locale of the fairies.

Oberon, king of the Fairies, has magical powers that affect the earth's seasons. Although a spirit, he possesses human traits such as jealousy and anger, which lead him to wreak his comic revenge on Titania. The love-juice he orders Puck to administer to Lysander and Demetrius is responsible for much of the play's confusion.

Titania, queen of the Fairies, is embroiled in a dispute with Oberon because she refuses to give him the orphaned human child of one of her devotees to be his attendant. Her touching loyalty mirrors the sentiments of friendship that Helena voices in an exchange with Hermia. Titania becomes a victim of Oberon's revenge when Oberon administers love-juice to her eyes and presents the newly transformed Nick Bottom, with whom she instantly falls in love. In spite of these goings-on, she and Oberon are reconciled at the end of the play.

Puck, or Robin Goodfellow, is Oberon's attendant and a household spirit. Acting on the king's commands, he carries out most of the play's mischief. Puck's first speech describes many of the tricks he plays on housewives. At the end of the play, he appears with a broom, ready to tidy the stage and restore order to the households of the newly married couples. He asks forgiveness for his trickery, reminding listeners that all he does is in good spirits.

Peaseblossom, Cobweb, Moth, and **Mustardseed** are Titania's fairy attendants, whom the queen orders to serve her new love. The descriptions of their duties illuminate the activities of the fairy world.

Nick Bottom, a weaver, is among the craftsmen who decide to put on a play for Theseus's wedding. While rehearsing in the woods for his role as Pyramus, Bottom becomes the vehicle of Oberon's revenge on Titania when Puck transforms the weaver into a creature with an ass's head and leads him into the enchanted Titania's sight. Bottom enjoys his status as Titania's beloved without realizing his transformation. When he is changed back, he is unsure of what has happened to him, and his speech reiterates the larger theme that things are never quite what they seem.

Peter Quince/Prologue, Francis Flute/Thisby, Tom Snout/Wall, Snug/ Lion, and **Robin Starveling/Moonshine** are the other members of the cast of the craftsmen's play. Speaking in prose (except for the absurd poetry of their play) and exhibiting a general lack of sophistication, the craftsmen stand in comic contrast to the play's other characters.

CRITICISM
THROUGH THE AGES
❧

Sources of
A Midsummer Night's Dream
ॐ

As the origins of *A Midsummer Night's Dream* are particularly complicated, a separate discussion of this play's foundation is in order. *A Midsummer Night's Dream* draws from a wide range of sources, from Greek mythology to the ancient English folklore tradition of fairies and spirits, as well as later English literary influences. The plot of *A Midsummer Night's Dream* is truly the product of Shakespeare's brilliant combination of the supernatural and his everyday world, not the dramatization of any single literary source or specific story. Had Shakespeare adhered to the classical rules of drama, which require writers to stick to a single time and place, a mythological Theseus and his courtiers would never have encountered the realistic Bottom the Weaver and his cohorts or Oberon and the fairies of English folklore.

According to Greek mythology, Theseus was the son of Aegeus, an Athenian king who fathered his son against the advice of the Delphic oracle. Theseus later became king of Athens and was responsible for uniting many small Attic towns into a single state. As to the love story of Theseus and Hippolyta depicted in Shakespeare's play, it was believed that following a successful expedition against the Amazons, Theseus won his future bride Hippolyta, the queen of a female race of warriors who reputedly despised men and were determined never to marry. The details of their love story may have been based on Chaucer's *Knight's Tale* combined with elements of the Theseus story from Sir Thomas North's translation of *Plutarch's Lives* (1579), both of which contain the story of Theseus's defeat of the Amazons and conquest of Hippolyta.

The story of the artisans' attempt to produce and perform a play to celebrate Theseus's wedding to Hippolyta may be based in part on a play by Anthony Munday titled *John a Kent and John a Cumber* (ca. 1587) in which a group of mechanicals are depicted in their humorous attempts to rehearse a play for an aristocratic audience. Furthermore, the story of a man being metamorphosed into an ass has several sources, including Reginald Scot's *The Discovery of Witchcraft* (1584), Apuleius' *The Golden Ass*, and the legend of King Midas.

The story of Pyramus and Thisby is found in Ovid's *Metamorphoses* and Chaucer's *The Legend of Good Women*. In Ovid's tale, Pyramus and Thisby are neighbors whose parents will not let them marry; however, they devise a way to speak to one another through a cracked wall. Ultimately they meet at Ninus's tomb, where Thisby, frightened by a lion, drops her cloak and runs while the lion mouths it. When her lover, Pyramus, finds her bloody clothing, he believes her to be dead and kills himself; afterwards, Thisby returns to the scene, finds Pyramus dead, and kills herself in response.

Within the British Isles, ideas about fairies vary from place to place. As a boy, Shakespeare would probably have heard local lore regarding these creatures, as he lived in a small market town where such stories were common. Fairies and similar spirits were also popular subjects in late sixteenth-century literature, such as Edmund Spenser's *The Faerie Queen*. Oberon, king of the fairies, can be founded in *Huon of Bordeaux*, a French romance translated by Lord Berners in 1540, while Titania is found in Ovid's *Metamorphoses*, and Puck in an English legend documented by Reginald Scot in *The Discovery of Witchcraft* (1584).

What appears to be without any known source is Shakespeare's imaginative story of the four lovers, Hermia, Helena, Lysander, and Demetrius, a story that exhibits the themes of mistaken identity and misguided love that appear in many of his comedies.

A MIDSUMMER NIGHT'S DREAM IN THE SEVENTEENTH CENTURY
✺

A Midsummer Night's Dream is believed to have been written sometime around 1595 and 1596, and though it is not known when, where, or exactly for whom it was first performed, scholars agree that it was most likely intended to be entertainment for the wedding of an aristocratic couple, quite possibly one in which Queen Elizabeth—who was often identified with the Fairy Queen—was in attendance. And although it may have been originally intended as a private performance, it nevertheless entered the public arena shortly thereafter. Modern commentators have pointed out that there is nothing within the play, beyond its lavish costumes and music, that would have required an elaborate stage or special effects. The audience would have been able to imagine the nighttime background based on Shakespeare's highly evocative language.

Not much notable commentary on the play was written in the seventeenth century. In 1633, the great poet John Milton published a poem titled "L'Allegro," the theme of which concerns the life of action as opposed to the life of contemplation depicted in the companion poem, "Il Penseroso." "L'Allegro," a study in merrymaking and good spirits, pays tribute to Shakespeare and the spirit of *A Midsummer Night's Dream*. The poem begins with the exiling of the figure of Melancholy, personified as a character in this poem, in a way very similar to Theseus's directions to Philostrate, "[t]urn melancholy forth to funerals / The pale companion is not for our pomp" (I.i.11-15). In "L'Allegro," Milton similarly consigns the unfortunate being to the hellish netherworld from whence it came: "Hence, loathed Melancholy, / Of Cerberus and blackest Midnight born, . . . / Find out some uncouth cell, / Where brooding Darkness spreads his jealous wings." Having removed Melancholy from the scene, Milton invokes the cheerful figures of Greek mythology, bidding them to come and inhabit his world with all their sensuality and carefree celebration of love. "But come, thou Goddess fair and free, / In heaven yclept Euphrosyne. . . . Zephyr, with Aurora playing, / As he met her once a-Maying. / There, on beds of violets blue, / And fresh-blown roses washed in dew, / Filled her with thee, a daughter fair, / So buxom, blithe, and debonair." Further on in the poem, Milton alludes specifically to *A Midsummer Night's Dream*, celebrating Shakespeare's beautiful and melodious paean to love and marriage. Milton first refers to Hymen, the Greek mythological god of marriage who was supposed to attend every wedding in order to ward off bad luck. In Milton's poem, Hymen is pictured wearing an orange-yellow robe while being entertained by a traditional masque, which is imagined to be a work by Shakespeare or Ben Jonson. Milton's comparison of Jonson, a classical playwright, to Shakespeare, described as "Fancy's child," is particularly interesting. The phrase "Jonson's learned sock" refers to a custom in which the sock, a low-heeled slipper, was worn by actors in classical comedy, as opposed to the buskin or high-heeled boot worn by actors in tragedy. Milton seems to make clear his preference for Shakespeare's dreamy pageant, as opposed to Jonson's more classical work, with the enchanting music near the poem's close that evokes the sounds of nature:

> There let Hymen oft appear
> In saffron robe, with taper clear,
> And pomp, and feast, and revelry,
> With mask and antique pageantry;
> Such sights as youthful poets dream
> On summer eves by haunted stream.
> Then to the well-trod stage anon,
> If Jonson's learned sock be on,
> Or sweetest Shakespeare, Fancy's child,
> Warble his native wood-notes wild . . .

In the next century, Thomas Percy would discuss the "Goblin" in the poem, which is similar to Shakespeare's Robin Goodfellow, or Puck.

The well-known diarist Samuel Pepys briefly mentioned seeing an adaptation of the play in his *Diary* entry for September 29, 1662. He declares it trite and utterly absurd, though he admits that the beautiful pageantry and attractive women were much to his liking.

A very different, semioperatic adaptation of *A Midsummer Night's Dream*, titled *The Fairy Queen*, was produced in 1692. It was thought to be the work of Elkanah Settle, though more recent scholars dispute that attribution, and it was set to Henry Purcell's music, though omitting Shakespeare's songs. The writer also cut many lines from the play, choosing to begin the play with Egeus's entrance on the stage, as well as altering and adding other lines, as Settle was apparently primarily interested in matters of decorum. This motive had the effect of creating an enervated version of some of the most memorable lines, such as Lysander's declaration to Hermia: "I have never found / By Observation, nor by History, / That Lovers run a smooth, and even course." Indeed, *The Fairy Queen* bears so little resemblance to *A Midsummer Night's Dream* that audiences would not have recognized Shakespeare's play. *The Fairy Queen* has not been an important part in the history of criticism of *A Midsummer Night's Dream*, since the score was lost in 1701 and not rediscovered until 1901. Nevertheless, we do have the benefit of a contemporary analysis from John Downes's *Roscius Anglicanus*, written in 1708 and discussed in the chapter on the eighteenth century.

1633—John Milton, from "L'Allegro"

John Milton (1608-1674) was one of the greatest English poets of all time. He was also a dramatist, essayist, and political activist. His most famous and celebrated work is his epic poem *Paradise Lost* (1667). Other notable works include *Paradise Regained* (1671), *Samson Agonistes* (1671) and several poems, including "Lycidas" and the companion poems, "L'Allegro" and "Il Penseroso."

HENCE, loathed Melancholy,
Of Cerberus and blackest Midnight born
In Stygian cave forlorn
'Mongst horrid shapes, and shrieks, and sights unholy!
Find out some uncouth cell,
Where brooding Darkness spreads his jealous wings,
And the night-raven sings;
There, under ebon shades and low-browed rocks,
As ragged as thy locks,
In dark Cimmerian desert ever dwell.
But come, thou Goddess fair and free,
In heaven yclept Euphrosyne,
And by men heart-easing Mirth;
Whom lovely Venus, at a birth,
With two sister Graces more,
To ivy-crowned Bacchus bore:
Or whether (as some sager sing)
The frolic wind that breathes the spring,
Zephyr, with Aurora playing,
As he met her once a-Maying,
There, on beds of violets blue,
And fresh-blown roses washed in dew,
Filled her with thee, a daughter fair,
So buxom, blithe, and debonair.
. . .
Hard by, a Cottage chimney smokes,
From betwixt two aged Okes,

Where Corydon and Thyrsis met,
Are at their savory dinner set
Of Hearbs, and other Country Messes,
Which the neat-handed Phillis dresses;
And then in haste her Bowre she leaves,
With Thestylis to bind the Sheaves;
Or if the earlier season lead
To the tann'd Haycock in the Mead,
Som times with secure delight
The up-land Hamlets will invite,
When the merry Bells ring round,
And the jocond rebecks sound
To many a youth, and many a maid,
Dancing in the Chequer'd shade;
And young and old com forth to play
On a Sunshine Holyday,
Till the live-long day-light fail,
Then to the Spicy Nut-brown Ale,
With stories told of many a feat,
How Faery Mab the junkets eat,
She was pincht, and pull'd the sed,
And he by Friars Lanthorn led
Tells how the drudging Goblin swet,
To ern his Cream-bowle duly set,
When in one night, ere glimps of morn,
His shadowy Flale hath thresh'd the Corn
That ten day-labourers could not end,
Then lies him down the Lubbar Fend,
And stretch'd out all the Chimney's length,
Basks at the fire his hairy strength;
And Crop-full out of dores he flings,
Ere the first Cock his Mattin rings.
Thus don the Tales, to bed they creep,
By whispering Windes soon lull'd asleep.
Towred Cities please us then,
And the busie humm of men,
Where throngs of Knights and Barons bold,
In weeds of Peace high triumphs hold,
With store of Ladies, whose bright eies
Rain influence, and judge the prise
Of Wit, or Arms, while both contend
To win her Grace, whom all commend.

There let Hymen oft appear
In saffron robe, with taper clear,
And pomp, and feast, and revelry,
With mask and antique pageantry;
Such sights as youthful poets dream
On summer eves by haunted stream.
Then to the well-trod stage anon,
If Jonson's learned sock be on,
Or sweetest Shakespeare, Fancy's child,
Warble his native wood-notes wild,
And ever against eating Cares,
Lap me in soft Lydian Aires,
Married to immortal verse
Such as the meeting soul may pierce
In notes, with many a winding bout
Of lincked sweetnes long drawn out,
With wanton heed, and giddy cunning,
The melting voice through mazes running;
Untwisting all the chains that ty
The hidden soul of harmony.
That Orpheus self may heave his head
From golden slumber on a bed
Of heapt Elysian flowres, and hear
Such streins as would have won the ear
Of Pluto, to have quite set free
His half regain'd Eurydice.
These delights, if thou canst give,
Mirth with thee, I mean to live.

1692—Samuel Pepys, from *The Diary of Samuel Pepys*

Samuel Pepys (1633–1703), an English naval administrator and member of Parliament, is most famous for his diary, which is considered an invaluable primary source about daily life in the Restoration period.

September 29, 1662

. . . and then to the King's Theatre, where we saw *Midsummer Night's Dream*, which I had never seen before, nor shall ever again, for it is the most insipid ridiculous play that ever I saw in my life. I saw, I confess, some good dancing and some handsome women, which was all my pleasure.

—⁓⁓— —⁓⁓— —⁓⁓—

1692—Anonymous (attributed to Elkanah Settle), from *The Fairy Queen*

This opera was a very liberal adaptation of *A Midsummer Night's Dream*, with music by Henry Purcell. The lines below show how the adaptor changed one of the most famous lines in the original, "The course of true love never did run smooth."

Lysander: O my true Hermia! I have never found
By Observation, nor by History,
That Lovers run a smooth, and even course:
Either they are unequal in their Birth—

Hermia. O cross too high to be imposed on Love!

Lysander. Or if there be a Simpathy in choice,
War, Sickness, or pale Death lay Siege to it,
Making it momentary as a sound,
Swift as the Lightning in the blackest night;
That at one Instant shews both Heav'n and Earth.
Yet ere a man can say, behold the Flame,
The jaws of darkness have devour'd it up;
So quick even brightest things run to Confusion.

Hermia. If then true Lovers have been ever cross'd,
It stands as a Decree in Destiny.
Then let us teach each other Patience,
Because it is a customary thing.

—⁓⁓— —⁓⁓— —⁓⁓—

A Midsummer Night's Dream in the Eighteenth Century

The eighteenth century marked the burgeoning of Shakespeare studies, as evidenced by the numerous editions of his complete works. The first standard collected edition of Shakespeare's plays was produced by Nicholas Rowe in 1709. This was followed by editions by Alexander Pope (1725), Lewis Theobald (1734), Samuel Johnson (1765–1768), George Steevens (1773 and 1778), and many others. However, true commentary on Shakespeare was mainly focused on his tragedies and histories and less so on comedies such as *A Midsummer Night's Dream*. In the first half of the century, the play only appeared onstage in a highly adapted form. In 1708, the writer John Downes discussed seeing *The Fairy Queen,* the operatic adaptation written in the late seventeenth century. Downes expressed his pleasure at the elaborate visual and sensual effects of the production but noted its prohibitive production costs.

Later in the century, David Garrick, the preeminent actor-manager of his time, staged three very different productions of *A Midsummer Night's Dream* during his tenure at the Drury Lane Theatre. The first of Garrick's productions was a 1755 opera (titled *The Fairies*) that omitted much of the original text; what was left of the text focused mainly on the fairies and the court. The next production, in 1763, was also operatic, but it included more of the original text and had some dialogue that was not set to music; it proved unpopular and did not last beyond its first performance. Three days later, Garrick's collaborator, George Coleman, presented yet another version, titled *A Fairy Tale*, which featured material on the artisans and the fairies but omitted the objectionable and uncouth Pyramus and Thisby play. This production met with greater success.

In his *Reliques of Ancient English Poetry*, a collection of popular songs, Thomas Percy traces the origins of Shakespeare's Robin Goodfellow, or Puck, back to an ancient English oral tradition of superstition and cheerful spirits who are variously named Puckie and Hobgoblin. "Indeed . . . the existence of Fairies and Goblins is alluded to in the most ancient British Bards, who mention them under various names, one of the most common of which signifies 'The spirits of the mountains.'" Percy then focuses on Milton's "L'Allegro," where, he says, Goodfellow is depicted as a spirit of supernatural strength who must work hard for his daily food in his nocturnal endeavors in the fields "[t]hat ten day-labourers could not end." It is notable that in the excerpt Percy quotes, Milton characterizes the imp as a "lubbar fiend," a big, clumsy fellow who lives in idleness and is therefore harmless. It's similar to how Robin Goodfellow is described as a "lob of spirits," meaning a clown or country bumpkin, in *A Midsummer Night's Dream* (II.i.16.)

Samuel Johnson in his commentary on *A Midsummer Night's Dream* expresses his disdain for Bottom. Branding Bottom as a histrionic lout "bred in a tiring-room," Johnson finds him overbearing and bent on stealing the stage from his cohorts. He says, "He is for engrossing every part and would exclude his inferiors from all possibility of distinction." Johnson also notes, "Bottom was perhaps the head of a rival house, and is therefore honoured with an ass's head." Nevertheless, Johnson concludes that the strange and disparate parts of *A Midsummer Night's Dream* manage to work together to provide the delightful experience that Shakespeare intended.

1708—John Downes, from *Roscius Anglicanus*

John Downes was a bookkeeper and prompter for Davenant's theater at Lincoln's Inn Fields from June 1661 through October 1706. Upon his retirement, Downes recorded his experience at the theater along with some impressions of the great actors with whom he worked. His work, *Roscius Anglicanus, or an Historical Review of the Stage,* was first published in 1708.

The Fairy Queen made into an Opera from a Comedy of Mr. *Shakespears*: This in Ornaments was Superior . . . especially in Cloaths, for all the Singers and Dancers, Scenes, Machines and Decorations, all most profusely set off; and excellently perform'd chiefly the Instrumental and Vocal part Compos'd by the said Mr *Purcel*, and Dances by Mr *Priest*. The Court and Town were wonderfully satisfy'd with it; but the Expences in setting it out being so great, the Company got very little by it.

1765—Thomas Percy, from *Reliques of Ancient English Poetry*

Thomas Percy (1729–1811), chaplain to King George III and, subsequently, Bishop of Dromore, was editor of the *Tatler*, *Guardian*, and

Spectator and the author of *Five Pieces of Runic Poetry* (1763). His most famous work, *Reliques of Ancient English Poetry* (1765), the first of the great ballad collections, contributed to the Romantic poets' interest in ballads, as evidenced by the *Lyrical Ballads* of William Wordsworth and Samuel Taylor Coleridge.

ROBIN GOODFELLOW, alias PUCKE, alias HOBGOBLIN, in the creed of ancient superstition, was a kind of merry sprite, whose character and achievements are recorded in this ballad, and in those well-known lines of Milton's L'Allegro, which the antiquarian Peck supposes to be owing to it:–

Tells how the drudging GOBLIN swet
To earn his cream-bowle duly set;
When in one night, ere glimpse of morne,
His shadowy flail hath thresh'd the corn
That ten day-labourers could not end;
Then lies him down the lubbar fiend,
And stretch'd out all the chimney's length,
Basks at the fire his hairy strength,
And crop-full out of doors he flings,
Ere the first cock his matins rings.

The reader had reduced all these whimsies to a kind of system, as regular, and perhaps more consistent, than many parts of classic mythology; a proof of the extensive influence and vast antiquity of these superstitions. Mankind, and especially the common people, could not everywhere have been so unanimously agreed concerning these arbitrary notions, if they had not prevailed among them for many ages. Indeed, a learned friend in Wales assures the editor that the existence of Fairies and Goblins is alluded to in the most ancient British Bards, who mention them under various names, one of the most common of which signifies 'The spirits of the mountains.'

——— ——— ———

1765—Samuel Johnson. "*A Midsummer Night's Dream*," from *Notes on Shakespeare's Plays*

Samuel Johnson (1709–1784) often referred to simply as Dr. Johnson, was one of England's greatest literary figures: a poet, essayist, biographer, and lexicographer. He is often considered the finest critic of

English literature and was a great wit and prose stylist. His work includes *Prefaces, Biographical and Critical, to the Works of the English Poets* (1779–1781). The following are among the most interesting notes he appended to the text of his edition of *A Midsummer Night's Dream*.

I.i.204 (13,6)

[Before the time I did Lysander see,
Seem'd Athens like a paradise to me]
Perhaps every reader may not discover the propriety of these lines. Hermia is willing to comfort Helena, and to avoid all appearance of triumph over her. She therefore bids her not to consider the power of pleasing, as an advantage to be much envied or much desired, since Hermia, whom she considers as possessing it in the supreme degree, has found no other effect of it than the loss of happiness.

I.ii (16,2)

[Enter Quince the carpenter, Snug the joiner. Bottom the weaver. Flute the bellows-mender. Snout the tinker, and Starveling the taylor]
In this scene Shakespeare takes advantage of his knowledge of the theatre, to ridicule the prejudices and competitions of the players. Bottom, who is generally acknowledged the principal actor, declares his inclination to be for a tyrant, for a part of fury, tumult, and noise, such as every young man pants to perform when he first steps upon the stage. The same Bottom, who seems bred in a tiring-room, has another histrionical passion. He is for engrossing every part, and would exclude his inferiors from all possibility of distinction. He is therefore desirous to play Pyramus, Thisbe, and the Lyon at the same time.

I.ii.52 (18,6)

[Flu. Nay, faith, let me not play a woman; I have a beard coming.
Quin. That's all one, you shall play it in a masque; and you may speak as small as you will]
This passage shews how the want of women on the old stage was supplied. If they had not a young man who could perform the part with a face that might pass for feminine, the character was acted in a mask, which was at that time part of a lady's dress so much in use that it did not give any unusual appearance to the scene: and he that could modulate his voice in a female tone might play the women very successfully. It is observed in Downes's Memoirs of the Playhouse, that one of these counterfeit heroines moved the passions more strongly than the women that have since been brought upon the stage. Some of the catastrophes of the old comedies, which make lovers marry the wrong women, are, by recollection of the common use of masks, brought nearer to probability.

I.ii.98 (20,8)
[Bot. I will discharge it in either your straw-coloured beard, your orange tawny beard, your purple-in grain beard, or your French crown-coloured beard; your perfect yellow]

Here Bottom again discovers a true genius for the stage by his solicitude for propriety of dress, and his deliberation which beard to choose among many beards, all unnatural.

II.i.40 (24,6)
[Those that Hobgoblin call you, and sweet Puck, You do their work]
To those traditionary opinions Milton has reference in L'Allegro,

> Then to the spicy nut-brown ale,
> With stories told of many a feat.
> How Fairy Mab the junkets eat;
> She was pinch'd and pull'd she said.
> And he by Frier's lapthorp led;
> Tells how the drudging goblin sweat
> To earn his cream-bowl duly set,
> When in one night ere glimpse of morn
> His shadowy flail had thresh'd the corn
> Which ten day-labourers could not end.
> Then lies him down the lubber fiend.

A like account of Puck is given by Drayton,

> He meeteth Puck, which most men call
> Hobgoblin, and on him doth fall.—
> This Puck seems but a dreaming dolt,
> Still walking like a ragged colt,
> And oft out of a bed doth bolt,
>   Of purpose to deceive us;
> And leading us makes us to stray.
> Long winter's nights out of the way.
> And when we stick in mire and clay.
>   He doth with laughter leave us.

It will be apparent to him that shall compare Drayton's poem with this play, that either one of the poets copied the other, or, as I rather believe, that there was then some system of the fairy empire generally received, which they both represented as accurately as they could. Whether Drayton or Shakespeare wrote first, I cannot discover.

II.i.42 (25,7)

[Puck. Thou speak'st aright]

. . .

It seems that in the Fairy mythology Puck, or Hobgoblin, was the trusty servant of Oberon, and always employed to watch or detect the intrigues of Queen Mab, called by Shakespeare Titania. For in Drayton's Nynphidia, the same fairies are engaged in the same business. Mab has an amour with Pigwiggen; Oberon being jealous, sends Hobgoblin to catch them, and one of Mab's nymphs opposes him by a spell.

II.i.100 (29,2)

[The human mortals want their winter here]

After all the endeavours of the editors, this passage still remains to me unintelligible. I cannot see why winter is, in the general confusion of the year now described, more wanted than any other season. Dr. Warburton observes that he alludes to our practice of singing carols in December; but though Shakespeare is no great chronologer in his dramas, I think he has never so mingled true and false religion, as to give us reason for believing that he would make the moon incensed for the omission of our carols. I therefore imagine him to have meant heathen rites of adoration. This is not all the difficulty. Titania's account of this calamity is not sufficiently consequential. Men find no winter, therefore they sing no hymns; the moon provoked by this omission, alters the seasons: that is, the alteration of the seasons produces the alteration of the seasons. I am far from supposing that Shakespeare might not sometimes think confusedly, and therefore am not sure that the passage is corrupted . . .

III.i (48,3)

In the time of Shakespeare, there were many companies of players, sometimes five at the same time, contending for the favour of the publick. Of these some were undoubtedly very unskilful and very poor, and it is probable that the design of this scene was to ridicule their ignorance, and the odd expedients to which they might be driven by the want of proper decorations. Bottom was perhaps the head of a rival house, and is therefore honoured with an ass's head.

III.i.173 (55,6)

[the fiery glow-worm's eyes]

I know not how Shakespeare, who commonly derived his knowledge of nature from his own observation, happened to place the glow-worm's light in his eyes, which is only in his tail.

IV.i (75,6)

I see no reason why the fourth act should begin here, when there seems no interruption of the action. In the old quartos of 1600, there is no division of acts, which seems to have been afterwards arbitrarily made in the first folio, and may therefore be altered at pleasure . . .

IV.i.107 (81,9)

[our observation is perform'd]
The honours due to the morning of May. I know not why Shakespear calls this play a Midsummer-Night's Dream, when he so carefully informs us that it happened on the night preceding May day.

V.i.147 (95,4)

[Whereat, with blade, with bloody blameful blade]
Mr. Upton rightly observes, that Shakespeare in this line ridicules the affectation of beginning many words with the same letter. He might have remarked the same of
  The raging rocks
  and shivering shocks.
Gascoigne, contemporary with our poet, remarks and blames the same affectation.

V.i.408 (106,6)

[Now, until the break of day]
This speech, which both the old quartos give to Oberon, is in the edition of 1623, and in all the following, printed as the song. I have restored it to Oberon, as it apparently contains not the blessing which he intends to bestow on the bed, but his declaration that he will bless it, and his orders to the fairies how to perform the necessary rites. But where then is the song?—I am afraid it is gone after many other things of greater value. The truth is that two songs are lost. The series of the scene is this; after the speech of Puck, Oberon enters, and calls his fairies to a song, which song is apparently wanting in all the copies. Next Titania leads another song, which is indeed lost like the former, tho' the editors have endeavoured to find it. Then Oberon dismisses his fairies to the dispatch of the ceremonies.

The songs, I suppose, were lost, because they were not inserted in the players parts, from which the drama was printed.

General Observation.

Of this play there are two editions in quarto; one printed for Thomas Fisher, the other for James Roberts, both in 1600. I have used the copy of Roberts, very carefully collated, as it seems, with that of Fisher. Neither of the editions approach to exactness. Fisher is sometimes preferable, but Roberts was followed, though not without some variations, by Hemings and Condel, and they by all the folios that succeeded them.

Wild and fantastical as this play is, all the parts in their various modes are well written, and give the kind of pleasure which the author designed. Fairies in his time were much in fashion; common tradition had made them familiar, and Spenser's poem had made them great.

A MIDSUMMER NIGHT'S DREAM
IN THE NINETEENTH CENTURY
❧

With the advent of the early nineteenth-century Romantic movement, the magical fantasy world of *A Midsummer Night's Dream* finally gained the appreciation and acclaim it deserved. August Wilhelm Schlegel's comments compare the play to *The Tempest*, which likewise presents "a wonderful world of spirits . . . interwoven with the turmoil of human passions and with the farcical adventures of folly," and refutes those critics who hold unreservedly that *The Tempest* is the superior work. Schlegel contends that in *A Midsummer Night's Dream* Shakespeare has worked his own magic as a playwright in his skillful and seemingly effortless combination of disparate elements, thus creating a "fairy world . . . [that] resembles those elegant pieces of arabesque, where little genii with butterfly wings rise, half embodied, above the flower-cups." Schlegel also praises *A Midsummer Night's Dream* for its presentation of an environment in which violence and threats of utmost cruelty are transformed into lighthearted fun. He insists that its disparate elements, including an odd mixture of the human and the fanciful as well as the seemingly gratuitous subplot of Pyramus and Thisby, are "necessary to each other for the formation of a whole."

The great essayist William Hazlitt extols the virtues of the beloved artisans in the play, especially the ever-resourceful and talented leader, Bottom the Weaver. He assigns to each character a social function within the little community: Snug the Joiner is the moral voice, proceeding with caution in all things, and Starveling the Tailor is the custodian of peace. But Hazlitt favors Bottom the Weaver above all others as the one who understands the dynamics of theatricality: "Bottom seems to have understood the subject of dramatic illusion at least as well as any modern essayist. If our holiday mechanic rules the roast among his fellows, he is no less at home in his new character of an ass, 'with amiable cheeks, and fair large ears.'" Hazlitt further states that Puck, the leader of the fairy band, is vastly different from Ariel, his counterpart in *The Tempest*, and he praises Shakespeare for having created such immensely different characters from the same imaginative material. While Puck is a fun-loving imp, "a most Epicurean little gentleman," who revels in his mischief, Ariel has a heavier and more determined nature.

Hazlitt concludes that those critics who find Shakespeare to be a gloomy writer have not seen or appreciated his genius for "delicacy and sportive gaiety."

In his commentary on *A Midsummer Night's Dream*, Thomas DeQuincey delights in the magic of Shakespeare's genius and his poetic representation of the fairy realm over which Oberon and Titania preside, comparing them to the much less delightful witches of *Macbeth*, who belong to a different and dangerous species of the supernatural. DeQuincey writes, "And in no other exhibition of this dreamy population of the moonlight forests and forest-lawns are the circumstantial proprieties of fairy life so exquisitely imagined, sustained, or expressed."

In his discussion of Shakespeare's humor in general, Edward Dowden focuses, like many other critics, on his favorite character in *A Midsummer Night's Dream*—Bottom the Weaver—whom he finds the most consummate representation of the absurd. Indeed, Dowden asserts that all his peers pale in comparison with this magnificent and ever-resourceful being: "With what a magnificent multiplicity of gifts he is endowed! . . . Bottom, though his chief humour is for a tyrant, knows not how to suppress his almost equal gift for playing a lady."

G.G. Gervinus pays tribute to Shakespeare's extraordinary originality in combining Saxon myths with other ancient religious and historical legends and investigates several critical issues essential to understanding the play's complexity. Gervinus identifies Cupid as the ultimate, albeit less obvious, cause of trouble in the play: "We have already said that the play of amorous caprice proceeded from no inner impulse of the soul, but from external powers, from the influence of gods and fairies, among whom Cupid, the demon of old mythology, only appears behind the scenes; while, on the other hand, the fairies, . . . occupy the main place upon the stage." Gervinus also offers a thoughtful analysis of the historical background of *A Midsummer Night's Dream*, acknowledging that although it was written with Queen Elizabeth in mind, Shakespeare does not lapse into the grandiose flattery found in Spenser's *The Faerie Queen* but, rather, renders Elizabeth inaccessible to the world of fancy, an important attribute for the head of state. Gervinus thus identifies this play as the allegory of dreams and the errors attendant to this realm when reason and consciousness are seduced by passion and Cupid's machinations. With respect to the world of fairies, Gervinus analyzes the possible sources from which Shakespeare may have drawn and, most importantly, the ways in which he transformed the various rudiments of English, Scottish, and German legends into a magical and powerful realm. He comments, "Shakespeare has given form and place to the fairy kingdom, and with the natural creative power of genius he has breathed a soul into his merry little citizens, thus imparting a living centre to their nature and their office, their behaviour and their doings."

Adopting a philosophical perspective, the American critic H.N. Hudson finds great merit in such instances as Theseus's speech at the beginning of Act V in which the Athenian king injects a cogent argument within what is seemingly a very childish play. After praising Theseus's insight into the similarities and distinctions of lunatics, lovers, and poets, Hudson finds a justification for the defects of *A Midsummer Night's Dream*, namely that it is set in a fairy world replete with elaborate and incredible conceits, and considers the plot as a carefully wrought plan in which the more profound elements are meant to balance and exonerate what may be deemed its silly or even offensive aspects. Hudson's essay continues with a discussion of some of the literary influences on *A Midsummer Night's Dream*, such as Ovid, Chaucer, and Golding, as well as a thoughtful analysis of the various characters, including an identification of Bottom as the one who comes closest to claiming human attributes. He concludes by praising Shakespeare's originality, as so many other critics do as well: "Besides that its very essence is irregularity, so that it cannot be fairly brought to the test of rules, the play forms properly a class by itself: literature has nothing else really like it; nothing therefore with which it may be compared, and its merits adjusted."

1809—August Wilhelm von Schlegel, from *A Course of Lectures on Dramatic Art and Literature*, tr. John Black

August Wilhelm Schlegel (1767–1845) was an influential German critic and poet and a key figure in the German Romantic movement. He translated a number of Shakespeare's plays into German.

The Midsummer Night's Dream and *The Tempest*, may be in so far compared together that in both the influence of a wonderful world of spirits is interwoven with the turmoil of human passions and with the farcical adventures of folly. *The Midsummer Night's Dream* is certainly an earlier production; but *The Tempest*, according to all appearance, was written in Shakspeare's later days: hence most critics, on the supposition that the poet must have continued to improve with increasing maturity of mind, have honoured the last piece with a marked preference. I cannot, however, altogether concur with them: the internal merit of these two works are, in my opinion, pretty nearly balanced, and a predilection for the one or the other can only be governed by personal taste. In profound and original characterization the superiority of *The Tempest* is obvious: as a whole we must always admire the masterly skill which he has here displayed in the economy of his means, and the dexterity with which he has disguised his preparations,—the scaffoldings for the wonderful aerial structure. In *The Midsummer Night's Dream*, on the other hand, there flows a luxuriant vein of the boldest and most fantastical invention; the most extraordinary combination of the most dissimilar ingredients seems to have been brought about without effort by some ingenious and lucky accident, and the colours are of such clear transparency that we think the whole of the variegated fabric may be blown away with a breath. The fairy world here described resembles those elegant pieces of arabesque, where little genii with butterfly wings rise, half embodied, above the flower-cups. Twilight, moonshine, dew, and spring perfumes, are the element of these tender spirits; they assist nature in embroidering her carpet with green leaves, many-coloured flowers, and glittering insects; in the human world they do but make sport childishly and waywardly with their beneficent or noxious influences. Their most violent rage dissolves in good-natured raillery; their passions, stripped of all earthly matter, are merely an ideal dream. To correspond with this, the loves of mortals are painted as a poetical enchantment, which, by a contrary enchantment, may be immediately suspended, and then renewed again. The different parts of the plot; the wedding of Theseus and Hippolyta, Oberon and Titania's quarrel, the flight of the two pair of lovers, and the theatrical manoeuvres of the mechanics, are so lightly and happily interwoven that they seem necessary to each other for the formation of a whole. Oberon is desirous of relieving the lovers from their perplexities, but greatly adds to them through the mistakes of his minister, till he at last comes really to the aid of their fruitless amorous pain, their inconstancy and jealousy, and restores fidelity to its old rights. The extremes of fanciful and vulgar are united when the enchanted Titania awakes and falls in love with a coarse mechanic with an ass's head, who represents, or rather disfigures, the part of a tragical lover. The droll wonder of Bottom's transformation is merely the translation of a metaphor in its literal sense; but in his behaviour during the tender homage of the Fairy Queen we have an amusing proof how much the consciousness of such a head-dress heightens the effect of his usual folly. Theseus and Hippolyta are, as it were, a splendid frame for the picture; they take no part in the action, but surround it with a stately pomp. The discourse of the hero and his Amazon, as they course through the forest with their noisy hunting-train, works upon the imagination like the fresh breath of morning, before which the shapes of night disappear. Pyramus and Thisbe is not unmeaningly chosen as the grotesque play within the play; it is exactly like the pathetic part of the piece, a secret meeting of two lovers in the forest, and their separation by an unfortunate accident, and closes the whole with the most amusing parody.

⸺ᴗᴠᴠᴧ⸺ ⸺ᴗᴠᴠᴧ⸺ ⸺ᴗᴠᴠᴧ⸺

1817—William Hazlitt. *"The Midsummer Night's Dream,"* from *Characters of Shakespear's Plays*

William Hazlitt (1778–1830) was an English essayist and one of the finest Shakespearean critics of the nineteenth century.

Bottom the Weaver is a character that has not had justice done him. He is the most romantic of mechanics. And what a list of companions he has—Quince the Carpenter, Snug the Joiner, Flute the Bellows-mender, Snout the Tinker, Starveling the Tailor; and then again, what a group of fairy attendants, Puck, Peaseblossom, Cobweb, Moth, and Mustard-seed! It has been observed that Shakespear's characters are constructed upon deep physiological principles; and there is something in this play which looks very like it. Bottom the Weaver, who takes the lead of

> This crew of patches, rude mechanicals,
> That work for bread upon Athenian stalls,

follows a sedentary trade, and he is accordingly represented as conceited, serious, and fantastical. He is ready to undertake any thing and every thing, as if it was as much a matter of course as the motion of his loom and shuttle. He is for playing the tyrant, the lover, the lady, the lion. 'He will roar that it shall do any man's heart good to hear him'; and this being objected to as improper, he still has a resource in his good opinion of himself, and 'will roar you an 'twere any nightingale.' Snug the Joiner is the moral man of the piece, who proceeds by measurement and discretion in all things. You see him with his rule and compasses in his hand. 'Have you the lion's part written? Pray you, if it be, give it me, for I am slow of study.'—'You may do it extempore,' says Quince, 'for it is nothing but roaring.' Starveling the Tailor keeps the peace, and objects to the lion and the drawn sword. 'I believe we must leave the killing out when all's done.' Starveling, however, does not start the objections himself, but seconds them when made by others, as if he had not spirit to express his fears without encouragement. It is too much to suppose all this intentional: but it very luckily falls out so. Nature includes all that is implied in the most subtle analytical distinctions; and the same distinctions will be found in Shakespear. Bottom, who is not only chief actor, but stage-manager for the occasion, has a device to obviate the danger of frightening the ladies: 'Write me a prologue, and let the prologue seem to say, we will do no harm with our swords, and that Pyramus is not killed indeed; and for better assurance, tell them that I, Pyramus, am not Pyramus, but Bottom the Weaver: this will put them out of fear.' Bottom seems to have understood the subject of dramatic illusion at least as well as any modern essayist. If our holiday mechanic rules the roast among his fellows, he is no less at home in his new character of an ass, 'with amiable cheeks, and fair large ears.' He instinctively acquires a most learned taste, and grows fastidious in the choice of dried peas and bottled hay. He is quite familiar with his new attendants, and assigns them their parts with all due gravity. 'Monsieur Cobweb, good Monsieur, get your weapon in your hand, and kill me a red-hipt humble bee on the top of a thistle, and, good

Monsieur, bring me the honey-bag.' What an exact knowledge is here shewn of natural history!

Puck, or Robin Goodfellow, is the leader of the fairy band. He is the Ariel of the *Midsummer Night's Dream;* and yet as unlike as can be to the Ariel in *The Tempest.* No other poet could have made two such different characters out of the same fanciful materials and situations. Ariel is a minister of retribution, who is touched with the sense of pity at the woes he inflicts. Puck is a mad-cap sprite, full of wantonness and mischief, who laughs at those whom he misleads—'Lord, what fools these mortals be!' Ariel cleaves the air, and executes his mission with the zeal of a winged messenger; Puck is borne along on his fairy errand like the light and glittering gossamer before the breeze. He is, indeed, a most Epicurean little gentleman, dealing in quaint devices, and faring in dainty delights. Prospero and his world of spirits are a set of moralists: but with Oberon and his fairies we are launched at once into the empire of the butterflies. How beautifully is this race of beings contrasted with the men and women actors in the scene, by a single epithet which Titania gives to the latter, 'the human mortals!' It is astonishing that Shakespear should be considered, not only by foreigners, but by many of our own critics, as a gloomy and heavy writer, who painted nothing but 'gorgons and hydras, and chimeras dire.' His subtlety exceeds that of all other dramatic writers, insomuch that a celebrated person of the present day said that he regarded him rather as a metaphysician than a poet. His delicacy and sportive gaiety are infinite. In the *Midsummer Night's Dream* alone, we should imagine, there is more sweetness and beauty of description than in the whole range of French poetry put together. What we mean is this, that we will produce out of that single play ten passages, to which we do not think any ten passages in the works of the French poets can be opposed, displaying equal fancy and imagery. Shall we mention the remonstrance of Helena to Hermia, or Titania's description of her fairy train, or her disputes with Oberon about the Indian boy, or Puck's account of himself and his employments, or the Fairy Queen's exhortation to the elves to pay due attendance upon her favourite, Bottom; or Hippolita's description of a chace, or Theseus's answer? The two last are as heroical and spirited as the others are full of luscious tenderness. The reading of this play is like wandering in a grove by moonlight: the descriptions breathe a sweetness like odours thrown from beds of flowers.

1838—Thomas DeQuincey, from "Shakspeare"

Thomas DeQuincey (1785-1859), an English essayist and critic, was the author of *Confessions of an English Opium-Eater*, a long essay "On Milton" and two essays on Pope, "The Poetry of Pope" and "Lord

Carlisle on Pope," as well as numerous articles for *London Magazine* and *Blackwood's*.

. . . In the *Midsummer-Night's Dream,* again, we have the old traditional fairy, a lovely mode of preternatural life, remodified by Shakspeare's eternal talisman. Oberon and Titania remind us at first glance of Ariel; they approach, but how far they recede: they are like—"like, but oh, how different!" And in no other exhibition of this dreamy population of the moonlight forests and forest-lawns are the circumstantial proprieties of fairy life so exquisitely imagined, sustained, or expressed. The dialogue between Oberon and Titania is, of itself, and taken separately from its connexion, one of the most delightful poetic scenes that literature affords. The witches in *Macbeth* are another variety of supernatural life in which Shakspeare's power to enchant and to disenchant are alike portentous.

1845—G.G. Gervinus. *"Midsummer-Night's Dream,"* from *Shakespeare Commentaries*

Georg Gottfried Gervinus (1805–1871) was a German literary and political historian who wrote extensively on Shakespeare. He also composed the first comprehensive history of German literature written both with scholarly erudition and literary skill.

If *All's Well That Ends Well* be read immediately between *Love's Labour's Lost* and the *Midsummer-Night's Dream,* we feel that in the former the matured hand of the poet was at work, while the two other pieces stand in closer connection. The performance of the comic parts by the clowns affords a resemblance between the two pieces, but this resemblance appears still more plainly in the mode of diction. Apart from the fairy songs, in which Shakespeare, in a masterly manner, preserves the popular tone of the style which existed before him, the play bears prominently the stamp of the Italian school. The language—picturesque, descriptive, and florid with conceits—the too apparent alliterations, the doggrel passages which extend over the passionate and impressive scenes, and the old mythology so suited to the subject; all this places the piece in a close, or at least not remote relation, to *Love's Labour's Lost.* As in this play, the story and the original combination of the characters of ancient, religious, and historical legends with those of the popular Saxon myths, are the property and invention of the poet. As in *Love's Labour's Lost,* utterly unlike the characterisation which we have just seen in *All's Well That Ends Well,* the acting characters are distinguished only by a very general outline; the strongest distinction is that between the little pert Hermia, shrewish and irritable even at school, and the slender yielding Helena, distrustful and reproachful of herself; the distinction is less apparent between the upright open Lysander and the somewhat malicious and inconstant Demetrius. The period of the origin of the play—which like *Henry VIII.* and the *Tempest* may have been written in honour of the nuptials of some noble couple—is placed at about 1594 or 1596. The marriage of Theseus is the turning-point of the action of the piece, which comprises the clowns, fairies, and the common race of men. The piece is a masque, one of those dramas for special occasions appointed for private representation, which Ben Jonson especially brought to perfection. In England this species of drama has as little a law of its own as the historical drama; compared to the ordinary drama it exhibits, according to Halpin, an insensible transition, undistinguishable by definition. As in the historical drama, its distinction from the free drama almost entirely arises from the nature and the mass of the matter; so in the masque, it proceeds from the occasion of its origin, from its necessary reference to it, and from the allegorical elements which are introduced. These latter, it must be admitted, have given a peculiar stamp to the *Midsummer-Night's Dream* among the rest of Shakespeare's works.

Upon the most superficial reading we perceive that the actions in the *Midsummer-Night's Dream,* still more than the characters themselves, are treated quite differently to those in other plays of Shakespeare. The presence of an underlying motive—the great art and true magic wand of the poet—has here been completely disregarded. Instead of reasonable inducements, instead of natural impulses arising from character and circumstance, caprice is master here. We meet with a double pair, who are entangled in strange mistakes, the motives to which we, however, seek for in vain in the nature of the actors themselves. Demetrius, like Proteus in the *Two Gentlemen of Verona,* has left a bride, and, like Proteus, woos the bride of his friend Lysander. This Lysander has fled with Hermia to seek a spot where the law of Athens cannot pursue them. Secretly, we are told, they both steal away into the wood; Demetrius in fury follows them, and, impelled by love, Helena fastens herself like a burr upon the heels of the latter. Alike devoid of conscience, Hermia errs at first through want of due obedience to her father, and Demetrius through faithlessness to his betrothed Helena, Helena through treachery to her friend Hermia, and Lysander through mockery of his father-in-law. The strife in the first act, in which we cannot trace any distinct moral motives, is in the third act changed into a perfect confusion owing to influences of an entirely external character. In the fairy world a similar disorder exists between Oberon and Titania. The play of Pyramus and Thisbe, enacted by the honest citizens, forms a comic-tragic counterpart to the tragic-comic point of the plot, depicting two lovers, who behind their parents' backs 'think no scorn to woo by moonlight,' and through a mere accident come to a tragic end.

The human beings in the main plot of the piece are apparently impelled by mere amorous caprice; Demetrius is betrothed, then Helena pleases him no longer, he trifles with Hermia, and at the close he remembers this breach of faith only as the trifling of youth. External powers and not inward impulses and feelings appear as the cause of these amorous caprices. In the first place, the brain is heated by the warm season, the first night in May, the ghost-hour of the mystic powers; for even elsewhere Shakespeare occasionally calls a piece of folly the madness of a midsummer-day, or a dog-day's fever; and in the 98th sonnet he speaks of April as the time which puts 'the spirit of youth in everything,' making even the 'heavy Saturn laugh and leap with him.' Then Cupid, who appears in the background of the piece as a real character, misleading the judgment and blinding the eyes, takes delight in causing a frivolous breach of faith. And last of all we see the lovers completely in the hands of the fairies, who ensnare their senses and bring them into that tumult of confusion, the unravelling of which, like the entanglement itself, is to come from without. These delusions of blind passion, this jugglery of the senses during the sleep of reason, these changes of mind and errors of 'seething brains,' these actions without any higher centre of a mental and moral bearing, are compared, as it were, to a dream which unrolls before us with its fearful complications, and from which there is no deliverance but in awaking and in the recovery of consciousness.

The piece is called a *Midsummer-Night's Dream;* the Epilogue expresses satisfaction, if the spectator will regard the piece as a dream; for in a dream time and locality are obliterated; a certain twilight and dusk is spread over the whole; Oberon desires that all shall regard the matter as a dream, and so it is. Titania speaks of her adventure as a vision, Bottom of his metamorphosis as a dream; all the rest awake at last out of a sleep of weariness, and the events leave upon them the impression of a dream. The sober Theseus esteems their stories as nothing else than dreams and fantasies. Indeed these allusions in the play must have suggested to Coleridge and others the idea that the poet had intentionally aimed at letting the piece glide by as a dream. We only wonder that, with this opinion, they have not reached the inner kernel in which this intention of the poet really lies enshrined—an intention which has not only given a name to the piece, but has called forth as by magic a free poetic creation of the greatest value. For it is indeed to be expected from our poet, that such an intention on his side were not to be sought for in the mere shell. If this intention were only shown in those poetical externals, in that fragrant charm of rhythm and verse, in that harassing suspense, and in that dusky twilight, then this were but a shallow work of superficial grace, by the sole use of which a poet like Shakespeare would never have dreamt of accomplishing anything worth the while.

We will now return to an examination of the play and its contents; and taking a higher and more commanding view, we will endeavour to reach the aim which Coleridge in truth only divined. We have already said that the play of amorous caprice proceeded from no inner impulse of the soul, but from external powers, from the influence of gods and fairies, among whom Cupid, the demon of the old mythology, only appears behind the scenes; while, on the other hand, the fairies, the spirits of later superstition, occupy the main place upon the stage. If we look at the functions which the poet has committed to both, namely to the god of love and to the fairies, we find to our surprise that they are perfectly similar. The workings of each upon the passions of men are the same. The infidelity of Theseus towards his many forsaken ones—Ariadne, Antiopa, and Perigenia—which according to the ancient myth, we should ascribe to Cupid and to the intoxication of sensuous love, are imputed in the *Midsummer-Night's Dream* to the elfin king. Even before the fairies appear in the play, Demetrius is prompted by the infatuation of blind love, and Puck expressly says that it is not he but Cupid who originated this madness of mortals; the same may be inferred also with Titania and the boy. The fairies pursue these errors still further, in the same manner as Cupid had begun them; they increase and heal them; the juice of a flower, Dian's bud, is employed to cure the perplexities of love in both Lysander and Titania; the juice of another flower (Cupid's) had caused them. This latter flower had received its wondrous power from a wound by Cupid's shaft. The power conveyed by the shaft was perceived by the elfin king, who knew how to use it; Oberon is closely initiated into the deepest secrets of the love-god, but not so his servant Puck.

The famous passage, in which Oberon orders Puck to fetch him this herb with its ensnaring charm, is as follows:

> My gentle Puck, come hither. Thou rememberest
> Since once I sat upon a promontory,
> And heard a mermaid on a dolphin's back
> Uttering such dulcet and harmonious breath
> That the rude sea grew civil at her song
> And certain stars shot madly from their spheres,
> To hear the sea-maid's music...
> That very time I saw (*but thou couldst not*)
> Flying between the cold moon and the earth,
> Cupid all arm'd: a certain aim he took
> At a fair vestal throned by the west,
> And loosed his love-shaft smartly from his bow,
> As it should pierce a hundred thousand hearts;
> But I might see young Cupid's fiery shaft
> Quench'd in the chaste beams of the watery moon,
> And the imperial votaress passed on,
> In maiden meditation, fancy-free.
> Yet mark'd I where the bolt of Cupid fell:
> It fell upon a little western flower,
> Before milk-white, now purple with love's wound,

And maidens call it love-in-idleness.
Fetch me that flower.

This passage has recently, in the writings of the Shakespeare Society, received a spirited interpretation by Halpin *(Oberon's Vision)*, which shows us that we can scarcely seek for too much in our poet; that even in the highest flight of his imagination, he never leaves the ground of reality; and that in every touch, however episodical it may appear, he ever inserts the profoundest allusions to his main subject. We know well that in the eyes of the dry critic this interpretation, though it has one firm basis of fact, has found little favour; to us this is not very conceivable: for every investigation has long proved how gladly this realistic poet maintained, in the smallest allusions as well as in the greatest designs, lively relations to the times and places round him; how in his freest tragic creations he loved to refer to historical circumstances, founding even the most foolish speeches and actions of his clowns, of his grave-diggers in *Hamlet*, or his patrols in *Much Ado about Nothing*, upon actual circumstances; and thus giving them by this very circumstance that value of indisputable truth to nature which distinguishes them so palpably beyond all other caricatures. Is it not natural that he should have been impelled to give to just such a sweet allegory as this the firmest possible basis of fact? To us, therefore, Halpin's interpretation of this passage is all the more unquestionable, as it gives a most definite purpose to the innermost spirit of the whole play. We must therefore, before we proceed further, first consider more narrowly this episodical narrative and its bearing upon the fundamental idea of the *Midsummer-Night's Dream.*

It has always been agreed that by the vestal, throned by the west, from whom Cupid's shaft glided off, Queen Elizabeth was intended; and the whole passage was in consequence esteemed as a delicate flattery of the maiden queen. But we see at once by this instance, that Shakespeare—extraordinary in this respect as in every other—knew how to make his courtly flatteries, of which he was on all occasions most sparing, subservient to the aesthetic or moral aims of his poetry, by the introduction of deeper poetic or moral bearings. It was thus with this passage, which has now received a much more extended interpretation. Cupid 'all armed' is referred to the Earl of Leicester's wooing of Elizabeth and to his great preparations at Kenilworth for this purpose (1575). From descriptions of these festivities (Gascoyne's *Princely Pleasures*, 1576, and Laneham's *Letter*, 1575), we know, that at the spectacles and fireworks which enlivened the rejoicings, a singing mermaid was introduced, swimming on smooth water upon a dolphin's back, amid shooting stars; these characteristics agree with those which Oberon specifies to Puck. The arrow aimed at the priestess of Diana, whose bud possesses the power of quenching love, and which had such force over Cupid's flower, rebounded. By the flower upon which it fell wounding, Halpin understands the Countess Lettice of Essex, with whom Leicester carried on a clandestine intercourse while her husband was absent in Ireland, who, apprised of the matter, returned in 1576, and was poisoned on the journey. The flower was milk-white, innocent, but purple with love's wound, which denoted her fall or the deeper blush of her husband's murder. The name is 'love in idleness,' which Halpin refers to the listlessness of her heart during the absence of her husband; for on other occasions also Shakespeare uses this popular denomination of the pansy, to denote a love which surprises and affects those who are indolent, unarmed, and devoid of all other feeling and aspiration. While Oberon declares to Puck that he marked the adventure, though the servant could not, the poet appears to denote the strict mystery which concealed this affair, and which might be known to him, because, as we may remember, the execution of his maternal relative, Edward Arden (1583), was closely connected with it; and because a son of that Lettice, the famous Robert Devereux, Earl of Essex, the favourite of Elizabeth, and subsequently the victim of her displeasure, was early a patron and protector of Shakespeare.

How significant then does this little allegorical episode become, which, even when regarded only as a poetic ornament, is full of grace and beauty! Whilst Spenser at that very time had extolled Elizabeth as the *Faerie Queen,* Shakespeare, on the contrary, represents her rather as a being unapproachable by this world of fancy. His courtesy to the queen becomes transformed into a very serious meaning: for, contrasting with this insanity of love, emphasis is placed upon the other extreme, the victory of Diana over Cupid, of the mind over the body, of maiden contemplativeness over the jugglery of love; and even in other passages of the piece those are extolled as 'thrice blessed, that master so their blood, to undergo such maiden pilgrimage.' But with regard to the bearing of the passage upon the actual purport of the *Midsummer-Night's Dream,* the poet carries back the mind to a circumstance in real life, which, like an integral part, lies in close parallel with the story of the piece. More criminal and more dissolute acts, prompted by the blind passion of love, were at that time committed in reality than were ever represented in the drama. The ensnaring charm, embodied in a flower, has an effect upon the entanglements of the lovers in the play. And whatever this representation might lack in probability and psychological completeness (for the sweet allegory of the poet was not to be overburdened with too much of the prose of characterisation), the spectator with poetic faith may explain by the magic sap of the flower, or with pragmatic soberness may interpret by analogy with the actual circumstance which the poet has converted into this exquisite allegory.

But it is time that we should return from this digression. We have before said that the piece appears designed to be treated as a dream; not merely in outer form and colouring, but also in inner signification. The errors of that blind intoxication of the senses, which form the main point of the play, appear to us to be an allegorical picture of the errors of a life of dreams. Reason and consciousness are cast aside in that intoxicating passion as in a dream; Cupid's delight in breach of faith and Jove's merriment at the perjury of the lovers cause the actions of those who are in the power of the God of Love to appear almost as unaccountable as the sins which we commit in a dream. We find moreover that the actions and occupations of Cupid and of the fairies throughout the piece are interwoven or alternate. And this appears to us to confirm most forcibly the intention of the poet to compare allegorically the sensuous life of love with a dream-life; the exchange of functions between Cupid and the fairies is therefore the true poetic embodiment of this comparison. For the realm of dreams is assigned to Shakespeare's fairies; they are essentially nothing else than personified dream-gods, children of the fantasy, which, as Mercutio says, is not only the idle producer of dreams, but also of the caprices of superficial love.

Vaguely, as in a dream, this significance of the fairies rests in the ancient popular belief of the Teutonic races, and Shakespeare, with the instinctive touch of genius, has fashioned this idea into exquisite form. In German *'Alp'* and *'Elfe'* are the same; 'Alp' is universally applied in Germany to a dream-goblin (nightmare). The name of the fairy king Oberon is only Frenchified from Alberon or Alberich, a dwarfish elf, a figure early appearing in old German poems. The character of Puck, or, as he is properly called, Robin Goodfellow, is literally no other than our own *'guter Knecht Ruprecht;* and it is curious that from this name in German the word 'Riipel' is derived, the only one by which we can give the idea of the English *clown,* the very part which, in Shakespeare, Puck plays in the kingdom of the fairies. This belief in fairies was far more diffused through Scandinavia than through England; and again in Scotland and England it was far more actively developed than in Germany. Robin Goodfellow especially, of whom we hear in England as early as the thirteenth century, was a favourite in popular traditions, and to his name all the cunning tricks were imputed which we relate of Eulenspiegel and other nations of others. His *Mad Pranks and Merry Jests* were printed in 1628 in a popular book, which Thorns has recently prepared for his little blue library. Collier places the origin of the book at least forty years earlier, so that Shakespeare might have been acquainted with it. Unquestionably this is the main source of his fairy kingdom; the lyric parts of the *Midsummer-Night's Dream* are in tone and colour a perfect imitation of the songs contained in it. In this popular book Robin appears, although only in a passing manner, as the sender of the dreams; the fairies and Oberon, who is here his father, speak to him by dreams before he is received into their community. But that which Shakespeare thus received in the rough form of fragmentary popular belief he developed in his playful creation into a beautiful and regulated world. He here in a measure deserves the merit which Herodotus ascribes to Homer; as the Greek poet has created the great abode of the gods and its Olympic inhabitants, so Shakespeare has given form and place to the fairy kingdom, and with the natural creative power of genius he has breathed a soul into his merry little citizens, thus imparting a living centre to their nature and their office, their behaviour and their doings. He has given embodied form to the invisible and life to the dead, and has thus striven for the poet's greatest glory; and it seems as if it was not without consciousness of this his work that he wrote in a strain of self-reliance that passage in this very play:—

> The poet's eye, in a fine frenzy rolling,
> Doth glance from heaven to earth, from earth to heaven;
> And as imagination bodies forth
> The forms of things unknown, the poet's pen
> Turns them to shapes, and gives to airy nothing
> A local habitation and a name.
> Such tricks hath strong imagination;
> That, if it would but apprehend some joy,
> It comprehends some bringer of that joy.

This he has here effected; he has clothed in bodily form those intangible phantoms, the bringers of dreams of provoking jugglery, of sweet soothing, and of tormenting raillery; and the task he has thus accomplished we shall only rightly estimate, when we have taken into account the severe design and inner congruity of this little world.

If it were Shakespeare's object expressly to remove from the fairies that dark ghost-like character (Act III. sc. 2), in which they appeared in Scandinavian and Scottish fable; if it were his desire to portray them as kindly beings in a merry and harmless relation to mortals; if he wished, in their essential office as bringers of dreams, to fashion them in their nature as personified dreams, he carried out this object in wonderful harmony both as regards their actions and their condition. The kingdom of the fairy beings is placed in the aromatic flower-scented Indies, in the land where mortals live in a half-dreamy state. From hence they come, 'following darkness,' as Puck says, 'like a dream.' Airy and swift, like the moon, they circle the earth; they avoid the sunlight without fearing it, and seek the darkness; they love the moon and dance in her beams; and above all they delight in the dusk and twilight, the very season for dreams, whether waking or asleep. They send and bring dreams to mortals; and we need only recall to mind the description of the fairies' midwife, Queen Mab, in *Romeo and Juliet*, a piece nearly of the same date with the *Midsummer-Night's Dream*, to discover that this is the charge essentially assigned to them, and the very means by which they influence mortals. The manner in which Shakespeare has fashioned their inner character in harmony with this outer function is full of profound thought. He depicts them as beings without delicate feeling and without morality, just as in dreams we meet with no check to our tender sensations and are without moral impulse and responsibility. Careless and unscrupulous, they tempt mortals to infidelity; the effects of the mistakes which they have contrived make no impression on their minds; they feel no sympathy for the deep affliction of the lovers, but only delight and marvel over their mistakes and their foolish demeanour. The poet farther depicts his fairies as beings of no high intellectual development. Whoever attentively reads their parts will find that nowhere is reflection imparted to them. Only in one exception does Puck make a sententious remark upon the infidelity of man, and whoever has penetrated into the nature of these beings will immediately feel that it is out of harmony. They can make no direct inward impression upon mortals; their influence over the mind is not spiritual, but throughout material; it is effected by means of vision, metamorphosis, and imitation. Titania has no spiritual association with her friend, but mere delight in her beauty, her 'swimming gait,' and her powers of imitation. When she awakes from her vision there is no reflection: 'Methought I was enamoured of an ass,' she says. 'Oh how mine eyes do hate this visage now!' She is only affected by the idea of the actual and the visible. There is no scene of reconciliation with her husband; her resentment consists in separation, her reconciliation in a dance; there is no trace of reflection, no indication of feeling. Thus, to remind Puck of a past event no abstract date sufficed, but an accompanying indication, perceptible to the senses, was required. They are represented, these little gods, as natural souls, without the higher human capacities of minds, lords of a kingdom, not of reason and morality, but of imagination and ideas conveyed by the senses; and thus they are uniformly the vehicle of the fancy which produces the delusions of love and dreams. Their will, therefore, only extends to the corporeal. They lead a luxurious, merry life, given up to the pleasure of the senses; the secrets of nature and the powers of flowers and herbs are confided to them. To sleep in flowers, lulled with dances and songs, with the wings of painted butterflies to fan the moonbeams from their eyes, this is their pleasure; the gorgeous apparel of flowers and dewdrops is their joy. When Titania wishes to allure her beloved, she offers him honey, apricots, purple grapes, and dancing. This life of sense and nature is seasoned by the power of fancy and by desire after all that is most choice, most beautiful, and agreeable. They harmonise with nightingales and butterflies; they wage war with all ugly creatures, with hedgehogs, spiders, and bats; dancing, play, and song are their greatest pleasures; they steal lovely children, and substitute changelings; they torment decrepit old age, toothless gossips, aunts, and the awkward company of the players of Pyramus and Thisbe, but they love and recompense all that is pure and pretty. Thus was it of old in the popular traditions; their characteristic trait of favouring honesty among mortals and persecuting crime was certainly borrowed by Shakespeare from these traditions in the *Merry Wives of Windsor,* though not in this play. The sense of the beautiful is the one thing which elevates the fairies not only above the beasts but also above the ordinary mortal, when he is devoid of all fancy and uninfluenced by beauty. Thus, in the spirit of the fairies, in which this sense of the beautiful is so refined, it is intensely ludicrous that the elegant Titania should fall in love with an ass's head. The only pain which agitates these beings is jealousy, the desire of possessing the beautiful sooner than others; they shun the distorting quarrel; their steadfast aim and longing is for undisturbed enjoyment. But in this sweet jugglery they neither appear constant to mortals nor do they carry on intercourse among themselves in monotonous harmony. They are full also of wanton tricks and railleries, playing upon themselves and upon mortals, pranks which never hurt, but which often torment. This is especially the property of Puck, who "jests to Oberon," who is the "lob" at this court, a coarser goblin, represented with broom or threshing-flail, in a leathern dress, and with a dark countenance, a roguish but awkward fellow, skilful at all transformation, practised in wilful tricks, but also clumsy enough to make mistakes and blunders contrary to his intention.

We mortals are unable to form anything out of the richest treasure of the imagination without the aid of actual human circumstances and qualities. Thus, even in this case, it is not difficult to discover in society the types of human nature which Shakespeare deemed especially suitable as the original of his fairies. There are, particularly among women of the middle and upper ranks, natures which are not accessible to higher spiritual necessities, which take their way through life with no serious and profound reference to the principles of morality or to intellectual objects, yet with a decided inclination and qualification for all that is beautiful, agreeable, and graceful, though without being able to reach even here the higher attainments of art. They grasp readily as occasion offers all that is tangible; they are ready, dexterous, disposed for tricks and raillery, ever skilful at acting parts, at assuming appearances, at disguises and deceptions, seeking to give a stimulant to life only by festivities, pleasures, sport and jest. These light, agreeable, rallying, and sylph-like natures, who live from day to day and have no spiritual consciousness of a common object in life, whose existence is a playful dream, full of grace and embellishment, but never a life of higher aim, have been chosen by Shakespeare with singular tact as the originals from whose fixed characteristics he gave form and life to his airy fairies.

We can now readily perceive why, in this work, the "rude mechanicals" and clowns, and the company of actors with their burlesque comedy, are placed in such rude contrast to the tender and delicate play of the fairies. Prominence is given to both by the contrast afforded between the material and the aerial, between the awkward and the beautiful, between the utterly unimaginative and that which, itself fancy, is entirely woven out of fancy. The play acted by the clowns is, as it were, the reverse of the poet's own work, which demands all the spectator's reflective and imitative fancy to open to him this aerial world, whilst in the other nothing at all is left to the imagination of the spectator. The homely mechanics, who compose and act merely for gain, and for the sake of so many pence a day, the ignorant players, with hard hands and thick heads, whose unskilful art consists in learning their parts by heart, these men believe themselves obliged to represent Moon and Moonshine by name in order to render them evident; they supply the lack of side-scenes by persons, and all that should take place behind the scenes they explain by disgressions. These rude doings are disturbed by the fairy chiefs with their utmost raillery, and the fantastical company of lovers mock at the performance. Theseus, however, draws quiet and thoughtful contemplation from these contrasts. He shrinks incredulously from the too-strange fables of love and its witchcraft; he enjoins that imagination should amend the play of the clowns, devoid as it is of all fancy. The real, that in this work of art has become "nothing," and the "airy nothing," which in the poet's hand has assumed this graceful form, are contrasted in the two extremes; in the centre is the intellectual man, who participates in both, who regards the one, namely, the stories of the lovers, the poets by nature, as art and poetry, and who receives the other, presented as art, only as a thanksworthy readiness to serve and as a simple offering.

It is the combination of these skilfully obtained contrasts into a whole which we especially admire in this work. The age subsequent to Shakespeare could not tolerate it, and divided it in twain. Thus sundered, the aesthetic fairy poetry and the burlesque caricature of the poet have made their own way. Yet in 1631 the *Midsummer-Night's Dream* appears to have been represented in its perfect form. We know that in this year it was acted at the bishop of Lincoln's house on a Sunday, and that a puritanical tribunal in consequence sentenced Bottom to sit for twelve hours in the porter's room belonging to the bishop's palace, wearing his ass's head. But even in the seventeenth century "the merry conceited humours of Bottom the weaver" were acted as a separate burlesque. The work was attributed to the actor Robert Cox, who, in the times of the civil wars, when the theatres were suppressed, wandered over the country, and, under cover of rope-dancing, provided the people thus depressed by religious hypocrisy with the enjoyment of small exhibitions, which he himself composed under the significant name of "drolls," and in which the stage returned as it were to the merry interludes of old. In the form in which Cox at this time produced the farce of Bottom, it was subsequently transplanted to Germany by our own Andreas Gryphius, the schoolmaster and pedant Squenz being the chief character. How expressive these burlesque parts of the piece must have been in Shakespeare's time to the public, who were acquainted with original drolleries of this kind, *we* now can scarcely imagine. Nor do we any longer understand how to perform them; the public at that time, on the contrary, had the types of the caricatured pageants in this play and in *Love's Labour's Lost* still existing among them.

On the other hand Shakespeare's fairy world became the source of a complete fairy literature. The kingdom of the fairies had indeed appeared, in the chivalric epics, many centuries before Shakespeare. The oldest Welsh tales and romances relate of the contact of mortals with this invisible world. The English of Shakespeare's time possessed a romance of this style written by Launfall, in a translation from the French. The romance of *Huon of Bordeaux* had been earlier (in 1570) translated by Lord Berners into English. From it, or from the popular book of *Robin Goodfellow,* Shakespeare may have borrowed the name of Oberon. From the reading of Ovid he probably gave to the fairy queen the name of Titania, while among his contemporaries, and even by Shakespeare, in *Romeo and Juliet,* she is called "Queen Mab." In those old chivalric romances, in Chaucer, in Spenser's allegorical *Faerie Queen,* the fairies are utterly different beings, without distinct character or office; they concur with the whole world of chivalry in the same monotonous description and want of character. But the Saxon fairy legends afforded Shakespeare a hold for renouncing the romantic art of the pastoral poets and for passing over to the rude popular taste of his fellow-countrymen. He could learn melodious language, descriptive art, the brilliancy of romantic pictures, and the sweetness of visionary images from Spenser's *Faerie Queen;* but he rejected his portrayal of this fairy world and grasped at the little pranks of Robin Goodfellow, where the simple faith of the people was preserved in pure and unassuming form. In a similar way in Germany, at the restoration of popular life at the time of the Reformation, the chivalric and romantic notions of the world of spirits were cast aside; men returned to popular belief, and we read nothing which reminds us so much of Shakespeare's fairy world as the theory of elementary spirits by our own Paracelsus. From the time that Shakespeare adopted the mysterious ideas of this mythology, and the homely expression of them in prose and verse, we may assert that the popular Saxon taste became more and more predominant in him. In *Romeo and Juliet* and in the *Merchant of Venice* there is an evident leaning towards both sides, and necessarily so, as the poet is here still occupied upon subjects completely Italian. Working, moreover, at the same time upon historical subjects, settled the poet, as it were, fully in his native soil, and the delineation of the lower orders of the people in *Henry IV.* and *V.* shows that he felt at home there. From the period of these pieces we find no longer the conceit-style, the love of rhyme, the insertion of sonnets, and similar forms of the artificial lyric; and that characteristic delight in simple popular songs, which shows itself even here in the fairy choruses, takes the place of the discarded taste. The example given in Shakespeare's formation of the fairy world had, however, little effect. Lilly, Drayton, Ben Jonson, and other contemporaries and successors, took full possession of the fairy world for their poems, in part evidently influenced by Shakespeare, but none of them has understood how to follow him even upon the path already cleared. Among the many productions of this kind Drayton's "Nymphidia" is the most distinguished. The poem turns upon Oberon's jealousy of the fairy knight Pigwiggen; it paints the fury of the king with quixotic colouring, and treats of the combat between the two in the style of the chivalric romances, seeking, like them, its main charm in the descriptions of the little dwellings, implements, and weapons of the fairies. If we compare this with Shakespeare's magic creation, which derives its charm entirely from the reverent thoughtfulness with which the poet clings with his natural earnestness to popular legends, leaving intact this childlike belief and preserving its object undesecrated; if we compare the two together, we shall perceive most clearly the immense distance at which our poet stood even from the best of his contemporaries.

We have frequently referred to the necessity of seeing Shakespeare's plays performed, in order to be able to estimate them fully, based as they are upon the joint effect of poetic and dramatic art. It will, therefore, be just to mention the representation which this most difficult of all theatrical tasks of a modern age has met with in all the great stages of Germany. And, that we may not be misunderstood, we will premise that, however strongly we insist upon this principle, we yet, in the present state of things, warn most decidedly against all overbold attempts at Shakespearian representation. If we would perform dramas in which such an independent position is assigned to the dramatic art as it is in these, we must before everything possess a histrionic art dependent and complete in itself. But this art has with us declined with poetic art, and amid the widely distracting concerns of the present time it is scarcely likely soon to revive. A rich, art-loving prince, endowed with feeling for the highest dramatic delights, and ready to make sacrifices on their behalf, could possibly effect much, were he to invite together to one place, during an annual holiday, the best artists from all theatres, and thus to re-cast the parts of a few of the Shakespearian pieces. Even then a profound judge of the poet must take the general management of the whole. If all this were done, a play like the *Midsummer-Night's Dream* might be at last attempted. This fairy play was produced upon the English stage when they had boys early trained for the characters; without this proviso it is ridiculous to desire the representation of the most difficult parts, with powers utterly inappropriate. When a girl's high treble utters the part of Oberon, a character justly represented by painters with abundant beard, and possessing all the dignity of the calm ruler of this hovering world; when the rude goblin Puck is performed by an affected actress, when Titania and her suite appear in ball-costume, without beauty or dignity, for ever moving about in the hopping motion of the dancing chorus, in the most offensive ballet-fashion that modern unnaturalness has created—what then becomes of the sweet charm of these scenes and figures which should appear in pure aerial drapery, which in their sport should retain a certain elevated simplicity, and which in the affair between Titania and Bottom, far from unnecessarily pushing the awkward fellow forward as the principal figure, should understand how to place the ludicrous character at a modest distance, and to give the whole scene the quiet charm of a picture? If it be impossible to act these fairy forms at the present day, it is equally so with the clowns. The common nature of the mechanics when they are themselves is perhaps intelligible to our actors; but when they perform their work of art few actors of the present day possess the self-denial that would lead them to represent this most foolish of all follies with solemn importance, as if in thorough earnestness, instead of overdoing its exaggeration, self-complacently working by laughter and smiling at themselves. Unless this self-denial be observed, the first and greatest object of these scenes, that of exciting laughter, is inevitably lost. Lastly, the middle class of mortals introduced between the fairies and the clowns, the lovers driven about by bewildering delusions, what sensation do they excite, when we see them in the frenzy of passion through the wood in kid-gloves, in knightly dress, conversing after the manner of the refined world, devoid of all warmth, and without a breath of this charming poetry? How can knightly accoutrements suit Theseus, the kinsman of Hercules, and the Amazonian Hippolyta? Certain it is that in the fantastic play of an unlimited dream, from which time and place are effaced, these characters ought not to appear in the strict costume of Greek antiquity; but still less, while one fixed attire is avoided, should we pass over to the other extreme, and transport to Athens a knightly dress, and a guard of Swiss halberdiers. We can only compare with this mistake one equally great, that of adding a disturbing musical accompaniment, inopportunely impeding the rapid course of the action, and interrupting this work of fancy, this delicate and refined action, this ethereal dream, with a march of kettledrums and trumpets, just at the point where Theseus is expressing his thoughts as to the unsubstantial nature of these visions. And amid all these modern accompaniments, the simple balcony of the Shakespearian stage was retained, as if in respect to stage apparatus we were to return to those days! This simplicity moreover was combined with all the magnificence customary at the present day. Elements thus contradictory and thus injudiciously united, tasks thus beautiful and thus imperfectly discharged, must always make the friend of Shakespearian performances desire that, under existing circumstances, they were rather utterly renounced.

⌇⌇⌇ ⌇⌇⌇ ⌇⌇⌇

1872—Edward Dowden,
from *Shakspere: A Critical Study of His Mind and Art*

Edward Dowden (1843–1913) was an Irish critic, university lecturer, and poet. His works include *New Studies in Literature* (1895), *The French Revolution and English Literature: Lectures Delivered in Connection with the Sesquicentennial Celebration of Princeton University* (1897), and *Shakespeare Primer* (1877).

In 'A Midsummer Night's Dream' Shakspere's humour has enriched itself by coalescing with the fancy. The comic is here no longer purely comic; it is a mingled web, shot through with the beautiful. Bottom and Titania meet; and this meeting of Bottom and Titania may be taken, by any lover of symbolism that pleases, as an undesigned symbol of the fact that the poet's faculties, which at first had stood apart, and were accustomed to go to work each faculty by itself, were not approaching one another. At a subsequent period, when the shocks of life had roused to highest energy every nerve, every fibre of the genius of Shakspere, the actions of all faculties were fused together in one. Bottom is incomparably a finer efflorescence of the absurd than any preceding character of Shakspere's invention. How lean and impoverished his fellows, the Athenian craftsmen, confess themselves in presence of the many-sided genius of Nick Bottom! Rarely is a great artist appreciated in the degree that Bottom is—"He hath simply the best wit of any handicraft man in Athens; yea, and the best person too; and he is a very paramour for a sweet voice." With what a magnificent multiplicity of gifts he is endowed! How vast has the bounty of nature been to him! The self-doubtful Snug hesitates to undertake the moderate duties assigned to the lion. Bottom, though his chief humour is for a tyrant, knows not how to suppress his almost equal gift for playing a lady. How, without a pang, can he deprive the world, through devotion to "the Ercles vein," of the monstrous little voice in which he can utter "Thisne, Thisne—Ah Pyramus, my lover dear! Thy Thisby dear and lady dear! And as to the part assigned to the too bashful Snug,—that Bottom can undertake in either of two styles, or in both, so that the Duke must say, "Let him roar again, let him roar again," or the ladies may be soothed by the "aggravated voice" in which he will "roar you as gently as any sucking dove." But from these dreams of universal ambition he is recalled by Quince to his most appropriate impersonation:—"You can play no part but Pyramus, for Pyramus is a sweet-faced man; a proper man as one shall see in a summer's day; a most lovely, gentleman-like man; therefore you must needs play Pyramus."

—◈— —◈— —◈—

1880—H. N. Hudson. "A Midsummer Night's Dream," from *Shakespeare: His Life, Art, and Characters*

Henry Norman Hudson (1814-86) was an American essayist and Shakespearean scholar. According to *The Cambridge History of English and American Literature*, his criticism was "popular rather than scholarly" and of the Romantic tradition of Coleridge, in that it "endeavours to set forth Shakespeare's inwardness, and pays comparatively little attention to his outwardness."

A Midsummer-Night's Dream was registered at the Stationers' October 8, 1600, and two quarto editions of it were published in the course of that year. The play is not known to have been printed again till it reappeared in the folio of 1623, where the repetition of certain misprints shows it to have been printed from one of the quarto copies. In all three of these copies, however, the printing is remarkably clear and correct for the time, insomuch that modern editors have little difficulty about the text. Probably none of the Poet's dramas has reached us in a more satisfactory state.

The play is first heard of in the list given by Francis Meres in his *Palladis Tamia*, 1598. But it was undoubtedly written several years before that time; and I am not aware that any editor places the writing at a later date than 1594. This brings it into the same period with *King John*, *King Richard the Second*, and the finished *Romeo and Juliet*; and the internal marks of style naturally sort it into that company. Our Mr. Verplanck, however, thinks there are some passages which relish strongly of an earlier time; while again there are others that with the prevailing sweetness of the whole have such an intertwisting of nerve and vigour, and such an energetic compactness of thought and imagery, mingled occasionally with the deeper tonings of "years that bring the philosophic mind," as to argue that they were wrought into the structure of the play not long before it came from the press. The part of the Athenian lovers certainly has a good deal that, viewed by itself, would scarce do credit even to such a boyhood as Shakespeare's must have been. On the other hand, there is a large philosophy in Theseus' discourse of "the lunatic, the lover, and the poet," a manly judgment in his reasons for preferring the "tedious brief scene of young Pyramus and his love Thisbe," and a bracing freshness in the short dialogue of the chase, all in the best style of the author's second period. Perhaps, however, what seem the defects of the former, the fanciful quirks and far-fetched conceits, were wisely designed, in order to invest the part with such an air of dreaminess and unreality as would better sort with the scope and spirit of the piece, and preclude a disproportionate resentment of some naughty acts into which those love-bewildered frailties are betrayed.

There is at least a rather curious coincidence, which used to be regarded as proving that the play was not written till after the Summer of 1594. I refer to Titania's superb description, in ii. 1, of the strange misbehaviour of the weather, which she ascribes to the fairy bickerings. I can quote but a part of it:

"The seasons alter: hoary-headed frosts
Fall in the fresh lap of the crimson rose;
And on old Hiems' thin and icy crown

An odorous chaplet of sweet summer buds
Is, as in mockery, set: the Spring, the Summer,
The childing Autumn, angry Winter, change
Their wonted liveries; and the mazèd world,
By their increase, now knows not which is which
And this same progeny of evils comes
From our debate, from our dissension."

For the other part of the coincidence, Strype in his *Annals* gives the following passage from a discourse by the Rev. Dr. King: "And see whether the Lord doth not threaten us much more, by sending such unseasonable weather and storms of rain among us; which if we will observe, and compare it with what is past, we may say that the course of nature is very much inverted. Our years are turned upside down: our Summers are no Summers; our harvests are no harvests; our seed-times are no seed-times. For a great space of time scant any day hath been seen that it hath not rained." Dyce indeed scouts the supposal that Shakespeare had any allusion to this eccentric conduct of the elements in the Summer of 1594, pronouncing it "ridiculous"; but I do not quite see it so; albeit I am apt enough to believe that most of the play was written before that date. And surely, the truth of the allusion being granted, all must admit that passing events have seldom been turned to better account in the service of poetry.

I can hardly imagine this play ever to have been very successful on the stage; and I am sure it could not be made to succeed there now. Still we are not without contemporary evidence that it had at least a fair amount of fame. And we have authentic information that it was performed at the house of Dr. John Williams, Bishop of Lincoln, on Sunday, the 27th of September, 1631. The actor of Bottom's part was on that occasion sentenced by a Puritan tribunal to sit twelve hours in the porter's room of the Bishop's palace, wearing the ass's head. This Dr. Williams was the very able but far from faultless man who was treated so harshly by Laud, and gave the King such crooked counsel in the case of Strafford, and spent his last years in mute sorrow at the death of his royal master, and had his life written by the wise, witty, good Bishop Hacket.

Some hints towards the part of Theseus and Hippolyta appear to have been taken from *The Knight's Tale* of Chaucer. The same poet's *Legend of Thisbe of Babylon*, and Golding's translation of the same story from Ovid, probably furnished the matter of the Interlude. So much as relates to Bottom and his fellows evidently came fresh from Nature as she had passed under the Poet's eye. The linking of these clowns with the ancient tragic tale of Pyramus and Thisbe, so as to draw the latter within the region of modern farce, is not less original than droll. How far it may have expressed the Poet's judgment touching the theatrical doings of the time, were perhaps a question more curious than profitable. The names of Oberon, Titania, and Robin Goodfellow were made familiar by the surviving relics of Gothic and Druidical mythology; as were also many particulars in their habits, mode of life, and influence in human affairs. Hints and allusions scattered through many preceding writers might be produced, showing that the old superstition had been grafted into the body of Christianity, where it had shaped itself into a regular system, so as to mingle in the lore of the nursery, and hold an influential place in the popular belief. Some reports of this ancient Fairydom are choicely translated into poetry by Chaucer in *The Wife of Bath's Tale.*

But, though Chaucer and others had spoken about the fairy nation, it was for Shakespeare to let them speak for themselves: until he clothed their life in apt forms, their thoughts in fitting words, they but floated unseen and unheard in the mental atmosphere of his fatherland. So that on this point there need be no scruple about receiving Hallam's statement of the matter: "*A Midsummer-Night's Dream* is, I believe, altogether original in one of the most beautiful conceptions that ever visited the mind of a poet,—the fairy machinery. A few before him had dealt in a vulgar and clumsy manner with popular superstitions; but the sportive, beneficent, invisible population of the air and earth, long since established in the creed of childhood, and of those simple as children, had never for a moment been blended with 'human mortals' among the personages of the drama." How much Shakespeare did as the friend and saviour of those sweet airy frolickers of the past from the relentless mowings of Time, has been charmingly set forth in our day in Hood's *Plea of the Midsummer Fairies.*

What, then, are the leading qualities which the Poet ascribes to these ideal or fanciful beings? Coleridge says he is "convinced that Shakespeare availed himself of the title of this play in his own mind, and worked upon it as a dream throughout." This remark no doubt rightly hits the true genius of the piece; and on no other ground can its merits be duly estimated. The whole play is indeed a sort of ideal dream; and it is from the fairy personages that its character as such mainly proceeds. All the materials of the piece are ordered and assimilated to that central and governing idea. This it is that explains and justifies the distinctive features of the work, such as the constant preponderance of the lyrical over the dramatic, and the free playing of the action unchecked by the conditions of outward fact and reality. Accordingly a sort of lawlessness is, as it ought to be, the very law of the performance. King Oberon is the sovereign who presides over the world of dreams; Puck is his prime minister; and all the other denizens of Fairydom are his subjects and the agents of his will in this capacity. Titania's nature and functions are precisely the same which Mercutio assigns to Queen Mab, whom he aptly describes as having for her office to deliver sleeping men's fancies of their dreams, those "children of an idle brain." In keeping with this central dream-idea, the actual order of things everywhere gives place to the spontaneous issues and capricious turnings of the dreaming mind; the lofty and the low, the beautiful and the grotesque, the world of fancy and of fact, all the strange diversities that enter into "such stuff as dreams are made of," running and frisking together, and interchanging their functions and properties; so that the whole seems confused, flitting, shadowy, and indistinct, as fading away in the remoteness and fascination of moonlight. The very scene is laid in a veritable dream-land, called Athens indeed, but only because Athens was the greatest beehive of beautiful visions then known; or rather it is laid in an ideal forest near an ideal Athens,—a forest peopled with sportive elves and sprites and fairies feeding on moonlight and music and fragrance; a place where Nature herself is preternatural; where everything is idealized, even to the sunbeams and the soil; where the vegetation proceeds by enchantment, and there is magic in the germination of the seed and secretion of the sap.

The characteristic attributes of the fairy people are, perhaps, most availably represented in Puck; who is apt to remind one of Ariel, though the two have little in common, save that both are preternatural, and therefore live no longer in the faith of reason. Puck is no such sweet-mannered, tender-hearted, music-breathing spirit, as Prospero's delicate prime-minister; there are no such fine interweavings of a sensitive moral soul in his nature, he has no such soft touches of compassion and pious awe of goodness, as link the dainty Ariel in so smoothly with our best sympathies. Though Goodfellow by name, his powers and aptitudes for mischief are quite unchecked by any gentle relentings of fellow-feeling: in whatever distresses he finds or occasions he sees much to laugh at, nothing to pity: to tease and vex poor human sufferers, and then to think "what fools these mortals be," is pure fun to him. Yet, notwithstanding his mad pranks, we cannot choose but love the little sinner, and let our fancy frolic with him, his sense of the ludicrous is so exquisite, he is so fond of sport, and so quaint and merry in his mischief; while at the same time such is the strange web of his nature as to keep him morally innocent. In all which I think he answers perfectly to the best idea we can frame of what a little dream-god should be.

In further explication of this peculiar people, it is to be noted that there is nothing of reflection or conscience or even of a spiritualized intelligence in their proper life: they have all the attributes of the merely natural and sensitive soul, but no attributes of the properly rational and moral soul. They worship the clean, the neat, the pretty, and the pleasant, whatever goes to make up the idea of purely sensuous beauty: this is a sort of religion with them; whatever of conscience they have adheres to this: so that herein they not unfitly represent the wholesome old notion which places cleanliness next to godliness. Every thing that is trim, dainty, elegant, graceful, agreeable, and sweet to the senses, they delight in: flowers, fragrances, dewdrops, and moonbeams, honey-bees, butterflies, and nightingales, dancing, play, and song,—these are their joy; out of these they weave their highest delectation; amid these they "fleet the time carelessly," without memory or forecast, and with no thought or aim beyond the passing pleasure of the moment. On the other hand, they have an instinctive repugnance to whatever is foul, ugly, sluttish, awkward, ungainly, or misshapen: they wage unrelenting war against bats, spiders, hedgehogs, spotted snakes, blindworms, long-legg'd spinners, beetles, and all such disagreeable creatures: to "kill cankers in the musk-rosebuds," and to "keep back the clamorous owl," are regular parts of their business. Their intense dislike of what is ugly and misshapen is the reason why they so much practise "the legerdemain of changelings," stealing away finished, handsome babies, and leaving blemished and defective ones in their stead. For the same cause they love to pester and persecute and play shrewd tricks upon decrepit old age, wise aunts, and toothless, chattering gossips, and especially such awkward "hempen home-spuns" as Bottom and his fellow-actors in the Interlude.

Thus these beings embody the ideal of the mere natural soul, or rather the purely sensuous fancy which shapes and governs the pleasing or the vexing delusions of sleep. They lead a merry, luxurious life, given up entirely to the pleasures of happy sensation,—a happiness that has no moral element, nothing of reason or conscience in it. They are indeed a sort of personified dreams; and so the Poet places them in a kindly or at least harmless relation to mortals as the bringers of dreams. Their very kingdom is located in the aromatic, flower-scented Indies, a land where mortals are supposed to live in a half-dreamy state. From thence they come, "following darkness," just as dreams naturally do; or, as Oberon words it, "tripping after the night's shade, swifter than the wandering Moon." It is their nature to shun the daylight, though they do not fear it, and to prefer the dark, as this is their appropriate work-time; but most of all they love the dusk and the twilight, because this is the best dreaming-time, whether the dreamer be asleep or awake. And all the shifting phantom-jugglery of dreams, all the sweet soothing witcheries, and all the teasing and tantalizing imagery of dream-land, rightly belong to their province.

It is a very noteworthy point that all their power or influence over the hearts and actions of mortals works through the medium of dreams, or of such fancies as are most allied to dreams. So that their whole inner character is fashioned in harmony with their external function. Nor is it without rare felicity that the Poet assigns to them the dominion over the workings of sensuous and superficial love, this being but as one of the courts of the dream-land kingdom; a region ordered, as it were, quite apart from the proper regards of duty and law, and where the natural soul of man moves free of moral thought and responsibility. Accordingly we have the King of this Fairydom endowed with the rights and powers both of the classical god of love and the classical goddess of chastity. Oberon commands alike the secret virtues of "Dian's bud" and of "Cupid's flower"; and he seems to use them both unchecked by any other law than his innate love of what is handsome and fair, and his native aversion to what is ugly and foul; that is, he owns no restraint but as he is inwardly held to apply either or both of them in such a way as to avoid all distortion or perversion from what is naturally graceful and pleasant. For everybody, I take it, knows that in the intoxications of a life of sensuous love reason and conscience have as little force as they have in a life of dreams. And so the Poet fitly ascribes to Oberon and his ministers both Cupid's delight in frivolous breaches of faith and Jove's laughter at lovers' perjuries; and this on the ground, apparently, that the doings of those in Cupid's power are as harmless and unaccountable as the freaks of a dream.

In pursuance of this idea he depicts the fairies as beings without any proper moral sense in what they do, but as having a very keen sense of what is ludicrous and absurd in the doings of men. They are careless and unscrupulous in their dealings in this behalf. The wayward follies and the teasing perplexities of the fancy-smitten persons are pure sport to them. If by their wanton mistakes they can bewilder and provoke the lovers into larger outcomes of the laughable, so much the higher runs their mirth. And as they have no fellow-feeling with the pains of those who thus feed their love of fun, so the effect of their roguish tricks makes no impression upon them: they have a feeling of simple delight and wonder at the harmless frettings and fumings which their merry mischief has a hand in bringing to pass: but then it is to be observed also, that they find just as much sport in tricking the poor lover out of his vexations as in tricking him into them; in fact, they never rest satisfied with the fun of the former so long as there is any chance of enjoying that of the latter also.

All readers of Shakespeare are of course familiar with the splendid passage in ii. 1, where Oberon describes to Puck how, on a certain occasion,

"I heard a mermaid, on a dolphin's back,
Uttering such dulcet and harmonious breath,
That the rude sea grew civil at her song."

And all are no doubt aware that the subsequent lines, referring to "a fair vestal throned by the west," are commonly understood to have been meant as a piece of delicate flattery to Queen Elizabeth. Mr. Halpin has recently given to this famous passage a new interpretation or application, which is at least curious enough to justify a brief statement of it. In his view, "Cupid all arm'd" refers to Leicester's wooing of Elizabeth, and his grand entertainment of her at Kenilworth in 1575. From authentic descriptions of that entertainment we learn, that among the spectacles and fireworks witnessed on the occasion was one of a singing mermaid on a dolphin's back gliding over smooth water amid shooting stars. The "love-shaft" which was aimed at the "fair vestal," that is, the Priestess of Diana, whose bud has such prevailing might over "Cupid's flower," glanced off; so that "the imperial votaress passed on, in maiden meditation, fancy-free."

Thus far, all is clear enough. But Halpin further interprets that the "little western flower" upon whom "the bolt of Cupid fell" refers to Lettice Countess of Essex, with whom Leicester carried on a secret intrigue while her husband was absent in Ireland. The Earl of Essex, on being apprised of the intrigue, set out to return the next year, but died of poison, as was thought, before he reached home. So Halpin understands the "western flower, before milk-white," that is, innocent, but "now purple with love's wound," as referring to the lady's fall, or to the deeper blush of her husband's murder. And the flower is called "love-in-idleness," to signify her listlessness of heart during the Earl's absence; as the Poet elsewhere uses similar terms of the pansy, as denoting the love that renders men pensive, dreamy, indolent, instead of toning up the soul with healthy and noble aspirations. The words of Oberon to Puck, "that very time I saw—but thou could'st not," are construed as referring to the strict mystery in which the affair was wrapped, and to the Poet's own knowledge of it, because a few years later the execution of Edward Arden, his maternal relative, was closely connected with it, and because the unfortunate Earl of Essex, so well known as for some time the Queen's favourite, and then the victim of her resentment, was the son of that Lettice, and was also the Poet's early friend and patron.

Such is, in substance, Halpin's view of the matter; which I give for what it may be worth; and freely acknowledge it to be ingenious and plausible enough. Gervinus regards it as "an interpretation full of spirit," and as "giving the most definite relation to the innermost sense of the whole piece." And I am very willing to believe that Shakespeare often took hints, perhaps something more than hints, for his poetry from the facts and doings of the time: nevertheless I rather fail to see how any real good is to be gained towards understanding the Poet from such interpretations of his scenes, or from tracing out such "definite relations" between his workmanship and the persons and particulars that may have come to his knowledge. For my own part, I doubt whether "the innermost sense" of the play is any the clearer to me for this ingenious piece of explanation.

Besides, I have yet to learn what proofs there are that the ill-fated Essex was an early patron and friend of Shakespeare. That great honour belongs to the Earls of Southampton and Pembroke. It was Lord Bacon, not Shakespeare, who enjoyed so richly the friendship and patronage of the generous Essex; and how he requited the same is known much too well for his credit. I am not unmindful that this may yield some comfort to those who would persuade us that Shakespeare's plays were written by Lord Bacon. Upon this point I have just four things to say: First, Bacon's requital of the Earl's bounty was such a piece of ingratitude as I can hardly conceive the author of *King Lear* to have been guilty of: Second, the author of Shakespeare's plays, whoever he may have been, certainly was not a scholar; he had indeed something vastly better than learning, but he had not that: Third, Shakespeare never philosophizes, Bacon never does anything else: Fourth, Bacon's mind, great as it was, might have been cut out of Shakespeare's without being missed.

Any very firm or strong delineation of character, any deep passion, earnest purpose, or working of powerful motives, would clearly go at odds with the spirit of such a performance as I have described this play to be. It has room but for love and beauty and delight, for whatever is most poetical in nature and fancy, and for such tranquil stirrings of thought and feeling as may flow out in musical expression. Any such tuggings of mind or heart as would ruffle and discompose the smoothness of lyrical division would be quite out of keeping in a course of dream-life. The characters here, accordingly, are drawn with light, delicate, vanishing touches; some of them being dreamy and sentimental, some gay and frolicsome, and others replete with amusing absurdities, while all are alike dipped in fancy or sprinkled with humour. And for the same reason the tender distresses of unrequited or forsaken love here touch not our moral sense at all, but only at the most our human sympathies; love itself being represented as but the effect of some visual enchantment, which the King of Fairydom can inspire, suspend, or reverse at pleasure. Even the heroic personages are fitly shown in an unheroic aspect: we see them but in their unbendings, when they have daffed their martial robes aside, to lead the train of day-dreamers, and have a nuptial jubilee. In their case, great care and art were required, to make the play what it has been blamed for being; that is, to keep the dramatic sufficiently under, and lest the law of a part should override the law of the whole.

So, likewise, in the transformation of Bottom and the dotage of Titania, all the resources of fancy were needed, to prevent the unpoetical from getting the upper hand, and thus swamping the genius of the piece. As it is, what words can fitly express the effect with which the extremes of the grotesque and the beautiful are here brought together? What an inward quiet laughter springs up and lubricates the fancy at Bottom's droll confusion of his two natures, when he talks, now as an ass, now as a man, and anon as a mixture of both; his thoughts running at the same time on honey-bags and thistles, the charms of music and of good dry oats! Who but Shakespeare or Nature could have so interfused the lyrical spirit, not only with, but into and through a series or cluster of the most irregular and fantastic drolleries? But indeed this embracing and kissing of the most ludicrous and the most poetical, the enchantment under which they meet, and the airy, dream-like grace that hovers over their union, are altogether inimitable and indescribable. In this singular wedlock, the very diversity of the elements seems to link them the closer, while this linking in turn heightens that diversity; Titania being thereby drawn on to finer issues of soul, and Bottom to larger expressions of stomach. The union is so very improbable as to seem quite natural: we cannot conceive how any thing but a dream could possibly have married things so contrary; and that they could not have come together save in a dream, is a sort of proof that they *were* dreamed together.

And so, throughout, the execution is in strict accordance with the plan. The play, from beginning to end, is a perfect festival of whatever dainties and delicacies poetry may command,—a continued revelry and jollification of soul, where the understanding is lulled asleep, that the fancy may run riot in unrestrained enjoyment. The bringing together of four parts so dissimilar as those of the Duke and his warrior Bride, of the Athenian ladies and their lovers, of the amateur players and their woodland rehearsal, and of the fairy bickerings and overreaching; and the carrying of them severally to a point where they all meet and blend in lyrical respondence; all this is done in the same freedom from the laws that govern the drama of character and life. Each group of persons is made to parody itself into concert with the others; while the frequent intershootings of fairy influence lift the whole into the softest regions of fancy. At last the Interlude comes in as an amusing burlesque on all that has gone before; as in our troubled dreams we sometimes end with a dream that we have been dreaming, and our perturbations sink to rest in the sweet assurance that they were but the phantoms and unrealities of a busy sleep.

Though, as I have already implied, the characterization is here quite secondary and subordinate, yet the play probably has as much of character as were compatible with so much of poetry. Theseus has been well described as a classic personage with romantic features and expression. The name is Greek, but the nature and spirit are essentially Gothic. Nor does the abundance of classical allusion and imagery in the story call for any qualification here; because whatsoever is taken is thoroughly steeped in the efficacy of the taker. This sort of anachronism, common to all modern writers before and during the age of Shakespeare, seems to have arisen in part from a comparative dearth of classical learning, which left men to contemplate the heroes of antiquity under the forms into which their own mind and manners had been cast. Thus their delineations became informed with the genius of romance; the condensed grace of ancient character giving way to the enlargement of chivalrous magnanimity and honour, with its "high-erected thoughts seated in the heart of courtesy." Such in Shakespeare's case appears to have been the no less beautiful than natural result of the small learning, so often smiled and sometimes barked at, by those more skilled in the ancient languages than in the mother-tongue of nature.

In the two pairs of lovers there are hardly any lines deep and firm enough to be rightly called characteristic. Their doings, even more than those of the other human persons, are marked by the dream-like freakishness and whimsicality which distinguish the piece. Perhaps the two ladies are slightly discriminated as individuals, in that Hermia, besides her brevity of person, is the more tart in temper, and the more pert and shrewish of speech, while Helena is of a rather milder and softer disposition, with less of confidence in herself. So too in the case of Demetrius and Lysander the lines of individuality are exceedingly faint; the former being perhaps a shade the more caustic and spiteful, and the latter somewhat the more open and candid. But there is really nothing of heart or soul in what any of them do: as we see them, they are not actuated by principle at all, or even by any thing striking so deep as motive: their conduct issues from the more superficial springs of capricious impulse and fancy, the "jugglery of the senses during the sleep of reason"; the higher forces of a mental and moral bearing having no hand in shaping their action. For the fairy influences do not reach so far as to the proper seat of motive and principle: they have but the skin-depth of amorous caprice; all the elements of character and all the vital springs of faith and loyalty and honour lying quite beyond their sphere. Even here the judgment or the genius of the Poet is very perceptible; the lovers being represented from the start as acting from no forces or inspirations too deep or strong for the powers of Fairydom to overcome. Thus the pre-condition of the two pairs in their whim-bewilderment is duly attempered to the purposed dream-play of the general action. Nor is the seeming stanchness of Hermia and Demetrius in the outset any exception to this view; for nothing is more wilful and obstinate than amorous caprice or skin-deep love during its brief tenure of the fancy.

Of all the characters in this play, Bottom descends by far the most into the realities of common experience, and is therefore much the most accessible to the grasp of prosaic and critical fingers. It has been thought that the Poet meant him as a satire on the envies and jealousies of the greenroom, as they had fallen under his keen yet kindly eye. But, surely, the qualities uppermost in Bottom the Weaver had forced themselves on his notice long before he entered the greenroom. It is indeed curious to observe the solicitude of this protean actor and critic, that all the parts of the forthcoming play may have the benefit of his execution; how great is his concern lest, if he be tied to one, the others may be "overdone or come tardy off"; and how he would fain engross them all to himself, to the end of course that all may succeed, to the honour of the stage and the pleasure of the spectators. But Bottom's metamorphosis is the most potent drawer-out of his genius. The sense of his new head-dress stirs up all the manhood within him, and lifts his character into ludicrous greatness at once.

Hitherto the seeming to be a man has made him content to be little better than an ass; but no sooner is he conscious of seeming an ass than he tries his best to be a man; while all his efforts that way only go to approve the fitness of his present seeming to his former being.

Schlegel happily remarks, that "the droll wonder of Bottom's metamorphosis is merely the translation of a metaphor in its literal sense." The turning of a figure of speech thus into visible form is a thing only to be thought of or imagined; so that probably no attempt to paint or represent it to the senses can ever succeed. We can bear—at least we often have to bear—that a man should seem an ass to the mind's eye; but that be should seem such to the eye of the body is rather too much, save as it is done in those fable-pictures which have long been among the playthings of the nursery. So a child, for instance, takes great pleasure in fancying the stick he is riding to be a horse, when he would be frightened out of his wits, were the stick to quicken and expand into an actual horse. In like manner we often delight in indulging fancies and giving names, when we should be shocked were our fancies to harden into facts: we enjoy visions in our sleep, that would only disgust or terrify us, should we awake and find them solidified into things. The effect of Bottom's transformation can hardly be much otherwise, if set forth in visible, animated shape. Delightful to think of, it is scarce tolerable to look upon: exquisitely true in idea, it has no truth, or even verisimilitude, when reduced to fact; so that, however gladly imagination receives it, sense and understanding revolt at it.

Partly for reasons already stated, and partly for others that I scarce know how to state, *A Midsummer-Night's Dream* is a most effectual poser to criticism. Besides that its very essence is irregularity, so that it cannot be fairly brought to the test of rules, the play forms properly a class by itself: literature has nothing else really like it; nothing therefore with which it may be compared, and its merits adjusted. For so the Poet has here exercised powers apparently differing even in kind, not only from those of any other writer, but from those displayed in any other of his own writings. Elsewhere, if his characters are penetrated with the ideal, their whereabout lies in the actual, and the work may in some measure be judged by that life which it claims to represent: here the whereabout is as ideal as the characters; all is in the land of dreams,—a place for dreamers, not for critics. For who can tell what a dream ought or ought not to be, or when the natural conditions of dream-life are or are not rightly observed? How can the laws of time and space, as involved in the transpiration of human character,—how can these be applied in a place where the mind is thus absolved from their proper jurisdiction? Besides, the whole thing swarms with enchantment: all the sweet witchery of Shakespeare's sweet genius is concentrated in it, yet disposed with so subtle and cunning a hand, that we can as little grasp it as get away from it: its charms, like those of a summer evening, are such as we may see and feel, but cannot locate or define; cannot say they are here, or they are there: the moment we yield ourselves up to them, they seem to be everywhere; the moment we go to master them, they seem to be nowhere.

A MIDSUMMER NIGHT'S DREAM IN THE TWENTIETH CENTURY

ဦ

Shakespearean criticism of the twentieth century is vast and rich, ranging from in-depth psychoanalytical studies of character to close examinations of the impact of historical and political facts and much more. The only trend to be identified among twentieth-century commentary on *A Midsummer Night's Dream* is its variety, though, as before, critics in this century consistently praised the originality of the play and delighted in the character of Bottom the Weaver.

Lauding the beautiful poetry in *A Midsummer Night's Dream*, the well-known Catholic critic and fiction writer G. K. Chesterton adopts a philosophical perspective by analyzing the "spiritual atmosphere" of the play, a spirituality which he identifies as a social commentary on a communal sense of belonging. Chesterton maintains that, like the great tragedies, there exists in *A Midsummer Night's Dream* a profound message about mankind: "the very soul and meaning of the great comedies is that of an uproarious communion between the public and the play. . . . " With respect to Bottom the Weaver, Chesterton maintains that he is more mystifying even than Hamlet because Bottom's interest "consists of a rich subconsciousness, and that of Hamlet in the comparatively superficial matter of a rich consciousness." Chesterton also says, "It is in our own homes and environments . . . in old nurses, and gentlemen with hobbies . . . that we may feel the presence of that blood of the gods. And this creature so hard to describe, so easy to remember, the august and memorable fool, has never been so sumptuously painted as in the Bottom of *A Midsummer Night's Dream*."

Mark Van Doren's essay evaluates *A Midsummer Night's Dream* as a type of parody of *Romeo and Juliet*, a tragedy written at approximately the same time. Declaring the lovers of the play to be mechanical beings to which no great harm can come, Van Doren nevertheless maintains that *A Midsummer Night's Dream* is anything but the "weak and idle" play for which Robin Goodfellow apologizes. He contends that despite its "tiny toy-shop" appearance, the world presented here is both genuine and expansive, a place where mortals and fairies interact and at times changes places with one another, and where all beings, both human and supernatural, are governed by the inconstant moon. Equally important to Van Doren is the beautiful music that surrounds this world, as exemplified in the passage where Theseus describes his hounds as "dew-lapp'd like Thessalian bulls; / Slow in pursuit, but match'd in mouth like bells, / . . . A cry more tuneable / Was never holla'd to, nor cheer'd with horn, / In Crete, in Sparta, nor in Thessaly." Having set forth the dynamic nature of *A Midsummer Night's Dream,* Van Doren concludes that Shakespeare has achieved the highest level of comedy in that this fantastic play is ultimately a parody of *Romeo and Juliet,* just like the mechanicals' rendition of Pyramus and Thisby.

Harold Goddard's essay praises Shakespeare for having presented, in a fanciful dream play, the underlying theme of his greatest tragedies, namely that a spirit world exists far beneath the surface of mortal existence, with a power to influence human history. For Goddard, that power resides within the imagination. He cites two important passages: Theseus's famous speech on the imagination in Act V, and also the lyrical passage in which Theseus and Hippolyta speak of the music of the hounds, a dialogue that Goddard characterizes as a "nearly perfect . . . metaphor" for the play, emphasizing the way in which all the problems attendant in combining British fairies with Athenian aristocracy are resolved through harmonious musical effects. Further on in his essay, Goddard discusses the significance of Bottom's waking from his dream. Bottom's redemption, Goddard maintains, offers nothing less than the potential for democracy. In sum, Goddard concludes that the play is a prophecy of the power of imagination to bring order out of pandemonium. It is "the story of the multifarious attempts of the divine faculty in man to ignore, to escape, to outwit, . . . to transmute into its own substance, as the case may be, the powers of disorder that possess the world."

C. L. Barber's essay, which Harold Bloom has praised as particularly illuminating, examines the pageantry of the play. He describes the usual events of a "May game," a pageant with which an Elizabethan audience would be familiar. The playful elements of such an event would include young lovers running into the woods at night, with all the emotional turmoil that accompanies falling in and out of love, as well as a clown like Puck who "manages" the commotion of the night. Barber emphasizes Shakespeare's originality in adding a supernatural element to a traditional English holiday celebration. The essay continues with a thorough analysis of *A Midsummer Night's Dream* as a representation of the workings of the human imagination, taking up such issues as ironic wit and burlesque as well as a discussion of the value of humor as a way of transforming gloom and melancholy: "*A Midsummer Night's Dream* is a play in the spirit of Mercutio: the dreaming in it includes the knowledge 'that dreamers often lie.' The comedy and tragedy are companion pieces: the one moves away from sadness as the other moves away from mirth."

Alexander Leggatt's essay focuses on a similar issue, the self-awareness in the confrontation of supernaturals and mortals. Beginning with the example of the interaction between Titania and Bottom, Leggatt finds a deeper logic to the way these two very different creatures respond to each other; Bottom has acquired a touch of magic while Titania is experiencing human passion. Leggatt's essay continues to examine the issue of misperception between the other sets of characters, all of whom are both susceptible to misapprehension and at the same time indispensable to the play's ultimate harmony. He notes Shakespeare's acute understanding that a presentation of the transcendent power of love must necessarily omit parts of reality: "Art, like love, is a limited and special vision; but like love it has by its very limits a transforming power, creating a small area of order in the vast chaos of the world . . . . [A]t the moment when the play most clearly declares itself to be trivial, we have the strongest appeal to our sympathy for it. . . ."

Ruth Nevo's essay "Fancy's Images" celebrates Shakespeare's originality in devising an intricate plot in order to reach a benign resolution to the conflict between folly and wisdom. According to Nevo, the core problem is that the various contenders in the love rivalries fail to understand what they actually want. Nevo argues that the resolution to the multilayered twists and turns of the plot, which produce a surfeit of misunderstandings and other foolish errors, is to set imagination straight: "But the whole question of corrected vision, of the tutored imagination, goes beyond the merely technical exigencics of plot. It is the essential mediator of the benign, non-disjunctive dialectic which conjures rejoicing out of mockery, and wisdom out of folly."

The Canadian Northrop Frye, one of the great critics of the twentieth century, wrote what Harold Bloom once called "a magisterial overview of the play, one that shows us the affinities of the wood-world with that part of the mind below the reason's encounter with objective reality, and yet connected with the hidden creative powers of the mind." Like so many other critics, Frye praises the character of Bottom, who "has been closer to the centre of this wonderful and mysterious play than any other of its characters."

In his introduction to a volume of the play in the Bloom's Notes series, Harold Bloom himself writes, "*A Midsummer Night's Dream* is unique in Shakespeare, because it is the most visionary of his dramas, beyond even *The Tempest* as a transcendental enterprise." His 1987 essay on the play centers on Puck and Bottom as the antithetical figures at the two limits of the drama's visions. Bloom notes his particular fondness for the "surpassingly amiable" Bottom.

Finally, toward the end of the century, David Wiles applies a modified notion of the "carnivalesque" in Shakespeare's time as a festive celebration more closely allied to the aristocracy than to the contemporary "popular audience" of *A Midsummer Night's Dream*, and he proceeds to analyze the play in terms of a very specific aristocratic holiday. Wiles argues that the particular occasion for which the play was written was an aristocratic wedding held on February 19, 1506, and, consequently, that the main action of the play should be understood within the context of a transitional, "dream-like space," in which the summertime setting is itself an inversion of the actual wedding date.

1904—Gilbert Keith Chesterton. "*A Midsummer Night's Dream*," from *Chesterton on Shakespeare*

G.K. Chesterton (1874–1936) was an influential English writer whose vast writings include journalism, philosophy, poetry, biography, Christian apologetics, fantasy, and detective fiction. His works include *The Man Who Was Thursday: A Nightmare* (1908), *Chaucer* (1932), and the *Father Brown* detective stories.

The greatest of Shakespeare's comedies is also, from a certain point of view, the greatest of his plays. No one would maintain that it occupied this position in the matter of psychological study if by psychological study we mean the study of individual characters in a play. No one would maintain that Puck was a character in the sense that Falstaff is a character, or that the critic stood awed before the psychology of Peaseblossom. But there is a sense in which the play is perhaps a greater triumph of psychology than *Hamlet* itself. It may well be questioned whether in any other literary work in the world is so vividly rendered a social and spiritual atmosphere. There is an atmosphere in *Hamlet*, for instance, a somewhat murky and even melodramatic one, but it is subordinate to the great character, and morally inferior to him; the darkness is only a background for the isolated star of intellect. But *A Midsummer Night's Dream* is a psychological study, not of a solitary man, but of a spirit that unites mankind. The six men may sit talking in an inn; they may not know each other's names or see each other's faces before or after, but night or wine or great stories, or some rich and branching discussion may make them all at one, if not absolutely with each other, at least with that invisible seventh man who is the harmony of all of them. That seventh man is the hero of *A Midsummer Night's Dream*.

A study of the play from a literary or philosophical point of view must therefore be founded upon some serious realisation of what this atmosphere is. In a lecture upon *As You Like It*, Mr. Bernard Shaw made a suggestion which is an admirable example of his amazing ingenuity and of his one most interesting limitation. In maintaining that the light sentiment and optimism of the comedy were regarded by Shakespeare merely as the characteristics of a more or less cynical pot-boiler, he actually suggested that the title "As You Like It" was a taunting address to the public in disparagement of their taste and the dramatist's own work. If Mr. Bernard Shaw had conceived of Shakespeare as insisting that Ben Jonson should wear Jaeger underclothing or join the Blue Ribbon Army, or distribute little pamphlets for the non-payment of rates, he could scarcely have conceived anything more violently opposed to the whole spirit of Elizabethan comedy than the spiteful and priggish modernism of such a taunt. Shakespeare might make the fastidious and cultivated Hamlet, moving in his own melancholy and purely mental world, warn players against an over-indulgence towards the rabble. But the very soul and meaning of the great comedies is that of an uproarious communion between the public and the play, a communion so chaotic that whole scenes of silliness and violence lead us almost to think that some of the "rowdies" from the pit have climbed over the footlights. The title "As you Like It", is, of course, an expression of utter carelessness, but it is not the bitter carelessness which Mr. Bernard Shaw fantastically reads into it; it is the god-like and inexhaustible carelessness of a happy man. And the simple proof of this is that there are scores of these genially taunting titles scattered through the whole of Elizabethan comedy. Is "As You Like It" a title demanding a dark and ironic explanation in a school of comedy which called its plays "What You Will", "A Mad World, My Masters", "If It Be Not Good, the Devil Is In It", "The Devil is an Ass", "An Humorous Day's Mirth", and "A Midsummer Night's Dream"? Every one of these titles is flung at the head of the public as a drunken lord might fling a purse at his footman. Would Mr. Shaw maintain that "If It Be Not Good, the Devil Is In It", was the opposite of "As You Like It", and was a solemn invocation of the supernatural powers to testify to the care and perfection of the literary workmanship? The one explanation is as Elizabethan as the other.

Now in the reason for this modern and pedantic error lies the whole secret and difficulty of such plays as *A Midsummer Night's Dream*. The sentiment of such a play, so far as it can be summed up at all, can be summed up in one sentence. It is the mysticism of happiness. That is to say, it is the conception that as man lives upon a borderland he may find himself in the spiritual or supernatural atmosphere, not only through being profoundly sad or meditative, but by being extravagantly happy. The soul might be rapt out of the body in an agony of sorrow, or a trance of ecstasy; but it might also be rapt out of the body in a paroxysm of laughter. Sorrow we know can go beyond itself; so, according to Shakespeare, can pleasure go beyond itself and become something dangerous and unknown. And the reason that the logical and destructive modern school, of which Mr. Bernard Shaw is an example, does not grasp this purely exuberant nature of the comedies is simply that their logical and destructive attitude have rendered impossible the very experience of this preternatural exuberance. We cannot realise *As You Like It* if we are always considering it as we understand it. We cannot have *A Midsummer's Night Dream* if our one object in life is to keep ourselves awake with the black coffee of criticism. The whole question which is balanced, and balanced nobly and fairly, in *A Midsummer Night's Dream*, is whether the life of waking, or the life of the vision, is the real life, the *sine quâ non* of man. But it is difficult to see what superiority for the purpose of judging is possessed by people whose pride it is not to live the life of vision at all. At least it is questionable whether the Elizabethan did not know more about both worlds than the modern intellectual. It is not altogether improbably that Shakespeare would not only have had a clearer vision of the fairies, but would have shot very much straighter at a deer and netted much more money for his performances than a member of the Stage Society.

In pure poetry and the intoxication of words, Shakespeare never rose higher than he rises in this play. But in spite of this fact, the supreme literary merit of *A Midsummer Night's Dream* is a merit of design. The amazing symmetry, the amazing artistic and moral beauty of that design, can be stated very briefly. The story opens in the sane and common world with the pleasant seriousness of very young lovers and very young friends. Then, as the figures advance into the tangled wood of young troubles and stolen happiness, a change and bewilderment begins to fall on them. They lose their way and their wits for they are in the heart of fairyland. Their words, their hungers, their very figures grow more and more dim and fantastic, like dreams within dreams, in the supernatural mist of Puck. Then the dream-fumes begin to clear, and characters and spectators begin to awaken together to the noise of horns and dogs and the clean and bracing morning. Theseus, the incarnation of a happy and generous rationalism, expounds in hackneyed and superb lines the sane view of such psychic experiences, pointing out with a reverent and sympathetic scepticism that all these fairies and spells are themselves but the emanations, the unconscious masterpieces, of man himself. The whole company falls back into a splendid human laughter. There is a rush for banqueting and private theatricals, and over all these things ripples one of those frivolous and inspired conversations in which every good saying seems to die in giving birth to another. If ever the son of a man in his wanderings was at home and drinking by the fireside, he is at home in the house of Theseus. All the dreams have been forgotten, as a melancholy dream remembered throughout the morning might be forgotten in the human certainty of any other triumphant evening party; and so the play seems naturally ended. It began on the earth and it ends on the earth. Thus to round off the whole midsummer night's dream in an eclipse of daylight is an effect of genius. But of this comedy, as I have said, the mark is that genius goes beyond itself; and one touch is added which makes the play colossal. Theseus and his train retire with a crashing finale, full of humour and wisdom and things set right, and silence falls on the house. Then there comes a faint sound of little feet, and for a moment, as it were, the' elves look into the house, asking which is the reality. "Suppose we are the realities and they the shadows." If that ending were acted properly any modern man would feel shaken to his marrow if he had to walk home from the theatre through a country lane.

It is a trite matter, of course, though in a general criticism a more or less indispensable one to comment upon another point of artistic perfection, the extraordinarily human and accurate manner in which the play catches the atmosphere of a dream. The chase and tangle and frustration of the incidents and personalities are well known to every one who has dreamt of perpetually falling over precipices or perpetually missing trains. While following out clearly and legally the necessary narrative of the drama, the author contrives to include every one of the main peculiarities of the exasperating dream. Here is the pursuit of the man we cannot catch, the flight from the man we cannot see; here is the perpetual returning to the same place, here is the crazy alteration in the very objects of our desire, the substitution of one face for another face, the putting of the wrong souls in the wrong bodies, the fantastic disloyalties of the night, all this is as obvious as it is important. It is perhaps somewhat more worth remarking that there is about this confusion of comedy yet another essential characteristic of dreams. A dream can commonly be described as possessing an utter discordance of incident combined with a curious unity of mood; everything changes but the dreamer. It may begin with anything and end with anything, but if the dreamer is sad at the end he will be sad as if by prescience at the beginning; if he is cheerful at the beginning he will be cheerful if the stars fall. *A Midsummer Night's Dream* has in a most singular degree effected this difficult, this almost desperate subtlety. The events in the wandering wood are in themselves, and regarded as in broad daylight, not merely melancholy but bitterly cruel and ignominious. But yet by the spreading of an atmosphere as magic as the fog of Puck, Shakespeare contrives to make the whole matter mysteriously hilarious while it is palpably tragic, and mysteriously charitable, while it is in itself cynical. He contrives somehow to rob tragedy and treachery of their full sharpness, just as a toothache or a deadly danger from a tiger, or a precipice, is robbed of its sharpness in a pleasant dream. The creation of a brooding sentiment like this, a sentiment not merely independent of but actually opposed to the events, is a much greater triumph of art than the creation of the character of Othello.

It is difficult to approach critically so great a figure as that of Bottom the Weaver. He is greater and more mysterious than Hamlet, because the interest of such men as Bottom consists of a rich subconsciousness, and that of Hamlet in the comparatively superficial matter of a rich consciousness. And it is especially difficult in the present age which has become hag-ridden with the mere intellect. We are the victims of a curious confusion whereby being great is supposed to have something to do with being clever, as if there were the smallest reason to suppose that Achilles was clever, as if there were not on the contrary a great deal of internal evidence to indicate that he was next door to a fool. Greatness is a certain indescribable but perfectly familiar and palpable quality of size in the personality, of steadfastness, of strong flavour, of easy and natural self-expression. Such a man is as firm as a tree and as unique as a rhinoceros, and he might quite easily be as stupid as either of them. Fully as much as the great poet towers above the small poet the great fool towers above the small fool. We have all of us known rustics like Bottom the Weaver, men whose faces would be blank with idiocy if we tried for -ten days to explain the meaning of the National Debt, but who are yet great men, akin to Sigurd and

Hercules, heroes of the morning of the earth, because their words were their own words, their memories their own memories, and their vanity as large and simple as a great hill. We have all of us known friends in our own circle, men whom the intellectuals might justly describe as brainless, but whose presence in a room was like a fire roaring in the grate changing everything, lights and shadows and the air, whose entrances and exits were in some strange fashion events, whose point of view once expressed haunts and persuades the mind and almost intimidates it, whose manifest absurdity clings to the fancy like the beauty of first-love, and whose follies are recounted like the legends of a paladin. These are great men, there are millions of them in the world, though very few perhaps in the House of Commons. It is not in the cold halls of cleverness where celebrities seem to be important that we should look for the great. An intellectual salon is merely a training-ground for one faculty, and is akin to a fencing class or a rifle corps. It is in our own homes and environments, from Croydon to St. John's Wood, in old nurses, and gentlemen with hobbies, and talkative spinsters and vast incomparable butlers, that we may feel the presence of that blood of the gods. And this creature so hard to describe, so easy to remember, the august and memorable fool, has never been so sumptuously painted as in the Bottom of *A Midsummer Night's Dream*.

Bottom has the supreme mark of this real greatness in that like the true saint or the true hero he only differs from humanity in being as it were more human than humanity. It is not true, as the idle materialists of today suggest, that compared to the majority of men the hero appears cold and dehumanised; it is the majority who appear cold and dehumanised in the presence of greatness. Bottom, like Don Quixote and Uncle Toby and Mr. Richard Swiveller and the rest of the Titans, has a huge and unfathomable weakness, his silliness is on a great scale, and when he blows his own trumpet it is like the trumpet of the Resurrection. The other rustics in the play accept his leadership not merely naturally but exuberantly; they have to the full that primary and savage unselfishness, that uproarious abnegation which makes simple men take pleasure in falling short of a hero, that unquestionable element of basic human nature which has never been expressed, outside this play, so perfectly as in the incomparable chapter at the beginning of *Evan Harrington* in which the praises of The Great Mel are sung with a lyric energy by the tradesmen whom he has cheated. Twopenny sceptics write of the egoism of primal human nature; it is reserved for great men like Shakespeare and Meredith to detect and make vivid this rude and subconscious unselfishness which is older than self. They alone with their insatiable tolerance can perceive all the spiritual devotion in the soul of a snob.

And it is this natural play between the rich simplicity of Bottom and the simple simplicity of his comrades which constitutes the unapproachable excellence of the farcical scenes in this play. Bottom's sensibility to literature is perfectly fiery and genuine, a great deal more genuine than that of a great many cultivated critics of literature—"the raging rocks, and shivering shocks shall break the locks of prison gates, and Phoebus' car shall shine from far, and make and mar the foolish fates", is exceedingly good poetical diction with a real throb and swell in it, and if it is slightly and almost imperceptibly deficient in the matter of sense, it is certainly every bit as sensible as a good many other rhetorical speeches in Shakespeare put into the mouths of kings and lovers and even the spirits of the dead. If Bottom liked cant for its own sake the fact only constitutes another point of sympathy between him and his literary creator. But the style of the thing, though deliberately bombastic and ludicrous, is quite literary, the alliteration falls like wave upon wave, and the whole verse, like a billow mounts higher and higher before it crashes. There is nothing mean about this folly; nor is there in the whole realm of literature a figure so free from vulgarity. The man vitally base and foolish sings "The Honeysuckle and the Bee"; he does not rant about "raging rocks" and "the car of Phibbus". Dickens, who more perhaps than any modern man had the mental hospitality and the thoughtless wisdom of Shakespeare, perceived and expressed admirably the same truth. He perceived, that is to say, that quite indefensible idiots have very often a real sense of, and enthusiasm for letters. Mr. Micawber loved eloquence and poetry with his whole immortal soul; words and visionary pictures kept him alive in the absence of food and money, as they might have kept a saint fasting in a desert. Dick Swiveller did not make his inimitable quotations from Moore and Byron merely as flippant digressions. He made them because he loved a great school of poetry. The sincere love of books has nothing to do with cleverness or stupidity any more than any other sincere love. It is a quality of character, a freshness, a power of pleasure, a power of faith. A silly person may delight in reading masterpieces just as a silly person may delight in picking flowers. A fool may be in love with a poet as he may be in love with a woman. And the triumph of Bottom is that he loves rhetoric and his own taste in the arts, and this is all that can be achieved by Theseus, or for the matter of that by Cosimo di Medici. It is worth remarking as an extremely fine touch in the picture of Bottom that his literary taste is almost everywhere concerned with sound rather than sense. He begins the rehearsal with a boisterous readiness, "Thisby, the flowers of odious savours sweete." "Odours, odours," says Quince, in remonstrance, and the word is accepted in accordance with the cold and heavy rules which require an element of meaning in a poetical passage. But "Thisby, the flowers of odious savours sweete", Bottom's version, is an immeasurably finer and more resonant line. The "i" which he inserts is an inspiration of metricism.

There is another aspect of this great play which ought to be kept familiarly in the mind. Extravagant as is the masquerade of the story, it is a very perfect aesthetic harmony down to such *coup-de-maître* as the name of Bottom, or the flower called Love in Idleness. In the whole matter it may be said that there

is one accidental discord; that is in the name of Theseus, and the whole city of
Athens in which the events take place. Shakespeare's description of Athens in
A Midsummer Night's Dream is the best description of England that he or any
one else ever wrote. Theseus is quite obviously only an English squire, fond
of hunting, kindly to his tenants, hospitable with a certain flamboyant vanity.
The mechanics are English mechanics, talking to each other with the queer
formality of the poor. Above all, the fairies are English; to compare them
with the beautiful patrician spirits of Irish legend, for instance, is suddenly to
discover that we have, after all, a folk-lore and a mythology, or had it at least in
Shakespeare's day. Robin Goodfellow, upsetting the old women's ale, or pulling
the stool from under them, has nothing of the poignant Celtic beauty; his is
the horse-play of the invisible world. Perhaps it is some debased inheritance
of English life which makes American ghosts so fond of quite undignified
practical jokes. But this union of mystery with farce is a note of the medieval
English. The play is the last glimpse of Merrie England, that distant but shining
and quite indubitable country. It would be difficult indeed to define wherein lay
the peculiar truth of the phrase "merrie England", though some conception of
it is quite necessary to the comprehension of *A Midsummer Night's Dream*. In
some cases at least, it may be said to lie in this, that the English of the Middle
Ages and the Renaissance, unlike the England of today, could conceive of the
idea of a merry supernaturalism. Amid all the great work of Puritanism the
damning indictment of it consists in one fact, that there was one only of the
fables of Christendom that it retained and renewed, and that was the belief in
witchcraft. It cast away the generous and wholesome superstition, it approved
only of the morbid and the dangerous. In their treatment of the great national
fairy-tale of good and evil, the Puritans killed St. George but carefully preserved
the Dragon. And this seventeenth-century tradition of dealing with the psychic
life still lies like a great shadow over England and America, so that if we glance
at a novel about occultism we may be perfectly certain that it deals with sad
or evil destiny. Whatever else we expect we certainly should never expect to
find in it spirits such as those in *Aylwin* as inspirers of a tale of tomfoolery
like the *Wrong Box* or *The Londoners*. That impossibility is the disappearance
of "merrie England" and Robin Goodfellow. It was a land to us incredible,
the land of a jolly occultism where the peasant cracked jokes with his patron
saint, and only cursed the fairies good-humouredly, as he might curse a lazy
servant. Shakespeare is English in everything, above all in his weaknesses. Just
as London, one of the greatest cities in the world, shows more slums and hides
more beauties than any other, so Shakespeare alone among the four giants of
poetry is a careless writer, and lets us come upon his splendours by accident, as
we come upon an old City church in the twist of a city street. He is English in
nothing so much as in that noble cosmopolitan unconsciousness which makes
him look eastward with the eyes of a child towards Athens or Verona. He loved

to talk of the glory of foreign lands, but he talked of them with the tongue and unquenchable spirit of England. It is too much the custom of a later patriotism to reverse this method and talk of England from morning till night, but to talk of her in a manner totally un-English. Casualness, incongruities, and a certain fine absence of mind are in the temper of England; the unconscious man with the ass's head is no bad type of the people. Materialistic philosophers and mechanical politicians have certainly succeeded in some cases in giving him a greater unity. The only question is, to which animal has he been thus successfully conformed?

1939—Mark Van Doren. "A Midsummer Night's Dream," from *Shakespeare*

Mark Van Doren (1894–1972) was a professor of literature at Columbia University, poet, critic, novelist, and short-story writer. He also served on the staff of *The Nation*. His *Collected Poems 1922–1938* won the Pulitzer Prize in 1940.

A Midsummer Night's Dream shines like *Romeo and Juliet* in darkness, but shines merrily. Lysander, one of the two nonentities who are its heroes, complains at the beginning about the brevity of love's course, and sums up his complaint with a line which would not be out of place in *Romeo and Juliet*:

So quick bright things come to confusion. [I. i. 149]

This, however, is at the beginning. Bright will come to clarity in a playful, sparkling night while fountains gush and spangled starlight betrays the presence in a wood near Athens of magic persons who can girdle the earth in forty minutes and bring any cure for human woe. Nor will the woe to be cured have any power to elicit our anxiety. The four lovers whose situation resembles so closely the situation created in *The Two Gentlemen of Verona* will come nowhere near the seriousness of that predicament; they will remain to the end four automatic creatures whose artificial and pretty fate it is to fall in and out of love like dolls, and like dolls they will go to sleep as soon as they are laid down. There will be no pretense that reason and love keep company, or that because they do not death lurks at the horizon. There is no death in *A Midsummer Night's Dream*, and the smiling horizon is immeasurably remote.

Robin Goodfellow ends the extravaganza with an apology to the audience for the "weak and idle theme" [V. i. 427] with which it has been entertained.

And Theseus, in honor of whose marriage with Hippolyta the entire action is occurring, dismisses most of it as a fairy toy, or such an airy nothing as some poet might give a local habitation and a name [V. i. 17]. But Robin is wrong about the theme, and Theseus does not describe the kind of poet Shakespeare is. For the world of this play is both veritable and large. It is not the tiny toy-shop that most such spectacles present, with quaint little people scampering on dry little errands, and with small music squeaking somewhere a childish accompaniment. There is room here for mortals no less than for fairies; both classes are at home, both groups move freely in a wide world where indeed they seem sometimes to have exchanged functions with one another. For these fairies do not sleep on flowers. Only Hermia can remember lying upon faint primrose-beds [I. i. 215], and only Bottom in the action as we have it ever dozes on pressed posies [III. i. 162]. The fairies themselves—Puck, Titania, Oberon—are too busy for that, and too hard-minded. The vocabulary of Puck is the most vernacular in the play; he talks of beans and crabs, dew-laps and ale, three-foot stools and sneezes [II. i. 42–57]. And with the king and queen of fairy-land he has immense spaces to travel. The three of them are citizens of all the universe there is, and as we listen to them the farthest portions of this universe stretch out, distant and glittering, like facets on a gem of infinite size. There is a specific geography, and the heavens are cold and high.

> *Oberon.* Thou rememb'rest
> Since once I sat upon a promontory,
> And heard a mermaid on a dolphin's back
> Uttering such dulcet and harmonious breath
> That the rude sea grew civil at her song,
> And certain stars shot madly from their spheres,
> To hear the sea-maid's music?
> *Robin.* I remember.
> *Oberon.* That very time I saw, but thou couldst not,
> Flying between the cold moon and the earth,
> Cupid all arm'd. A certain aim he took
> At a fair vestal throned by the west,
> And loos'd his love-shaft smartly from his bow,
> As it should pierce a hundred thousand hearts;
> But I might see young Cupid's fiery shaft
> Quench'd in the chaste beams of the watery moon,
> And the imperial votaress passed on,
> In maiden meditation, fancy-free.
> Yet mark'd I where the bolt of Cupid fell.
> It fell upon a little western flower. . . .

Fetch me that flower, the herb I shew'd thee once. . . .
Fetch me this herb; and be thou here again
Ere the leviathan can swim a league.
Robin. I'll put a girdle round about the earth
In forty minutes. [II. i. 148–76]

The business may be trivial, but the world is as big and as real as any world
we know. The promontory long ago; the rude sea that grew—not smooth,
not gentle, not anything pretty or poetical, but (the prosaic word is one of
Shakespeare's best) civil; the mermaid that is also a sea-maid; the direction west;
and the cold watery moon that rides so high above the earth—these are the signs
of its bigness, and they are so clear that we shall respect the prowess implied in
Robin's speed, nor shall we fail to be impressed by the news that Oberon has just
arrived from the farthest steep of India [II. i. 69].

Dr. [Samuel] Johnson and [William] Hazlitt copied [Joseph] Addison in
saying that if there could be persons like these they would act like this. Their
tribute was to the naturalness of Shakespeare's supernature. [John] Dryden's
tribute to its charm:

But Shakespeare's magic could not copied be;
Within that circle none durst walk but he

has an identical source: wonder that such things can be at all, and be so genuine.
The explanation is the size and the concreteness of Shakespeare's setting. And
the key to the structure of that setting is the watery moon to which Oberon so
casually referred.

The poetry of the play is dominated by the words moon and water. Theseus
and Hippolyta carve the moon in our memory with the strong, fresh strokes of
their opening dialogue:

Theseus. Now, fair Hippolyta, our nuptial hour
Draws on apace. Four happy days bring in
Another moon; but, O, methinks, how slow
This old moon wanes! She lingers my desires,
Like to a step-dame or a dowager
Long withering out a young man's revenue.
Hippolyta. Four days will quickly steep themselves in night;
Four nights will quickly dream away the time;
And then the moon, like to a silver bow
New-bent in heaven, shall behold the night
Of our solemnities. [I. i. 1–11]

This is not the sensuous, softer orb of *Antony and Cleopatra*, nor is it the sweet sleeping friend of Lorenzo and Jessica. It is brilliant and brisk, silver-distant, and an occasion for comedy in Theseus's worldly thought. Later on in the same scene he will call it cold and fruitless [I. 73], and Lysander will look forward to

> Tomorrow night, when Phoebe doth behold
> Her silver visage in the watery glass,
> Decking with liquid pearl the bladed grass. [I. i. 209–11]

Lysander has connected the image of the moon with the image of cool water on which it shines, and hereafter they will be inseparable. *A Midsummer Night's Dream* is drenched with dew when it is not saturated with rain. A film of water spreads over it, enhances and enlarges it miraculously. The fairy whom Robin hails as the second act opens wanders swifter than the moon's sphere through fire and flood. The moon, says Titania, is governess of floods, and in anger at Oberon's brawls has sucked up from the sea contagious fogs, made every river overflow, drowned the fields and rotted the green corn:

> The nine men's morris is fill'd up with mud,
> And the quaint mazes in the wanton green
> For lack of tread are undistinguishable. [II. i. 98–100]

Here in the west there has been a deluge, and every object still drips moisture. But even in the east there are waves and seas. The little changeling boy whom Titania will not surrender to Oberon is the son of a votaress on the other side of the earth:

> And, in the spiced Indian air, by night,
> Full often hath she gossip'd by my side,
> And sat with me on Neptune's yellow sands,
> Marking the embarked traders on the flood. [II. i. 124–27]

The jewels she promises Bottom will be fetched "from the deep" [III. i. 161]. And Oberon is addicted to treading seaside groves

> Even till the eastern gate, all fiery-red,
> Opening on Neptune with fair blessed beams,
> Turns into yellow gold his salt green streams. [III. ii. 391–93]

So by a kind of logic the mortals of the play continue to be washed with copious weeping. The roses in Hermia's cheeks fade fast "for want of rain" [I. i. 130], but rain will come. Demetrius "hails" and "showers" oaths on Helena [I. i. 245], whose eyes are bathed with salt tears [II. ii. 92–3]; and Hermia takes comfort in the tempest of her eyes [I. i. 131].

When the moon weeps, says Titania to Bottom, "weeps every little flower" [III. i. 204]. The flowers of *A Midsummer Night's Dream* are not the warm, sweet, dry ones of Perdita's garden, or even the daytime ones with which Fidele's brothers will strew her forest grave [in *The Winter's Tale*]. They are the damp flowers that hide among ferns and drip with dew. A pearl is hung in every cowslip's ear [II. i. 15]; the little western flower which Puck is sent to fetch is rich with juice; and luscious woodbine canopies the bank of wild thyme where Titania sleeps—not on but "in" musk-roses and eglantine. Moon, water, and wet flowers conspire to extend the world of *A Midsummer Night's Dream* until it is as large as all imaginable life. That is why the play is both so natural and so mysterious.

Nor do its regions fail to echo with an ample music. The mermaid on the promontory with her dulcet and harmonious breath sang distantly and long ago, but the world we walk in is filled with present sound.

> *Theseus.* Go, one of you, find out the forester,
> For now our observation is perform'd,
> And since we have the vaward of the day,
> My love shall hear the music of my hounds.
> Uncouple in the western valley, let them go.
> Dispatch, I say, and find the forester.
> We will, fair queen, up to the mountain's top
> And mark the musical confusion
> Of hounds and echo in conjunction.
> *Hippolyta.* I was with Hercules and Cadmus once,
> When in a wood of Crete they bay'd the bear
> With hounds of Sparta. Never did I hear
> Such gallant chiding; for, besides the groves,
> The skies, the fountains, every region near
> Seem'd all one mutual cry. I never heard
> So musical a discord, such sweet thunder.
> *Theseus.* My hounds are bred out of the Spartan kind.
> So flew'd, so sanded, and their heads are hung
> With ears that sweep away the morning dew;
> Crook-knee'd, and dew-lapp'd like Thessalian bulls;
> Slow in pursuit, but match'd in mouth like bells,
> Each under each. A cry more tuneable
> Was never holla'd to, nor cheer'd with horn,
> In Crete, in Sparta, nor in Thessaly.
> Judge when you hear. [IV. i. 107–31]

Had Shakespeare written nothing else than this he still might be the best of English poets. Most poetry which tries to be music also is less than poetry. This is absolute. The melody which commences with such spirit in Theseus's fifth line has already reached the complexity of counterpoint in his eight and ninth; Hippolyta carries it to a like limit in the line with which she closes; and Theseus, taking it back from her, hugely increases its volume, first by reminding us that the hounds have form and muscle, and then by daring the grand dissonance, the mixed thunder, of bulls and bells. The passage sets a forest ringing, and supplies a play with the music it has deserved.

But Shakespeare is still more a poet because the passage is incidental to his creation. The creation with which he is now busy is not a passage, a single effect; it is a play, and though this one contribution has been mighty there are many others. And none of the others is mightier than bully Bottom's.

Bottom likes music too. "I have a reasonable good ear," he tells Titania. "Let's have the tongs and the bones" [IV. i. 28–9]. So does he take an interest in moonshine, if only among the pages of an almanac. "A calendar, a calendar!" he calls. "Find out moonshine, find out moonshine" [III. i. 53–4]. When they find the moon, those Athenian mechanics of whom he is king, it has in it what the cold fairy moon cannot be conceived as having, the familiar man of folklore. Bottom and his fellows domesticate the moon, as they domesticate every other element of which Shakespeare has made poetry. And the final effect is parody. Bottom's amazed oration concerning his dream follows hard upon the lovers' discourse concerning dreams and delusions; but it is in prose, and the speaker is utterly literal when he pronounces that it will be called Bottom's dream because it hath no bottom [IV. i. 220]. Nor is the story of Pyramus and Thisbe as the mechanics act it anything but a burlesque of *Romeo and Juliet*.

> O night, which ever art when day is not! . . .
> And thou, O wall, O sweet, O lovely wall,
> That stand'st between her father's ground and mine!
> Thou wall, O wall,
> O sweet and lovely wall. [V. i. 172–7]

Shakespeare has come, even this early, to the farthest limit of comedy. The end of comedy is self-parody, and its wisdom is self-understanding. Never again will he work without a full comprehension of the thing he is working at; of the probability that other and contrary things are of equal importance; of the certainty that his being a poet who can do anything he wants to do is not the only thing to be, or the best possible thing; of the axiom that the whole is greater than the part—the part in his instance being one play among many thinkable plays, or one man, himself, among the multitude that populate a world for whose size and variety he with such giant strides is reaching respect. Bully Bottom and his friends have lived three centuries to good purpose, but to no better purpose at any time than the one they first had—namely, in their sublime innocence, their earthbound, idiot openness and charity of soul, to bring it about that their creator should become not only the finest of poets but the one who makes the fewest claims for poetry.

―――――――――

1951—Harold Goddard. *"A Midsummer-Night's Dream,"* from *The Meaning of Shakespeare*

Harold Goddard (1878-1950) was head of the English Department at Swarthmore College. One of the most important twentieth-century books on Shakespeare is his *The Meaning of Shakespeare*, published after his death.

A Midsummer-Night's Dream is one of the lightest and in many respects the most purely playful of Shakespeare's plays. Yet it is surpassed by few if any of his early works in its importance for an understanding of the unfolding of his genius. It is characteristic of its author that he should have chosen this fanciful dream-play through which to announce for the first time in overt and unmistakable fashion the conviction that underlies every one of his supreme Tragedies: that this world of sense in which we live is but the surface of a vaster unseen world by which the actions of men are affected or overruled. He had already in *The Comedy of Errors* hinted at a witchcraft at work behind events. But that at the moment seemed little more than the author's apology for the amount of coincidence in his plot. Now he begins to explore the causes of coincidence. Not until the end of his career, in *The Tempest*, was he to treat this theme with such directness, not even in *Macbeth*. It may be objected that this is taking a mere dream or fantasy quite too seriously. It is of course possible to hold that in *A Midsummer-Night's Dream* Shakespeare is not so much giving utterance to convictions of his own as recording a folklore which itself carries certain metaphysical implications. There is doubtless some truth in this view—how much it is hard to tell. But it makes little difference. For the implications, in the latter case, were the seeds of the convictions, and our mistake, if any, is merely that of finding the oak in the acorn. The congruity, in spite of their differences, of *A Midsummer-Night's Dream* with *The Tempest* is one of the most striking demonstrations of the continuity and integrity of Shakespeare's genius that his works afford.

There are two passages, as distinct from incidents, in *A Midsummer-Night's Dream* that perhaps above all others embody its central theme. Each enhances the other. One of them, Theseus' well-known speech on the imagination at the beginning of Act V, has always been accorded due importance. The other, oddly, though almost as universally praised, has generally been looked on as a kind of digression, a purple patch that justifies itself by its own beauty rather than through any particular pertinence to the rest of the play. The lines have been widely and deservedly acclaimed for their sound. But their euphony is only one aspect of their miraculous quality. The passage is the one in the first scene of Act IV where Theseus and Hippolyta, just as the dogs are about to be released for the hunt, speak of the music of the hounds in words that by some magic catch and echo that very music itself:

> *The.*: My love shall hear the music of my hounds.
> Uncouple in the western valley; let them go:
> Dispatch, I say, and find the forester.
> We will, fair queen, up to the mountain's top,
> And mark the musical confusion
> Of hounds and echo in conjunction.
> *Hip.*: I was with Hercules and Cadmus once,
> When in a wood of Crete they bay'd the bear
> With hounds of Sparta: never did I hear
> Such gallant chiding; for, besides the groves,
> The skies, the fountains, every region near
> Seem'd all one mutual cry. I never heard
> So musical a discord, such sweet thunder.
> *The.*: My hounds are bred out of the Spartan kind,
> So flew'd, so sanded; and their heads are hung
> With ears that sweep away the morning dew;
> Crook-knee'd, and dew-lapp'd like Thessalian bulls;
> Slow in pursuit, but match'd in mouth like bells,
> Each under each. A cry more tuneable
> Was never holla'd to, nor cheer'd with horn,
> In Crete, in Sparta, nor in Thessaly:
> Judge, when you hear.

This a digression! On the contrary it is as nearly perfect a metaphor as could be conceived for *A Midsummer-Night's Dream* itself and for the incomparable counterpoint with which its own confusions and discords are melted into the "sweet thunder" of a single musical effect. How can British fairies and Athenian nobility be mingled with decency in the same play? As easily as the "confusion" of hounds and echoes can make "conjunction." How can the crossings and bewilderments of the four lovers lead to their happy reunion at the end? As easily as discord can contribute to harmony in music. How can the foolish and awkward pranks of the rustics adorn the wedding celebration of a great duke? As easily, to turn things the other way around, as a fairy dream can enter the head of an ass or as animals who are like bulls can emit sounds that are like bells—as easily as thunder can be sweet.

The very incongruities, anachronisms, contradictions, and impossible juxtapositions of *A Midsummer-Night's Dream*, and the triumphant manner in which the poet reduces them to a harmony, are what more than anything else make this play a masterpiece. The hounds are symbols of the hunt, and so of death. But their voices are transmuted by distance, in the ear of the listener, to symbols of harmony and life. The hunt is called off; the will of the cruel father is overborne; a triple wedding is substituted for it:

> Our purpos'd hunting shall be set aside.
> Away with us to Athens: three and three,
> We'll hold a feast in great solemnity.

We might discover the whole history of humanity, past and future, in those lines.

It is right here that the passage about the hounds links with Theseus' speech on the imagination. The Duke, in words too well known to need quotation, tells of the power of this faculty, whether in the lunatic, the lover, or the poet, to create something out of nothing. The poet alone, however, has power to capture this "airy nothing" and anchor it, as it were, to reality, even as Shakespeare gives actuality to fairies in this very play. Yet Theseus is suspicious of the "tricks" of imagination, conscious of its illusory quality. He hints that it must be brought to the test of "cool reason." Strictly, what Theseus is talking about is not imagination at all in its proper sense, but fantasy. Hippolyta catches just this distinction and for once seems wiser than her lover. She holds that the miracles of love are even greater than those of fancy, and because the same miracle takes place at the same time in more than one mind she believes that they testify to something solid and lasting that emerges from this "airy nothing." Theseus had called this faculty more strange than true. Hippolyta holds it both strange and true:

> But all the story of the night told over,
> And all their minds transfigur'd so together,
> More witnesseth than fancy's images,
> And grows to something of great constancy,
> But, howsoever, strange and admirable.

In practice Theseus agrees with this exactly, as is shown later in the same scene when he insists on hearing the play that the craftsmen have prepared. The master of revels, Philostrate, protests against its selection:

> *Phi.*: in all the play
> There is not one word apt, one player fitted.
> . . . No, my noble lord,
> It is not for you. I have heard it over,
> And it is nothing, nothing in the world. . . .
> *The.*: I will hear that play;
> For never anything can be amiss,
> When simpleness and duty tender it. . . .
> *Hip.*: He says they can do nothing in this kind.
> *The.*: The kinder we, to give them thanks for nothing.

That four-times reiterated "nothing" is Shakespeare's way of sending our minds back to the "airy nothing" of Theseus' earlier speech which, he then said and now proves, imagination has power to turn into something actual. It is Hippolyta this time who fails.

> This is the silliest stuff that ever I heard,[1]

she protests as the play proceeds. Appropriately, now that it is a question of art, Theseus turns out to be wiser than she, as she was wiser than he when it was a question of love. "The best in this kind are but shadows," he reminds her, "and the worst are no worse, if imagination amend them." At last, Theseus is using "imagination" in its proper sense, and in his words we seem to catch the very accent and secret of the poet's own tolerance and sympathy.

Shakespeare, in this play and elsewhere, was only too well aware how frail imagination can appear in the face of ineluctable fact. "The course of true love never did run smooth." "So quick bright things come to confusion."

> These things seem small and undistinguishable,
> Like far-off mountains turned into clouds.

What, indeed, is more insubstantial than a midsummer-night's dream? And yet from about this time, if not from the beginning, he never lost faith in "bright things," in the power of the imagination to transmute the lead of life into its own gold. More and more, if with some ebbings, some descents into the valleys, this faith grew in him, in Hippolyta's words, to "something of great constancy." Is it any wonder, after the miracle that Imagination had performed through him in this very play?

A Midsummer-Night's Dream is a kind of fugue with four voices

> match'd in mouth like bells,
> Each under each.

There are the fairies. There are the lovers. There are the rustics. There is the court. What metaphysical as well as social gulfs divide them! But Imagination bridges them all. Imagination makes them all one.

And the play has four voices in another and profounder sense.

A Midsummer-Night's Dream is itself, as its title says, a dream. Its action occurs mostly at night. Its atmosphere is that of moonlight and shadows. Its characters are forever falling asleep and dreaming. And at the end Puck invites the audience to believe that as they have been sitting there they have nodded and slumbered and that all that has passed before them has been a vision.

But as the other part of its title suggests, *A Midsummer-Night's Dream* is not only a dream, it is "play" in the quite literal sense of that term, a piece pervaded with the atmosphere of innocent idleness and joy befitting a midsummer night. It is not merely a play; it is the spirit of play in its essence. From the pranks of Puck and the frolics of the fairies, through the hide-and-seek of the lovers in the wood and the rehearsals of the rustics, on to the wedding festivities of the court and the final presentation of the masque of Pyramus and Thisbe, the tone of the piece is that of love-in-idleness, of activity for the sheer fun of it and for its own sake.

And because *A Midsummer-Night's Dream* is permeated with this spirit of doing things just for the love of doing them or for the love of the one for whom they are done, because the drama opens and closes on the wedding note and what comes between is just an interweaving of love stories, the piece may be said to be not only *dream* from end to end, and *play* from end to end, but also *love* from end to end.

And finally *A Midsummer-Night's Dream* is art from end to end—not just a work of art itself, which of course it is, but dedicated in good measure to the theme of art and made up of many little works of art of varying degrees of merit: its innumerable songs, its perpetual references to music, its rehearsal and presentation of the story of Pyramus and Thisbe, to say nothing of its many quotable passages, which, like the one about the hounds, the one about the superiority of silence to eloquence, the one about true love, the one about the mermaid on the dolphin's back, when lifted from their context seem like poems or pictures complete in themselves, whatever subtler values they may have in relation to the whole.

Dream, play, love, art. Surely it is no coincidence that these four "subjects" which are here interwoven with such consummate polyphony represent the four main aspects under which Imagination reveals itself in human life. Dream: what is that but a name for the world out of which man emerges into conscious life, the world of the unconscious as we have a habit of calling it today? Play: the instrument by which the child instinctively repeats the experience of the race and so by rehearsal prepares himself for the drama of life. Love: a revelation to each of the sexes that it is but a fragment of Another, which, by combined truth and illusion, seems at first concentrated in a person of the opposite sex. Art: the dream become conscious of itself, play grown to an adult estate, love freed of its illusion and transferred to wider and higher than personal ends. Dream, play, love, art: these four. Is there a fifth?

The fifth perhaps is what we finally have in this play, a union of the other four, Imagination in its quintessence—not just dream, nor play, nor love, nor art, but something above and beyond them all. With the attainment of it, the first becomes last, dream comes full circle as Vision, an immediate conscious apprehension of an invisible world, or, if you will, transubstantiation of the world of sense into something beyond itself.[2]

The example of Bottom and his transformation will serve to bring these un-Shakespearean abstractions back to the concrete. To the average reader, Puck and Bottom are probably the most memorable characters in the play, Bottom especially. This instinct is right. Bottom is as much the master-character here as Launce is in *The Two Gentlemen of Verona*. Bottom symbolizes the earthy, the ponderous, the slow, in contrast with Puck, who is all that is quick, light, and aerial. Bottom is substance, the real in the common acceptation of that term. If Puck is the apex, Bottom is the base without whose four-square foundation the pyramid of life would topple over. He is the antithesis of the thesis of the play, the ballast that keeps the elfin bark of it from capsizing. He is literally what goes to the bottom. Like all heavy things he is content with his place in life, but his egotism is the unconscious selfishness of a child, both a sense and a consequence of his own individuality, not greed but pride in the good significance of that word. His realistic conception of stagecraft is in character. To Puck, Bottom is an ass. Yet Titania falls in love with him, ass's head and all.

> And I will purge thy mortal grossness so
> That thou shalt like an airy spirit go,

she promises. And she keeps her promise by sending him Bottom's dream.

The moment when Bottom awakens from this dream is the supreme moment of the play."[3] There is nothing more wonderful in the poet's early works and few things more wonderful in any of them. For what Shakespeare has caught here in perfection is the original miracle of the Imagination, the awakening of spiritual life in the animal man. Bottom is an ass. If Bottom can be redeemed, matter itself and man in all his materiality can be redeemed also. Democracy becomes possible. Nothing less than this is what this incident implies. Yet when it is acted, so far as my experience in the theater goes, this divine insight is reduced to nothing but an occasion for roars of laughter. Laughter of course there should be, but laughter shot through with a beauty and pathos close to tears. Only an actor of genius could do justice to it. Bottom himself best indicates its quality when he declares that the dream deserves to be *sung* at the conclusion of a play and that it should be called Bottom's dream "because it hath no bottom." It is the same thought that Thoreau expounds when he shows why men persist in believing in bottomless ponds. For a moment in this scene, however far over the horizon, we sense the Shakespeare who was to describe the death of Falstaff, compose *King Lear*, and create Caliban.

Indeed, *A Midsummer-Night's Dream* as a whole is prophetic, in one respect at least, as is no other of the earlier plays, of the course the poet's genius was to take. There are few more fruitful ways of regarding his works than to think of them as an account of the warfare between Imagination and Chaos—or, if you will, between Imagination and the World—the story of the multifarious attempts of the divine faculty in man to ignore, to escape, to outwit, to surmount, to combat, to subdue, to forgive, to convert, to redeem, to transmute into its own substance, as the case may be, the powers of disorder that possess the world. Taken retrospectively, *A Midsummer-Night's Dream* seems like the argument of this story, like an overture to the vast musical composition which the poet's later masterpieces make up, like a seed from which the Shakespearean flower developed and unfolded.

NOTES

1. Just what Samuel Pepys said of *A Midsummer-Night's Dream* itself, "The most insipid ridiculous play that ever I saw."

2. I refrain from using the word Religion for this ultimate phase of the Imagination. A word so contaminated with theological, ecclesiastic, and moral considerations can lead only to confusion. If the word were only uncontaminated, it might be a near synonym for Vision as I use it.

3. "I have had a most rare vision. I have had a dream, past the wit of man to say what dream it was. Man is but an ass, if he go about to expound this dream. Methought I was—there is no man can tell what. Methought I was,—and methought I had,—but man is but a patch'd fool, if he will offer to say what methought I had. The eye of man hath not heard, the ear of man hath not seen, man's hand is not able to taste, his tongue to conceive, nor his heart to report, what my dream was. I will get Peter Quince to write a ballad of this dream. It shall be called 'Bottom's Dream,' because it hath no bottom; and I will sing it in the latter end of a play, before the Duke; peradventure, to make it the more gracious, I shall sing it at her death."

1959—C. L. Barber. "May Games and Metamorphoses on a Midsummer Night," from *Shakespeare's Festive Comedy: A Study of Dramatic Form and its Relation to Social Custom*

C. L. Barber was a professor of literature at the University of California, Santa Cruz. He is also the co-author, with Richard P. Wheeler, of *The Whole Journey: Shakespeare's Power of Development* and *The Story of Language*.

Such shaping fantasies, that apprehend
More than cool reason ever comprehends.

If Shakespeare had called *A Midsummer Night's Dream* by a title that referred to pageantry and May games, the aspects of it with which I shall be chiefly concerned would be more often discussed. To honor a noble wedding, Shakespeare gathered up in a play the sort of pageantry which was usually presented piece-meal at aristocratic entertainments, in park and court as well as in hall. And the May game, everybody's pastime, gave the pattern for his whole action, which moves "from the town to the grove" and back again, bringing in summer to the bridal. These things were familiar and did not need to be stressed by a title.

Shakespeare's young men and maids, like those Stubbes described in May games, "run gadding over night to the woods, . . . where they spend the whole night in pleasant pastimes—" and in the fierce vexation which often goes with the pastimes of falling in and out of love and threatening to fight about it. "And no marvel," Stubbes exclaimed about such headlong business, "for there is a great Lord present among them, as superintendent and Lord over their pastimes and sports, namely, Satan, prince of hell."[1] In making Oberon, prince of fairies, into the May king, Shakespeare urbanely plays with the notion of a supernatural power at work in holiday: he presents the common May game presided over by an aristocratic garden god. Titania is a Summer Lady who "waxeth wounder proud":

I am a spirit of no common rate,
The summer still doth tend upon my state . . . (III.i.157–158)

And Puck, as jester, promotes the "night-rule" version of misrule over which Oberon is superintendent and lord in the "haunted grove." The lovers originally meet

in the wood, a league without the town,
Where I did meet thee once with Helena
To do observance to a morn of May. (I.i.165–167)

Next morning, when Theseus and Hippolyta find the lovers sleeping, it is after their own early "observation is performed"—presumably some May-game observance, of a suitably aristocratic kind, for Theseus jumps to the conclusion that

> No doubt they rose up early to observe
> The rite of May; and, hearing our intent,
> Came here in grace of our solemnity. (IV.i.135–137)

These lines need not mean that the play's action happens on May Day. Shakespeare does not make himself accountable for exact chronological inferences; the moon that will be new according to Hippolyta will shine according to Bottom's almanac. And in any case, people went Maying at various times, "Against May, Whitsunday, and other time" is the way Stubbes puts it. This Maying can be thought of as happening on a midsummer night, even on Midsummer Eve itself, so that its accidents are complicated by the delusions of a magic time. (May Week at Cambridge University still comes in June.) The point of the allusions is not the date, but the *kind* of holiday occasion.[2] The Maying is completed when Oberon and Titania with their trains come into the great chamber to bring the blessings of fertility. They are at once common and special, a May king and queen making their good luck visit to the manor house, and a pair of country gods, half-English and half-Ovid, come to bring their powers in tribute to great lords and ladies.

The play's relationship to pageantry is most prominent in the scene where the fairies are introduced by our seeing their quarrel. This encounter is the sort of thing that Elizabeth and the wedding party might have happened on while walking about in the park during the long summer dusk. The fairy couple accuse each other of the usual weakness of pageant personages—a compelling love for royal personages:

> Why art thou here,
> Come from the farthest steep of India,
> But that, forsooth, the bouncing Amazon,
> Your buskin'd mistress and your warrior love,
> To Theseus must be wedded, and you come
> To give their bed joy and prosperity? (II.i.68–73)

Oberon describes an earlier entertainment, very likely one in which the family of the real-life bride or groom had been concerned:

> My gentle Puck, come hither. Thou rememb'rest
> Since once I sat upon a promontory

And heard a mermaid, on a dolphin's back . . .
That very time I saw (but thou couldst not)
Flying between the cold moon and the earth
Cupid, all arm'd. A certain aim he took
At a fair Vestal, throned by the West,
And loos'd his love-shaft smartly from his bow,
As it should pierce a hundred thousand hearts.
But I might see young Cupid's fiery shaft
Quench'd in the chaste beams of the wat'ry moon,
And the imperial vot'ress passed on,
In maiden meditation, fancy-free. (II.i.147–164)

At the entertainment at Elvetham in 1591, Elizabeth was throned by the west side of a garden lake to listen to music from the water; the fairy queen came with a round of dancers and spoke of herself as wife to Auberon. These and other similarities make it quite possible, but not necessary, that Shakespeare was referring to the Elvetham occasion.[3] There has been speculation, from Warburton on down, aimed at identifying the mermaid and discovering in Cupid's fiery shaft a particular bid for Elizabeth's affections; Leicester's Kenilworth entertainment in 1575 was usually taken as the occasion alluded to, despite the twenty years that had gone by when Shakespeare wrote.[4] No one, however, has cogently demonstrated any reference to court intrigue—which is to be expected in view of the fact that the play, after its original performance, was on the public stage. The same need for discretion probably accounts for the lack of internal evidence as to the particular marriage the comedy originally celebrated.[5] But what is not in doubt, and what matters for our purpose here, is the *kind* of occasion Oberon's speech refers to, the kind of occasion Shakespeare's scene is shaped by. The speech describes, in retrospect, just such a joyous overflow of pleasure into music and make-believe as is happening in Shakespeare's own play. The fact that what Shakespeare handled with supreme skill was just what was most commonplace no doubt contributes to our inability to connect what he produced with particular historical circumstances.

As we have seen, it was commonplace to imitate Ovid. Ovidian fancies pervade *A Midsummer Night's Dream*, and especially the scene of the fairy quarrel: the description of the way Cupid "loos'd his love shaft" at Elizabeth parallels the Metamorphoses' account of the god's shooting "his best arrow, with the golden head" at Apollo; Helena, later in the scene, exclaims that "The story shall be chang'd: / Apollo flies, and Daphne holds the chase"—and proceeds to invert animal images from Ovid.[6] The game was not so much to lift things gracefully from Ovid as it was to make up fresh things in Ovid's manner, as Shakespeare here, by playful mythopoesis, explains the bad weather by his fairies' quarrel and makes up a metamorphosis of the little Western flower to motivate the play's follies and place Elizabeth superbly above them.[7] The pervasive Ovidian influence accounts for Theseus' putting fables and fairies in the same breath when he says, punning on ancient and antic,

> I never may believe
> These antique fables nor these fairy toys. (V.i.2–3)

The humor of the play relates superstition, magic and passionate delusion as "fancy's images." The actual title emphasizes a sceptical attitude by calling the comedy a "dream." It seems unlikely that the title's characterization of the dream, "a midsummer night's dream," implies association with the specific customs of Midsummer Eve, the shortest night of the year, except as "midsummer night" would carry suggestions of a magic time. The observance of Midsummer Eve in England centered on building bonfires or "bonefires," of which there is nothing in Shakespeare's moonlight play. It was a time when maids might find out who their true love would be by dreams or divinations. There were customs of decking houses with greenery and hanging lights, which just possibly might connect with the fairies' torches at the comedy's end. And when people gathered fern seed at midnight, sometimes they spoke of spirits whizzing invisibly past. If one ranges through the eclectic pages of *The Golden Bough*, guided by the index for Midsummer Eve, one finds other customs suggestive of Shakespeare's play, involving moonlight, seeing the moon in water, gathering dew, and so on, but in Sweden, Bavaria, or still more remote places, rather than England.[8] One can assume that parallel English customs have been lost, or one can assume that Shakespeare's imagination found its way to similarities with folk cult, starting from the custom of Maying and the general feeling that spirits may be abroad in the long dusks and short nights of midsummer. Olivia in *Twelfth Night* speaks of "midsummer madness" (III.iv.61). In the absence of evidence, there is no way to settle just how much comes from tradition. But what *is* clear is that Shakespeare was not *simply* writing out folklore which he heard in his youth, as Romantic critics liked to assume. On the contrary, his fairies are produced by a complex fusion of pageantry and popular game, as well as popular fancy. Moreover, as we shall see, they are not serious in the menacing way in which the people's fairies were serious. Instead they are serious in a very different way, as embodiments of the May-game experience of eros in men and women and trees and flowers, while any superstitious tendency to believe in their literal reality is mocked. The whole night's action is presented as a release of shaping fantasy which brings clarification about the tricks of strong imagination. We watch a dream; but we are awake, thanks to pervasive humor about the tendency to take fantasy literally, whether in love, in superstition, or in Bottom's mechanical dramatics. As in *Love's Labour's Lost* the folly of wit becomes the generalized comic subject in the course of an astonishing release of witty invention, so here in the course of a more inclusive release of imagination, the folly of fantasy becomes the general subject, echoed back and forth between the strains of the play's imitative counterpoint.

The Fond Pageant

We can best follow first the strain of the lovers; then the fairies, their persuasive and then their humorous aspects; and finally the broadly comic strain of the clowns. We feel what happens to the young lovers in relation to the wedding of the Duke. Theseus and Hippolyta have a quite special sort of role: they are principals without being protagonists; the play happens for them rather than to them. This relation goes with their being stand-ins for the noble couple whose marriage the play originally honored. In expressing the prospect of Theseus' marriage, Shakespeare can fix in ideal form, so that it can be felt later at performance in the theater, the mood that would obtain in a palace as the "nuptial hour / Draws on apace." Theseus looks towards the hour with masculine impatience, Hippolyta with a woman's happy willingness to dream away the time. Theseus gives directions for the "four happy days" to his "usual manager of mirth," his Master of the Revels, Philostrate:

> Go, Philostrate,
> Stir up the Athenian youth to merriments,
> Awake the pert and nimble spirit of mirth,
> Turn melancholy forth to funerals;
> The pale companion is not for our pomp. (I.i.11–15)

The whole community is to observe a decorum of the passions, with Philostrate as choreographer of a pageant where Melancholy's float will not appear. After the war in which he won Hippolyta, the Duke announces that he is going to wed her

> in another key,
> With pomp, with triumph, and with revelling. (I.i.18–19)

But his large, poised line is interrupted by Egeus, panting out vexation. After the initial invocation of nuptial festivity, we are confronted by the sort of tension from which merriment is a release. Here is Age, standing in the way of Athenian youth; here are the locked conflicts of everyday. By the dwelling here on "the sharp Athenian law," on the fate of nuns "in shady cloister mew'd," we are led to feel the outgoing to the woods as an escape from the inhibitions imposed by parents and the organized community. And this sense of release is also prepared by looking for just a moment at the tragic potentialities of passion. Lysander and Hermia, left alone in their predicament, speak a plaintive, symmetrical duet on the theme, learned "from tale or history," that "The course of true love never did run smooth":

> *Lysander.* But, either it was different in blood—
> *Hermia.* O cross! too high to be enthrall'd to low!
> *Lysander.* Or else misgraffed in respect of years—
> *Hermia.* O spite! too old to be engag'd to young! (I.i.135–138)

Suddenly the tone changes, as Lysander describes in little the sort of tragedy presented in *Romeo and Juliet*, where Juliet exclaimed that their love was "Too like the lightning, which doth cease to be / Ere one can say 'It lightens'" (II.ii.119–120).

> *Lysander.* Or, if there were a sympathy in choice,
> War, death, or sickness did lay siege to it,
> Making it momentary as a sound,
> Swift as a shadow, short as any dream,
> Brief as the lightning in the collied night,
> That, in a spleen, unfolds both heaven and earth,
> And ere a man hath power to say 'Behold!'
> The jaws of darkness do devour it up:
> So quick bright things come to confusion. (I.i.141–149)

But Hermia shakes herself free of the tragic vision, and they turn to thoughts of stealing forth tomorrow night to meet in the Maying wood and go on to the dowager aunt, where "the sharp Athenian law / Cannot pursue us."

If they had reached the wealthy aunt, the play would be a romance. But it is a change of heart, not a change of fortune, which lets love have its way. The merriments Philostrate was to have directed happen inadvertently, the lovers walking into them blind, so to speak. This is characteristic of the way game is transformed into drama in this play, by contrast with the disabling of the fictions in *Love's Labour's Lost*. Here the roles which the young people might play in a wooing game, they carry out in earnest. And nobody is shown setting about to play the parts of Oberon or Titania. Instead the pageant fictions are presented as "actually" happening—at least so it seems at first glance.

We see the fairies meet by moonlight in the woods before we see the lovers arrive there, and so are prepared to see the mortals lose themselves. In *The Winter's Tale*, Perdita describes explicitly the transforming and liberating powers of the spring festival which in *A Midsummer Night's Dream* are embodied in the nightwood world the lovers enter. After Perdita has described the spring flowers, she concludes with

> O, these I lack
> To make you garlands of; and my sweet friend,
> To strew him o'er and o'er!
> *Florizel.* What, like a corse?
> *Perdita.* No, like a bank for love to lie and play on;
> Not like a corse; or if—not to be buried,
> But quick, and in mine arms. Come, take your flowers.
> Methinks I play as I have seen them do
> In Whitsun pastorals. Sure this robe of mine
> Does change my disposition. (*WT* IV.iv.127–135)

Her recovery is as exquisite as her impulse towards surrender: she comes back to herself by seeing her gesture as the expression of the occasion. She makes the festive clothes she wears mean its transforming power. Florizel has told her that

> These your unusual weeds to each part of you
> Do give a life—no shepherdess but Flora
> Peering in April's front! (IV.iv.1–3)

Holiday disguising, her humility suggests, would be embarrassing but for the license of the sheep-shearing feast:

> But that our feasts
> In every mess have folly, and the feeders
> Digest it with a custom, I should blush
> To see you so attired. (IV.iv.10–13)

The lovers in *A Midsummer Night's Dream* play "as in Whitsun pastorals," but they are entirely without this sort of consciousness of their folly. They are unreservedly *in* the passionate protestations which they rhyme at each other as they change partners:

> *Helena.* Lysander, if you live, good sir, awake.
> *Lysander.* And run through fire I will for thy sweet sake
> Transparent Helena! (II.ii.102–104)

The result of this lack of consciousness is that they are often rather dull and undignified, since however energetically they elaborate conceits, there is usually no qualifying irony, nothing withheld. And only accidental differences can be exhibited, Helena tall, Hermia short. Although the men think that "reason says" now Hermia, now Helena, is "the worthier maid," personalities have nothing to do with the case: it is the flowers that bloom in the spring. The life in the lovers' parts is not to be caught in individual speeches, but by regarding the whole movement of the farce, which swings and spins each in turn through a common pattern, an evolution that seems to have an impersonal power of its own. Miss Enid Welsford describes the play's movement as a dance:

> The plot is a pattern, a figure, rather than a series of human events occasioned by character and passion, and this pattern, especially in the moonlight parts of the play, is the pattern of a dance.
> "Enter a Fairie at one doore, and Robin Goodfellow at another. . . . Enter the King of Fairies, at one doore, with his traine; and the Queene, at another with hers."
> The appearance and disappearance and reappearance of the various lovers, the will-o'-the-wisp movement of the elusive Puck, form a kind of figured ballet. The lovers quarrel in a dance pattern: first, there are two men to one woman and the other woman alone, then a brief space of circular movement, each one pursuing and pursued, then a return to the first figure with the position of the woman reversed, then a cross-movement, man quarrelling with man and woman with woman, and then, as finale, a general setting to partners, including not only the lovers but fairies and royal personages as well.[9]

This is fine and right, except that one must add that the lovers' evolutions have a headlong and helpless quality that depends on their not being *intended* as dance, by contrast with those of the fairies. (One can also contrast the courtly circle's intended though abortive dances in *Love's Labour's Lost*.) The farce is funniest, and most meaningful, in the climactic scene where the lovers are most unwilling, where they try their hardest to use personality to break free, and still are willy-nilly swept along to end in pitch darkness, trying to fight. When both men have arrived at wooing Helena, she assumes it must be voluntary mockery, a "false sport" fashioned "in spite." She appeals to Hermia on the basis of their relation as particular individuals, their "sister's vows." But Hermia is at sea, too; names no longer work: "Am I not Hermia? Are not you Lysander?" So in the end Hermia too, though she has held off, is swept into the whirl, attacking Helena as a thief of love. She grasps at straws to explain what has happened by something manageably related to their individual identities:

> *Helena.* Fie, fie! You counterfeit, you puppet you.
> *Hermia.* Puppet? Why so! Ay, that way goes the game.
> Now I perceive that she hath made compare

Between our statures; she hath urg'd her height . . .
How low am I, thou painted maypole? Speak! (III.ii.289–296)

In exhibiting a more drastic helplessness of will and mind than anyone experienced in *Love's Labour's Lost*, this farce conveys a sense of people being tossed about by a force which puts them beside themselves to take them beyond themselves. The change that happens is presented simply, with little suggestion that it involves a growth in insight—Demetrius is not led to realize something false in his diverted affection for Hermia. But one psychological change, fundamental in growing up, is presented. Helena tries at first to move Hermia by an appeal to "schooldays friendship, childhood innocence," described at length in lovely, generous lines:

> So we grew together,
> Like to a double cherry, seeming parted,
> But yet an union in partition—
> Two lovely berries molded on one stem . . .
> And will you rent our ancient love asunder
> To join with men in scorning your poor friend? (III.ii.208–216)

"To join with men" has a plaintive girlishness about it. But before the scramble is over, the two girls have broken the double-cherry bond, to fight each without reserve for her man. So they move from the loyalties of one stage of life to those of another. When it has happened, when they wake up, the changes in affections seem mysterious. So Demetrius says

> But, my good lord, I wot not by what power
> (But by some power it is) my love to Hermia,
> Melted as the snow, seems to me now
> As the remembrance of an idle gaud
> Which in my childhood I did dote upon . . . (IV.i.167–171)

The comedy's irony about love's motives and choices expresses love's power not as an attribute of special personality but as an impersonal force beyond the persons concerned. The tragedies of love, by isolating Romeo and Juliet, Antony and Cleopatra, enlist our concern for love as it enters into unique destinies, and convey its subjective immensity in individual experience. The festive comedies, in presenting love's effect on a group, convey a different sense of its power, less intense but also less precarious.

In *Love's Labour's Lost* it was one of the lovers, Berowne, who was aware, in the midst of folly's game, that it was folly and a game; such consciousness, in *A Midsummer Night's Dream*, is lodged outside the lovers, in Puck. It is he who knows "which way goes the game," as poor Hermia only thought she did.

As a jester, and as Robin Goodfellow, games and practical jokes are his great delight: his lines express for the audience the mastery that comes from seeing folly as a pattern:

> Then will two at once woo one.
> That must needs be sport alone. (III.ii.118–119)

Like Berowne, he counts up the sacks as they come to Cupid's mill:

> Yet but three? Come one more.
> Two of both kinds makes up four.
> Here she comes, curst and sad.
> Cupid is a knavish lad
> Thus to make poor females mad. (III.ii.437–441)

Females, ordinarily a graceless word, works nicely here because it includes *every* girl. The same effect is got by using the names Jack and Jill, *any* boy and *any* girl:

> And the country proverb known,
> That every man should take his own,
> In your waking shall be shown:
>> Jack shall have Jill;
>> Nought shall go ill:
> The man shall have his mare again and all shall be well. (III.ii.457–463)

The trailing off into rollicking doggerel is exactly right to convey a country-proverb confidence in common humanity and in what humanity have in common. The proverb is on the lovers' side, as it was not for Berowne, who had ruefully to accept an ending in which "Jack hath not Jill." A festive confidence that things will ultimately go right supports the perfect gayety and detachment with which Puck relishes the preposterous course they take:

> Shall we their fond pageant see?
> Lord, what fools these mortals be! (III.ii.114–115)

The pageant is "fond" because the mortals do not realize they are in it, nor that it is sure to come out right, since nature will have its way.

Bringing in Summer to the Bridal

Spenser's *Epithalamion*, written at about the same time as *A Midsummer Night's Dream*, about 1595, is very like Shakespeare's play in the way it uses a complex literary heritage to express native English customs. In the course of fetching the bride to church and home again, Spenser makes the marriage a fulfillment of the whole countryside and community:

> So goodly all agree with sweet consent,
> To this dayes merriment. (83–84)

A gathering in, like that of the May game, is part of this confluence:

> Bring with you all the Nymphes that you can heare
> Both of the riuers and the forrests greene:
> And of the sea that neighbours to her neare,
> Al with gay girlands goodly well beseene. (37–40)

The church of course is decked with garlands, and the bride, "being crowned with a girland greene," seems "lyke some mayden Queene." It is Midsummer. The pervasive feeling for the kinship of men and nature is what rings in the refrain:

> That all the woods them answer and their echo ring.

Shakespeare, in developing a May-game action at length to express the will in nature that is consummated in marriage, brings out underlying magical meanings of the ritual while keeping always a sense of what it is humanly, as an experience. The way nature is felt is shaped, as we noticed in an earlier chapter, by the things that are done in encountering it.[10] The woods are a region of passionate excitement where, as Berowne said, love "adds a precious seeing to the eye." This precious seeing was talked about but never realized in *Love's Labour's Lost*; instead we got wit. But now it is realized; we get poetry. Poetry conveys the experience of amorous tendency diffused in nature; and poetry, dance, gesture, dramatic fiction, combine to create, in the fairies, creatures who embody the passionate mind's elated sense of its own omnipotence. The woods are established as a region, of metamorphosis, where in liquid moonlight or glimmering starlight, things can change, merge and melt into each other. Metamorphosis expresses both what love sees and what it seeks to do.

The opening scene, like an overture, announces this theme of dissolving, in unobtrusive but persuasive imagery. Hippolyta says that the four days until the wedding will "quickly *steep* themselves in night" and the nights "quickly *dream* away the time" (I.i.6–7)—night will dissolve day in dream. Then an imagery of wax develops as Egeus complains that Lysander has bewitched his daughter

Hermia, "stol'n the *impression* of her fantasy" (I.i.32). Theseus backs up Egeus
by telling Hermia that

> To you your father should be as a god;
> One that compos'd your beauties; yea, and one
> To whom you are but as a form in wax,
> By him imprinted, and within his power
> To leave the figure, or disfigure it. (I.i.47–51)

The supposedly moral threat is incongruously communicated in lines that relish
the joy of composing beauties and suggests a godlike, almost inhuman freedom
to do as one pleases in such creation. The metaphor of sealing as procreation
is picked up again when Theseus requires Hermia to decide "by the next new
moon, / The sealing day betwixt my love and me" (I.i.84–85). The consummation
in prospect with marriage is envisaged as a melting into a new form and a new
meaning. Helena says to Hermia that she would give the world "to be to you
translated" (I.i.191), and in another image describes meanings that melt from
love's transforming power:

> ere Demetrius look'd on Hermia's eyes,
> He hail'd down oaths that he was only mine;
> And when this hail some heat from Hermia felt,
> So he dissolv'd, and show'rs of oaths did melt. (I.i.242–245)

The most general statement, and one that perfectly fits what we are to see in the
wood when Titania meets Bottom, is

> Things base and vile, holding no quantity,
> Love can transpose to form and dignity. (I.i.232–233)

"The glimmering night" promotes transpositions by an effect not simply of
light, but also of a half-liquid medium in or through which things are seen:

> Tomorrow night, when Phoebe doth behold
> Her silver visage in the wat'ry glass,
> Decking with liquid pearl the bladed grass,
> (A time that lovers' flights doth still conceal) . . . (I.i.209–213)

Miss Caroline Spurgeon pointed to the moonlight in this play as one of the
earliest sustained effects of "iterative imagery."[11] To realize how the effect is

achieved, we have to recognize that the imagery is not used simply to paint an external scene but to convey human attitudes. We do not get simply "the glimmering night," but

> Didst thou not lead him through the glimmering night
> From Perigouna, whom he ravished? (II.i.77–78)

The liquid imagery conveys an experience of the skin, as well as the eye's confusion by refraction. The moon "looks with a wat'ry eye" (III.i.203) and "washes all the air" (II.i.104); its sheen, becoming liquid pearl as it mingles with dew, seems to get onto the eyeballs of the lovers, altering them to reshape what they see, like the juice of the flower with which they are "streaked" by Oberon and Puck. The climax of unreason comes when Puck overcasts the night to make it "black as Acheron" (III.ii.357); the lovers now experience only sound and touch, running blind over uneven ground, through bog and brake, "bedabbled with the dew and torn with briers" (III.ii.442). There is nothing more they can do until the return of light permits a return of control: light is anticipated as "comforts from the East" (III.ii.432), "the Morning's love" (III. ii.389). The sun announces its coming in a triumph of red and gold over salt green, an entire change of key from the moon's "silver visage in her wat'ry glass":

> the eastern gate, all fiery red,
> Opening on Neptune, with fair blessed beams
> Turns into yellow gold his salt green streams. (III.ii.391–393)

Finally Theseus comes with his hounds and his horns in the morning, and the lovers are startled awake. They find as they come to themselves that

> These things seem small and undistinguishable,
> Like far-off mountains turned into clouds. (IV.i.190–191)

The teeming metamorphoses which we encounter are placed, in this way, in a medium and in a moment where the perceived structure of the outer world breaks down, where the body and its environment interpenetrate in unaccustomed ways, so that the seeming separateness and stability of identity is lost.

The action of metaphor is itself a process of transposing, a kind of metamorphosis. There is less direct description of external nature *in* the play than one would suppose: much of the effect of being in nature comes from imagery which endows it with anthropomorphic love, hanging a wanton pearl in every cowslip's ear. Titania laments that

the green corn
Hath rotted ere his youth attain'd a beard;

while

Hoary-headed frosts
Fall in the fresh lap of the crimson rose . . . (II.i.94–95, 107–108)

By a complementary movement of imagination, human love is treated in terms of growing things. Theseus warns Hermia against becoming a nun, because

earthlier happy is the rose distill'd
Than that which, withering on the virgin thorn
Grows, lives and dies in single blessedness. (I.i.76–78)

Titania, embracing Bottom, describes herself in terms that fit her surroundings and uses the association of ivy with women of the songs traditional at Christmas:[12]

So doth the woodbine the sweet honeysuckle
Gently entwist; the female ivy so
Enrings the barky fingers of the elm. (IV.i.45–47)

One could go on and on in instancing metamorphic metaphors. But one of the most beautiful bravura speeches can serve as an epitome of the metamorphic action in the play, Titania's astonishing answer when Oberon asks for the changeling boy:

Set your heart at rest.
The fairyland buys not the child of me.
His mother was a vot'ress of my order;
And in the spiced Indian air, by night,
Full often hath she gossip'd by my side,
And sat with me on Neptune's yellow sands,
Marking th'embarked traders on the flood;
When we have laugh'd to see the sails conceive
And grow big-bellied with the wanton wind;
Which she, with pretty and with swimming gait
Following (her womb then rich with my young squire)
Would imitate, and sail upon the land
To fetch me trifles, and return again,

As from a voyage, rich with merchandise.
But she, being mortal, of that boy did die,
And for her sake do I rear up her boy;
And for her sake I will not part from him. (II.i.121–137)

The memory of a moment seemingly so remote expresses with plastic felicity the present moment when Titania speaks and we watch. It suits Titania's immediate mood, for it is a glimpse of women who gossip alone, apart from men and feeling now no need of them, rejoicing in their own special part of life's power. At such moments, the child, not the lover, is their object—as this young squire is still the object for Titania, who "crowns him with flowers, and makes him all her joy." The passage conveys a wanton joy in achieved sexuality, in fertility; and a gay acceptance of the waxing of the body (like joy in the varying moon). At leisure in the spiced night air, when the proximate senses of touch and smell are most alive, this joy finds sport in projecting images of love and growth where they are not. The mother, having laughed to see the ship a woman with child, imitates it so as to go the other way about and herself become a ship. She fetches trifles, but she is also actually "rich with merchandise," for her womb is "rich with my young squire." The secure quality of the play's pleasure is conveyed by having the ships out on the flood while she sails, safely, upon the *land*, with a pretty and swimming gait that is an overflowing of the security of make-believe. The next line brings a poignant glance out beyond this gamesome world:

But she, being mortal, of that boy did die.

It is when the flower magic leads Titania to find a new object that she gives up the child (who goes now from her bower to the man's world of Oberon). So here is another sort of change of heart that contributes to the expression of what is consummated in marriage, this one a part of the rhythm of adult life, as opposed to the change in the young lovers that goes with growing up. Once Titania has made this transition, their ritual marriage is renewed:

Now thou and I are new in amity,
And will to-morrow midnight solemnly
Dance in Duke Theseus' house triumphantly
And bless it to all fair prosperity. (IV.i.90–93)

The final dancing blessing of the fairies, "Through the house with glimmering light" (V.i.398), after the lovers are abed, has been given meaning by the symbolic action we have been describing: the fairies have been made into tutelary spirits of fertility, so that they can promise that

> the blots of Nature's hand
> Shall not in their issue stand. (V.i.416–417)

When merely read, the text of this episode seems somewhat bare, but its clipped quality differentiates the fairy speakers from the mortals, and anyway richer language would be in the way. Shakespeare has changed from a fully dramatic medium to conclude, in a manner appropriate to festival, with dance and song. It seems likely that, as Dr. Johnson argued, there were two songs which have been lost, one led by Oberon and the other by Titania.[13] There were probably two dance evolutions also, the first a processional dance led by the king and the second a round led by the queen: Oberon's lines direct the fairies to dance and sing "through the house," "by the fire," "after me"; Titania seems to start a circling dance with "First rehearse your song by rote"; by contrast with Oberon's "after me," she calls for "hand in hand." This combination of processional and round dances is the obvious one for the occasion: to get the fairies in and give them something to do. But these two forms of dance are associated in origin with just the sort of festival use of them which Shakespeare is making. "The customs of the village festival," Chambers writes, "gave rise by natural development to two types of dance. One was the processional dance of a band of worshippers in progress round their boundaries and from field to field, house to house. . . . The other type of folk dance, the *ronde* or 'round,' is derived from the comparatively stationary dance of the group of worshippers around the more especially sacred objects of the festival, such as the tree or fire. The custom of dancing round the Maypole has been more or less preserved wherever the Maypole is known. But 'Thread the Needle' (a type of surviving processional dance) itself often winds up with a circular dance or *ronde*. . . ."[14] One can make too much of such analogies. But they do illustrate the rich traditional meanings available in the materials Shakespeare was handling.

Puck's broom is another case in point: it is his property as a housemaid's sprite, "to sweep the dust behind the door" (V.i.397); also it permits him to make "room," in the manner of the presenter of a holiday mummers' group. And with the dust, out go evil spirits. Puck refers to "evil sprites" let forth by graves, developing a momentary sense of midnight terrors, of spirits that walk by night; then he promises that no mouse shall disturb "this hallowed house." The exorcism of evil powers complements the invocation of good. With their "field dew consecrate," the fairies enact a lustration. Fertilizing and beneficent virtues are in festival custom persistently attributed to dew gathered on May mornings.[15] Shakespeare's handling of nature has infused dew in this play with the vital spirit of moist and verdant woods. The dew is "consecrate" in this sense. But the religious associations inevitably attaching to the word suggest also the sanctification of love by marriage. It was customary for the clergy, at least in important marriages, to bless the bed and bridal couple with holy water. The benediction included exorcism, in the Manual for the use of Salisbury a prayer to protect them from what Spenser called "evill sprights" and "things that be not" (*ab omnibus fantasmaticis demonum illusionibus*).[16] This custom may itself be an ecclesiastical adaptation of a more primitive bridal lustration, a water charm of which dew-gathering on May Day is one variant. Such a play as *A Midsummer Night's Dream* is possible because the May and Summer Spirit, despite its pagan affinities, is not conceived as necessarily in opposition to the wholeness of traditional Christian life.

Magic as Imagination: The Ironic Wit

In promoting the mastery of passion by expression, dramatic art can provide a civilized equivalent for exorcism. The exorcism represented as magically accomplished at the conclusion of the comedy is accomplished, in another sense, by the whole dramatic action, as it keeps moving through release to clarification. By embodying in the fairies the mind's proclivity to court its own omnipotence, Shakespeare draws this tendency, this "spirit," out into the open. They have the meaning they do only because we see them in the midst of the metamorphic region we have just considered—removed from this particular wood, most of their significance evaporates, as for example in *Nymphidia* and other pretty floral miniatures. One might summarize their role by saying that they represent the power of imagination. But to say what they *are* is to short-circuit the life of them and the humor. They present themselves moment by moment as actual persons; the humor keeps *recognizing* that the person is a personification, that the magic is imagination.

The sceptical side of the play has been badly neglected because romantic taste, which first made it popular, wanted to believe in fairies. Romantic criticism usually praised *A Midsummer Night's Dream* on the assumption that its spell should be complete, and that the absolute persuasiveness of the poetry should be taken as the measure of its success. This expectation of unreserved illusion finds a characteristic expression in Hazlitt:

> All that is finest in the play is lost in the representation. The spectacle is grand; but the spirit was evaporated, the genius was fled. Poetry and the stage do not agree well together. . . . Where all is left to the imagination (as is the case in reading) every circumstance, near or remote, has an equal chance of being kept in mind and tells according to the mixed impression of all that has been suggested. But the imagination cannot sufficiently qualify the actual impressions of the senses. Any offense

given to the eye is not to be got rid of by explanation. Thus Bottom's head in the play is a fantastic illusion, produced by magic spells; on the stage it is an ass's head, and nothing more; certainly a very strange costume for a gentleman to appear in. Fancy cannot be embodied any more than a simile can be painted; and it is as idle to attempt it as to personate *Wall* or *Moonshine*. Fairies are not incredible, but Fairies six feet high are so.[17]

Hazlitt's objections were no doubt partly justified by the elaborate methods of nineteenth-century production. A superfluity of "actual impressions of the senses" came into conflict with the poetry by attempting to reduplicate it. But Hazlitt looks for a complete illusion of a kind which Shakespeare's theater did not provide and Shakespeare's play was not designed to exploit; failing to find it on the stage, he retires to his study, where he is free of the discrepancy between imagination and sense which he finds troublesome. The result is the nineteenth-century's characteristic misreading, which regards "the play" as a series of real supernatural events, with a real ass's head and real fairies, and, by excluding all awareness that "the play" is a play, misses its most important humor.

The extravagant subject matter actually led the dramatist to rely more heavily than elsewhere on a flexible attitude toward representation. The circumstances of the original production made this all the more inevitable: Puck stood in a hall familiar to the audience. We have noticed how in holiday shows, it was customary to make game with the difference between art and life by witty transitions back and forth between them. The aim was not to make the auditors "forget they are in a theater," but to extend reality into fiction. The general Renaissance tendency frankly to accept and relish the artificiality of art, and the vogue of formal rhetoric and "conceited" love poetry, also made for sophistication about the artistic process. The sonneteers mock their mythological machinery, only to insist the more on the reality of what it represents:

It is most true, what we call Cupid's dart,
An image is, which for ourselves we carve.

Yet it is

True and most true, that I must Stella love.[18]

Shakespeare's auditors had not been conditioned by a century and a half of effort to achieve sincerity by denying art. Coleridge has a remark about the advantages that Shakespeare enjoyed as a dramatist which is particularly illuminating in connection with this feeling for art in *A Midsummer Night's Dream*. He observes that "the circumstances of acting were altogether different from ours; it was more of recitation," with the result that "the idea of the poet was always present."[19]

The nearly bare stage worked as Proust observed that the bare walls of an art gallery work, to isolate "the essential thing, the act of mind."

It is "the act of mind" and "the idea of the poet" which are brought into focus when, at the beginning of the relaxed fifth act, Theseus comments on what the lovers have reported of their night in the woods. I shall quote the passage in full, despite its familiarity, to consider the complex attitude it conveys:

> The lunatic, the lover, and the poet
> Are of imagination all compact.
> One sees more devils than vast hell can hold:
> That is the madman. The lover, all as frantic,
> Sees Helen's beauty in a brow of Egypt.
> The poet's eye, in a fine frenzy rolling,
> Doth glance from heaven to earth, from earth to heaven;
> And as imagination bodies forth
> The forms of things unknown, the poet's pen
> Turns them to shapes, and gives to airy nothing
> A local habitation and a name.
> Such tricks hath strong imagination
> That, if it would but apprehend some joy,
> It comprehends some bringer of that joy;
> Or in the night, imagining some fear,
> How easy is a bush suppos'd a bear! (V.i.7–22)

The description of the power of poetic creation is so beautiful that these lines are generally taken out of context and instanced simply as glorification of the poet. But the praise of the poet is qualified in conformity with the tone Theseus adopts towards the lover and the madman. In his comment there is wonder, wonderfully expressed, at the power of the mind to create from airy nothing; but also recognition that the creation may be founded, after all, merely on airy nothing. Neither awareness cancels out the other. A sense of the plausible life and energy of fancy goes with the knowledge that often its productions are more strange than true.

Scepticism is explicitly crystallized out in the *détente* of Theseus' speech; but scepticism is in solution throughout the play. There is a delicate humor about the unreality of the fairies even while they are walking about in a local habitation with proper names. The usual production, even now, rides rough-shod over this humor by trying to act the fairies in a "vivid" way that will compel belief—with much fluttery expressiveness that has led many to conclude that the fairies are naïve and silly. Quite the contrary—the fairy business is exceedingly sophisticated. The literal and figurative aspects of what is presented are both deliberately kept open to view. The effect is well described by Hermia's remark when she looks back at her dream:

> Methinks I see these things with parted eye,
> When everything seems double. (IV.i.192–193)

As we watch the dream, the doubleness is made explicit to keep us aware that strong imagination is at work:

> And I serve the Fairy Queen,
> To dew her orbs upon the green.
> The cowslips tall her pensioners be;
> In their gold coats spots you see.
> Those be rubies, fairy favours;
> In those freckles live their savours. (II.i.8–13)

These conceits, half botany, half personification, are explicit about remaking nature's economy after the pattern of man's: "spots you see. / Those be rubies . . ." The same conscious double vision appears when Puck introduces himself:

>   sometime lurk I in a gossip's bowl
> In very likeness of a roasted crab . . .
> The wisest aunt, telling the saddest tale,
> Sometime for three-foot stool mistaketh me (II.i.47–52)

The plain implication of the lines, though Puck speaks them, is that Puck does not really exist—that he is a figment of naïve imagination, projected to motivate the little accidents of household life.

This scepticism goes with social remoteness from the folk whose superstitions the poet is here enjoying. Puck's description has the aloof detachment of genre painting, where the grotesqueries of the subject are seen across lines of class difference. As a matter of fact there is much less popular lore in these fairies than is generally assumed in talking about them. The fairies do, it is true, show all the main characteristics of fairies in popular belief: they appear in the forest, at midnight, and leave at sunrise; they take children, dance in ringlets. But as I have remarked already, their whole quality is drastically different from that of the fairies "of the villagery," creatures who, as Dr. Minor White Latham has shown, were dangerous to meddle with, large enough to harm, often malicious, sometimes the consorts of witches.[20] One can speak of Shakespeare's having changed the fairies of popular superstition, as Miss Latham does. Or one can look at what he did in relation to the traditions of holiday and pageantry and see his creatures as pageant nymphs and holiday celebrants, colored by touches from popular superstition, but shaped primarily by a very different provenance. Most of the detailed popular lore concerns Puck, not properly a fairy at all; even he is several parts Cupid and several parts mischievous stage page (a cousin of Moth in *Love's Labour's Lost* and no doubt played by the same small, agile boy). And Puck is only *using* the credulity of the folk as a jester, to amuse a king.

Titania and Oberon and their trains are very different creatures from the *gemütlich* fairies of middle-class folklore enthusiasm in the nineteenth century. The spectrum of Shakespeare's imagination includes some of the warm domestic tones which the later century cherished. But the whole attitude of self-abnegating humility before the mystery of folk imagination is wrong for interpreting this play. His fairies are creatures of pastoral, varied by adapting folk superstitions so as to make a new sort of arcadia. Though they are not shepherds, they lead a life similarly occupied with the pleasures of song and dance and, for king and queen, the vexations and pleasures of love. They have not the pastoral "labours" of tending flocks, but equivalent duties are suggested in the tending of nature's fragile beauties, killing "cankers in the musk-rose buds." They have a freedom like that of shepherds in arcadias, but raised to a higher power: they are free not only of the limitations of place and purse but of space and time.

The settled content of regular pastoral is possible because it is a "low" content, foregoing wealth and position; Shakespeare's fairies too can have their fine freedom because their sphere is limited. At times their tiny size limits them, though this is less important than is generally suggested by summary descriptions of "Shakespeare's fairy race." The poet plays the game of diminution delightfully, but never with Titania and Oberon, only with their attendants, and not all the time with them. It seems quite possible that Peaseblossom, Cobweb, Moth, and Mustardseed were originally played by children of the family—their parts seem designed to be foolproof for little children: "Ready.—And I.—And I.—And I." Diminutiveness is *the* characteristic of the Queen Mab Mercutio describes in *Romeo and Juliet*, and, as Dr. Latham has shown, it quickly became the hallmark of the progeny of literary fairies that followed;[21] but it is only occasionally at issue in *A Midsummer Night's Dream*. More fundamental is their limited time. Oberon can boast that, by contrast with horrors who must "wilfully themselves exile from light,"

> we are spirits of another sort.
> I with the Morning's love have oft made sport;
> And, like a forester, the groves may tread
> Even till the eastern gate, all fiery red,
> Opening on Neptune, with fair blessed beams
> Turns into yellow gold his salt green streams. (III.ii.388–393)

But for all his pride, full daylight is beyond him: "But notwithstanding, haste; . . . We must effect this business yet ere day." The enjoyment of any sort of pastoral depends on an implicit recognition that it presents a hypothetical case as if it were actual. Puck's lines about the way the fairies run

> From the presence of the sun,
> > Following darkness like a dream, (V.i.392–393)

summarizes the relation between their special time and their limited sort of existence.

This explicit summary comes at the close, when the whole machinery is being distanced to end with "If we shadows have offended. . . ." But the consciousness and humor which I am concerned to underline are present throughout the presentation of the fairies. It has been easy for production and criticism to ignore, just because usually amusement is not precipitated out in laughter but remains in solution with wonder and delight. In the scene of the quarrel between Titania and Oberon, the fragility of the conceits correspond finely to the half-reality of their world and specialness of their values. The factitiousness of the causes Titania lays out for the weather is gently mocked by the repeated *therefore's*: "Therefore the winds . . . Therefore the moon . . . The ox hath therefore. . . ." Her account makes it explicit that she and Oberon are tutelary gods of fertility, but with an implicit recognition like Sidney's about Cupid's dart—"an image . . . which for ourselves we carve." And her emphasis makes the wheat blight a disaster felt most keenly not for men who go hungry but for the green wheat itself, because it never achieves manhood:

> and the green corn
> Hath rotted ere his youth attain'd a beard. (II.i.94–95)

Her concern for the holiday aspect of nature is presented in lines which are poised between sympathy and amusement:

> The human mortals want their winter cheer;
> No night is now with hymn or carol blest . . .
> The seasons alter. Hoary-headed frosts
> Fall in the fresh lap of the crimson rose;
> And on old Hiems' thin and icy crown
> An odorous chaplet of sweet summer buds
> Is, as in mockery, set. (II.i.101–102, 107–111)

Part of the delight of this poetry is that we can enjoy without agitation imaginative action of the highest order. It is like gazing in a crystal: what you see is clear and vivid, but on the other side of the glass. Almost unnoticed, the lines have a positive effect through the amorous suggestion implicit in the imagery, even while letting it be manifest that those concerned are only personifications of flowers and a pageant figure wearing the livery of the wrong season. Titania can speak of "the human mortals" as very far off indeed; the phrase crystallizes what has been achieved in imaginative distance and freedom. But Titania is as far off from us as we are from her.

The effect of wit which in such passages goes along with great imaginative power is abetted by the absence of any compelling interest in passion or plot. Producers utterly ruin the scene when they have the fairy couple mouth their lines at each other as expressively as possible. Titania, after all, leaves before that point is reached: "Fairies, away! / We shall chide downright if I longer stay" (II.i.144–145). At moments of dramatic intensity, the most violent distortion can go unnoticed; what the poet is doing is ignored in responding to what his people are doing. But here a great part of the point is that we *should* notice the distortion, the action of the poet, the wit. Plot tension launches flights of witty poetry which use it up, so to speak, just as the tensions in broad comedy are discharged in laughter. Rhetorical schematizations, or patterns of rhyme, are often used in *A Midsummer Night's Dream* to mark off the units of such verse. But blank verse paragraphs are also constructed so as to form autonomous bravura passages which reach a climax and come to rest while actor and audience catch their breath. Oberon's description of the mermaid, and his tribute to Elizabeth (II.i.148–164), are two such flights, each a rhythmical unit, the first punctuated by Puck's "I remember," the second by Oberon's change of tone at "Yet mark'd I where the bolt of Cupid fell." The formal and emotional isolation of the two passages is calculated to make the audience respond with wonder to the effortless reach of imagination which brings the stars madly shooting from their spheres. In a tribute to Elizabeth, the prominence of "the idea of the poet" in the poetry obviously was all to the good. By Oberon's remark to Puck, "that very time I saw, but thou couldst not," courtly Shakespeare contrived to place the mythology he was creating about Elizabeth on a level appropriately more sublime and occult than that about the mermaid.

Moonlight and Moonshine: The Ironic Burlesque

The consciousness of the creative or poetic act itself, which pervades the main action, explains the subject-matter of the burlesque accompaniment provided by the clowns. If Shakespeare were chiefly concerned with the nature of love, the clowns would be in love, after their fashion. But instead, they are putting on a play. That some commoners should honor the wedding, in their own way, along with the figures from pageantry, is of course in keeping with the purpose of gathering into a play the several sorts of entertainments usually presented separately. But an organic purpose is served too: the clowns provide a broad burlesque of the mimetic impulse to become something by acting it, the impulse which in the main action is fulfilled by imagination and understood by humor. Bottom feels he can be anything: "What is Pyramus, a lover, or a tyrant? . . . An I may hide my face, let me play Thisby too . . . Let me play the lion too." His soul would like to fly out into them all; but he is *not* Puck! In dealing with dramatic illusion, he and the other mechanicals are invincibly literal-minded, carrying to absurdity the tendency to treat the imaginary as though it were real. They exhibit just the all-or-nothing attitude towards fancy which would be fatal to the play as a whole.

When the clowns think that Bottom's transformation has deprived them of their chief actor, their lament seems pointedly allusive to Shakespeare's company and their play.

> *Snug.* Masters, the Duke is coming from the temple, and there is two or three lords and ladies more married. If our sport had gone forward, we had all been made men.
> *Flute.* O sweet bully Bottom! Thus hath he lost sixpence a day during his life. He could not have scaped sixpence a day. An the Duke had not given him sixpence a day for playing Pyramus, I'll be hanged! He would have deserved it. Sixpence a day in Pyramus, or nothing! (IV.ii.15–24)

The repetition of "sixpence a day" seems loaded: if Bottom in Pyramus is worth sixpence, what is Kempe in Bottom worth? For Bottom is to Theseus as Kempe was to the nobleman for whom the play was first produced. The business about moonshine brings this out

> *Quince.* . . . But there is two hard things: that is, to bring the moonlight into a chamber; for, you know, Pyramus and Thisby meet by moonlight.
> *Snout.* Doth the moon shine that night we play our play?
> *Bottom.* A calendar, a calendar! Look in the almanac. Find out moonshine, find out moonshine!
> *Quince.* Yes, it doth shine that night.
> *Bottom.* Why, then may you leave a casement of the great chamber window, where we play, open, and the moon may shine in at the casement.
> *Quince.* Ay; or else one must come in with a bush of thorns and a lantern, and say he comes to disfigure, or to present, the person of Moonshine. (III.i.47–63)

Shakespeare, in *his* play, triumphantly accomplishes just this hard thing, "to bring the moonlight into a chamber." The moonshine, here and later, shows how aware Shakespeare was of what his plastic imagination was doing with moonlight. Since the great chamber Bottom speaks of was, at the initial private performance, the very chamber in which the Chamberlain's men were playing, "Pyramus and Thisby" adorns Theseus' fictitious wedding just as *A Midsummer Night's Dream* adorns the real wedding. Bottom's proposal to open a casement reduces the desire for realism to the absurdity of producing the genuine article. Translated out of irony, it suggests, that "if you want real moonlight, you put yourself in Bottom's class." It is amusing how later producers have labored with ever greater technical resources to achieve Bottom's ideal: Hollywood's Max Reinhardt version omitted most of the poetry to make room for cellophane-spangled fairies standing in rows on ninety-foot moonbeams.

The difference between art and life is also what the clowns forget in their parlous fear lest "the ladies be afeared of the lion" and the killing. Bottom's solution is to tell the ladies in plain language that fiction is not fact:

> Write me a prologue; and let the prologue seem to say, we will do no
> harm with our swords, and that Pyramus is not kill'd indeed; and for the
> more better assurance, tell them that I Pyramus am not Pyramus, but
> Bottom the weaver. This will put them out of fear. (III.i.18–23)

Now this expresses Bottom's vanity, too. But producers and actors, bent on showing "character," can lose the structural, ironic point if they let the lines get lost in Bottom's strutting. What the clowns forget, having "never labour'd in their minds till now," is that a killing or a lion in a play, however plausibly presented, is a mental event.[22] Because, like children, they do not discriminate between imaginary and real events, they are literal about fiction. But they are not *un*imaginative: on the contrary they embody the stage of mental development before the discipline of facts has curbed the tendency to equate what is "in" the mind with what is "outside" it. They apply to drama the same sort of mentality that supports superstition—it is in keeping that the frightening sort of folk beliefs about changelings are for them an accepted part of life: "Out of doubt he is transported."[23] Because this uncritical imaginativeness is the protoplasm from which all art develops, the clowns are as delightful and stimulating as they are ridiculous. Even while we are laughing at them, we recover sympathetically the power of fantasy enjoyed by children, who, like Bottom, can be anything, a train, an Indian or a lion.

In the performance of *Pyramus and Thisby*, Shakespeare captures the naïveté of folk dramatics and makes it serve his controlling purpose as a final variant of imaginative aberration. The story from Ovid, appropriate for a burlesque in an Ovidian play, is scarcely the kind of thing the simple people would have presented in life; but their method and spirit in putting it on, and the spirit in which the noble company take it, are not unlike what is suggested by Laneham's account of the bride-ale show at Kenilworth. "If we imagine no worse of them than they of themselves," Theseus observes of the Athenian artisans, "they may pass for excellent men" (V.i.218). The comedy of the piece centers not so much on what is acted in it as in the continual failure to translate actor into character. Shakespeare's skill is devoted to keeping both the players and their would-be play before us at the same time, so that we watch, not Pyramus alone, nor Bottom alone, but Bottom "in Pyramus," the fact of the one doing violence to the fiction of the other.

Almost half of *Pyramus and Thisby* is taken up with prologues of the sort one gets in the mummers' plays:

> I am king of England,
> As you may plainly see.[24]

Such prologues suit Shakespeare's purpose, because they present the performer openly climbing in the window of aesthetic illusion, where he can get stuck midway:

> In this same enterlude it doth befall
> That I, one Snout by name, present a wall . . .
> This loam, this roughcast, and this stone doth show
> That I am that same wall. The truth is so. (V.i.156–163)

"The truth is so," by warranting that fiction is fact, asks for a laugh, as does the Prologue's "At the which let no man wonder," or Moon's

> Myself the man i' the moon *do seem to be*.

The incarnation of Wall is a particularly "happy-unhappy" inspiration, because the more Wall does, the less he is a wall and the more he is Snout.

There is a great deal of incidental amusement in the parody and burlesque with which *Pyramus and Thisby* is loaded. It burlesques the substance of the death scene in *Romeo and Juliet* in a style which combines ineptitudes from Golding's translation of Ovid with locutions from the crudest doggerel drama.[25] What is most remarkable about it, however, is the way it fits hilarious fun into the whole comedy's development of attitude and understanding. After the exigent poise of the humorous fantasy, laughs now explode one after another; and yet they are still on the subject, even though now we are romping reassuringly through easy-to-make distinctions. Theseus can say blandly

> The best in this kind are but shadows; and the worst are no worse, if
> imagination amend them. (V.i.214–216)

Although we need not agree (Hippolyta says "It must be your imagination then, and not theirs."), Theseus expresses part of our response—a growing detachment

towards imagination, moving towards the distance from the dream expressed in
Puck's epilogue.

The meeting in the woods of Bottom and Titania is the climax of the
polyphonic interplay; it comes in the middle of the dream, when the humor has
the most work to do. Bottom in the ass's head provides a literal metamorphosis,
and in the process brings in the element of grotesque fantasy which the Savage
Man or Woodwose furnished at Kenilworth, a comic version of an animal-
headed dancer or of the sort of figure Shakespeare used in Herne the Hunter,
"with great ragged horns," at the oak in *The Merry Wives of Windsor*. At the same
time he is the theatrical company's clown "thrust in by head and shoulder to play
a part in majestical matters" and remaining uproariously literal and antipoetic as
he does so. Titania and he are fancy against fact, not beauty and the beast. She
makes all the advances while he remains very respectful, desiring nothing bestial
but "a peck of provender." Clownish oblivion to languishing beauty is sure-fire
comedy on any vaudeville stage. Here it is elaborated in such a way that when
Titania is frustrated, so is the transforming power of poetry:

> *Titania.* I pray thee, gentle mortal, sing again.
> Mine ear is much enamoured of thy note;
> So is mine eye enthralled to thy shape;
> And thy fair virtue's force (perforce) doth move me,
> On the first view, to say, to swear, I love thee.
> *Bottom.* Methinks, mistress, you should have little reason for that. And
> yet, to say the truth, reason and love keep little company together now-
> a-days. The more the pity that some honest neighbours will not make
> them friends. Nay, I can gleek, upon occasion.
> *Titania.* Thou art as wise as thou art beautiful.
> *Bottom.* Not so, neither . . . (III.i.140–152)

From a vantage below romance, the clown makes the same point as sceptical
Theseus, that reason and love do not go together. Titania tells him that she

> . . . will purge thy mortal grossness so
> That thou shalt like an airy spirit go. (III.i.163–164)

But even her magic cannot "transpose" Bottom.

The "low" or "realistic" effect which he produces when juxtaposed with her
is much less a matter of accurate imitation of common life than one assumes
at first glance. Of course the homely touches are telling—forms of address like
"Methinks, mistress" or words like *gleek* suggest a social world remote from the
elegant queen's. But the realistic effect does not depend on Bottom's being like
real weavers, but on the *détente* of imaginative tension, on a downward movement

which counters imaginative lift. This anti-poetic action involves, like the poetic, a high degree of abstraction from real life, including the control of rhythm which can establish a blank verse movement in as little as a single line, "Thou art as wise as thou art beautiful," and so be able to break the ardent progression of the queen's speech with "Not so, neither." When Bottom encounters the fairy attendants, he reduces the fiction of their existence to fact:

> *Bottom.* I cry your worships merry, heartily. I beseech your worship's
> name.
> *Cobweb.* Cobweb.
> *Bottom.* I shall desire you of more acquaintance, good Master Cobweb.
> If I cut my finger, I shall make bold with you. (III.i.182–187)

Cobwebs served the Elizabethans for adhesive plaster, so that when Bottom proposes to "make bold with" Cobweb, he treats him as a *thing*, undoing the personification on which the little fellow's life depends. To take hold of Cobweb in this way is of course a witty thing to do, when one thinks about it. But since the wit is in the service of a literal tendency, we can take it as the expression of a "hempen homespun." There is usually a similar incongruity between the "stupidity" of a clown and the imagination and wit required to express such stupidity. Bottom's charming combination of ignorant exuberance and oblivious imaginativeness make him the most humanly credible and appealing personality Shakespeare had yet created from the incongruous qualities required for the clown's role. The only trouble with the part, in practice, is that performers become so preoccupied with bringing out the weaver's vanity as an actor that they lose track of what the role is expressing as part of the larger imaginative design.

For there is an impersonal, imaginative interaction between the clowning and the rest of the play which makes the clowns mean more than they themselves know and more than they are as personalities. Bottom serves to represent, in so aware a play, the limits of awareness, limits as limitations—and also, at moments, limits as form and so strength.

> *Bottom.* Where are these lads? Where are these hearts?
> *Quince.* Bottom! O most courageous day! O most happy hour!
> *Bottom.* Masters, I am to discourse wonders; but ask me not what. For
> if I tell you, I am no true Athenian. I will tell you everything, right as it
> fell out.
> *Quince.* Let us hear, sweet Bottom.
> *Bottom.* Not a word of me. All that I will tell you is, that the Duke
> hath dined. Get your apparel together, good strings to your beards . . .
> (IV.ii.26–36)

It is ludicrous for Bottom to be so utterly unable to cope with the "wonders," especially where he is shown boggling in astonishment as he wordlessly remembers them: "I have had a most rare vision. I have had a dream past the wit of man to say what dream it was" (IV.i.207–209). But there is something splendid, too, in the way he exuberantly rejoins "these lads" and takes up his particular, positive life as a "true Athenian." Metamorphosis cannot faze him for long. His imperviousness, indeed, is what is most delightful about him with Titania: he remains so completely himself, even in her arms, and despite the outward change of his head and ears; his confident, self-satisfied tone is a triumph of consistency, persistence, existence.

The Sense of Reality

The value of humor, and the finest pleasure in it, depends on the seriousness of what it makes into fun. It is easy to be gay by taking a trivial theme, or by trivializing an important theme. The greatness of comedy, as of every other art form, must rest, to use Henry James' phrase, on the amount of "felt life" with which it deals in its proper fashion. After examining the structure and artifice of *A Midsummer Night's Dream*, we can now ask how much reality it masters by its mirth. This comedy is the first that is completely, triumphantly successful; but it has the limitations, as well as the strength, of a youthful play.

The role of imagination in experience is a major preoccupation in other plays of the same period. Dreams are several times presented as oracles of irrational powers shaping life, and inspire dread and awe. In the death scene of Clarence, in *Richard III*, the poet had presented the experience of oppression and helplessness on waking from the grip of nightmare. *A Midsummer Night's Dream* presents a resolution of the dream forces which so often augur conflict. To indulge dreamlike irrationality with impunity is, as Freud pointed out, one of the basic satisfactions of wit. The action of *A Midsummer Night's Dream* shows the same pattern on a large scale: it suggests the compulsion of dream, and then reconciles night's motives with the day's as the lovers conclude, "Why then, we are awake":

> *Demetrius.* These things seem small and undistinguishable,
> Like far-off mountains turned into clouds . . .
> *Helena.* And I have found Demetrius like a jewel,
> Mine own, and not mine own.
> *Demetrius.* Are you sure
> That we are awake? It seems to me
> That yet we sleep, we dream. Do not you think
> The Duke was here, and bid us follow him?

Hermia. Yea, and my father.
Helena. And Hippolyta.
Lysander. And he did bid us follow to the temple.
Demetrius. Why then, we are awake. Let's follow him,
And by the way let us recount our dreams. (IV.i.190–202)

The fun which Mercutio makes of dreams and fairies in *Romeo and Juliet* is an attempt to do in a single speech what the whole action does in *A Midsummer Night's Dream*. His excursion on Queen Mab is designed to laugh away Romeo's dream-born misgivings about their fatal visit to the Capulets.

Romeo. . . . we mean well, in going to this masque;
But 'tis no wit to go.
Mercutio. Why, may one ask?
Romeo. I dreamt a dream to-night.
Mercutio. And so did I.
Romeo. Well, what was yours?
Mercutio. That dreamers often lie.
Romeo. In bed asleep, while they do dream things true.
Mercutio. O, then I see Queen Mab hath been with you.
          (*Romeo* I.iv.47–53)

—and then follow the delightfully plausible impossibilities about the fairies' midwife, implying that dreams accord with the dreamer's wishes, and huddled rapidly one on another, to prevent Romeo's interrupting. The implication is that to believe in dreams is as foolish as to believe in Queen Mab's hazel-nut chariot. When Romeo finally interrupts, Mercutio dismisses his own fairy toys almost in the spirit of Duke Theseus:

Romeo. Peace, peace, Mercutio, peace!
Thou talk'st of nothing.
Mercutio. True, I talk of dreams;
Which are the children of an idle brain,
Begot of nothing but vain fantasy;
Which is as thin of substance as the air . . . (I.iv.95–99)

Romeo's dream, however, in spite of Mercutio, is not to be dismissed so easily as airy nothing:

          . . . my mind misgives
Some consequence, yet hanging in the stars . . . (I.iv.106–107)

A Midsummer Night's Dream is a play in the spirit of Mercutio: the dreaming in it includes the knowledge "that dreamers often lie." The comedy and tragedy are companion pieces: the one moves away from sadness as the other moves away from mirth.

One can feel, indeed, that in the comedy, as compared with Shakespeare's later works, mastery comes a little too easily, because the imaginary and the real are too easy to separate. The same thing can be said of the other plays of the period, *Titus Andronicus*, *Romeo and Juliet*, and *Richard II*. Theseus makes a generalization that

> The lunatic, the lover, and the poet
> Are of imagination all compact. (*Dream* V.i.7–8)

In all these plays the young author gives dramatic urgency to poetic language by putting his heroes in situations which give the lie to what their minds imagine under the influence of passion. Tragedy is conceived chiefly as the contradiction between a warm inner world of feeling and impulse and a cold outer world of fact. Imagination, as the voice of this inner world, has a crucial significance, but its felt reality is limited by the way the imaginary and the real are commonly presented as separate realms. Imagination tends to be *merely* expressive, an evidence of passion rather than a mode of perception. This is true almost without qualification of *Titus Andronicus*, the earliest play of the group. In presenting the madness of Titus, Shakespeare's assumptions about reality are altogether those of Theseus' speech, empirical and fact-minded. The psychological factor is always kept in the foreground when the young poet, following, with more imagination but less profundity, Kyd's method in *The Spanish Tragedy*, expresses the intensity of Titus' grief by having his distraction take literally hyperboles and imaginative identifications. His delusions are very deliberately manipulated to conform to his predominant emotion; in the almost comical scene about killing the fly, Titus first bemoans the act because the fly is a fellow victim, then exults at the creature's death because its blackness links it with the Moor who has wronged him. Even in *Romeo and Juliet*, while the emotional reality of love is triumphantly affirmed we remain always aware of what in the expression is factual and what imaginary, and of how the poetry is lifting us from one plane to the other:

> A grave? O, no, a lanthorn, slaught'red youth,
> For here lies Juliet, and her beauty makes
> This vault a feasting presence full of light. (*Romeo* V.iii.84–86)

In the poetry of this period, there is room beside metaphor and hyperbole to insert a phrase like "so to speak." Marcus exclaims of Titus' distraction:

> Alas, poor man! Grief has so wrought on him
> He takes false shadows for true substances. (*Tit.* III.ii.79–80)

The same remark could be made about Richard II, whose hosts of grief-begotten angels prove so inadequate against the "true substances" mobilized by Bolingbroke. The plays present passionate expression or delusion by the use of relatively simple contrasts between fact and fiction, reason and feeling, keeping an orientation outside the passionate characters' imaginative expression.

In *Richard II*, however, the simple shadow-substance antithesis becomes something more: the divine right of kings gives one sort of objective validity to Richard's imaginings—although his guardian angels are ineffective immediately, they are grounded in moral perception, and Bolingbroke eventually finds their avenging power. Later in Shakespeare's work, the imagination becomes in its own right a way of knowing "more things in heaven and earth" than cool reason ever comprehends. Contrasts between real and imaginary are included in and superseded by contrasts between appearance and reality, as these unfold at various levels of awareness. How different Shakespeare's sense of reality finally became is evident if we set the proud scepticism of Theseus beside the humble scepticism of Prospero. The presiding genius of Shakespeare's latest fantasy also turns from a pageant-like work of imagination to reflect on its relation to life. But for him life itself is like the insubstantial pageant, and we, not just the Titanias and Oberons, are such stuff as dreams are made on.

The greater profundity of the later work, however, should not blind us to the different virtues of the earlier: The confident assumption dominant in *A Midsummer Night's Dream*, that substance and shadow can be kept separate, determines the peculiarly unshadowed gaiety of the fun it makes with fancy. Its organization by polarities—everyday–holiday, town–grove, day–night, waking–dreaming—provides a remarkable resource for mastering passionate experience. By a curious paradox, the full dramatization of holiday affirmations permitted "that side" of experience to be boxed off by Theseus. If we take our stand shoulder to shoulder with Theseus, the play can be an agency for distinguishing what is merely "apprehended" from what is "comprehended." Shakespeare's method of structuring is as powerful, in its way, as Descartes' distinction between mind and body, the formidable engine by which the philosopher swept away "secondary qualities" so that mathematical mind might manipulate geometrical extension. If we do not in our age want to rest in Theseus' rationalistic position (any more than in Descartes'), it remains a great achievement to have got there, and wherever we are going in our sense of reality, we have come via that standing place.

Theseus, moreover, dares not quite have the last word; even in this play: his position is only one stage in a dialectic. Hippolyta will not be reasoned out of her wonder, and answers her new Lord with

But all the story of the night told over,
And all their minds transfigur'd so together,

More witnesseth than fancy's images
And grows to something of great constancy;
But howsoever, strange and admirable. (V.i.23–27)

Did it happen, or didn't it happen? The doubt is justified by what Shakespeare
has shown us. We are not asked to think that fairies exist. But imagination, by
presenting these figments, has reached to something, a creative tendency and
process. What is this process? Where is it? What shall we call it? It is what
happens in the play. It is what happens in marriage. To name it requires many
words, words in motion—the words of *A Midsummer Night's Dream*.

NOTES

1. The passage in Stubbes is quoted more fully previously in the course of a
summary of May day custom.

2. A great deal of misunderstanding has come from the assumption of commentators that a Maying must necessarily come on May Day, May 1. The confusion that results is apparent throughout Furness' discussion of the title and date
in his preface to the *Variorum* edition. He begins by quoting Dr. Johnson downright "I know not why Shakespeare calls this play 'A *Midsummer* Night's Dream'
when he so carefully informs us that it happened on the night preceding *May
day*" (p. v.).

3. See E. K. Chambers, *Shakespearean Gleanings* (Oxford, 1944), pp. 63–64;
and Venezky, *Pageantry*, pp. 140ff.

4. The conjectures are summarized in *Variorum*, pp. 75–91.

5. Chambers, *Gleanings*, pp. 61–67.

6. Ovid, *Metamorphoses*, with an English translation by Frank Justus Miller
(New York, 1916), pp. 34 and 36–37, Bk. I, 11. 465–474 and 505–506.

7. See above, pp. 83f., for a similar compliment to the Queen by Nashe in
Summer's Last Will and Testament. Nashe also elaborates meteorology into make-
believe: Summer blames the drying up of the Thames and earlier flooding of it on
the pageant figure, Sol (McKerrow, *Nashe*, III, 250, 11. 541–565).

8. A good summary of English Midsummer Eve customs is in *Brand's
Antiquities*, ed. Ellis, pp. 298–337, which gives simply and briefly examples of
almost all the English customs included in Frazer's far more complete survey (see
The Golden Bough, Vol. XII, *Bibliography and General Index*, London, 1915, pp.
370–371). Ellis cites (p. 319) a song from Penzance which describes what is in
many respects a Maying, held on Midsummer Eve with a Midsummer bonfire
for the men and maids to dance around (such a local combination of the customs
is to be expected):

> Bright Luna spreads its light around,
> The gallants for to cheer,
>
> As they lay sporting on the ground,
> At the fair June bonfire.
>
> All on the pleasant dewy mead,
> They shared each other's charms,

> Till Phoebus' beams began to spread,
> And coming day alarms.

Although reported as "sung for a long series of years at Penzance and the neighbourhood," the piece obviously was written after Shakespeare's period. But the customs it describes in its rather crude way are interesting in relation to *A Midsummer Night's Dream*, particularly the moonlight and dew, and the sun's beams coming to end it all.

9. *The Court Masque*, pp. 331–332. Although Miss Welsford's perceptions about dance and revel make her account of *A Midsummer Night's Dream* extremely effective, the court masque, to which she chiefly refers it, is not really a formal prototype for this play. It is a direct and large influence in shaping *The Tempest*, and her account of that play brings out fundamental structure such as the early masterpiece gets from entertainment and outdoor holiday, not the court masque.

10. See above, p. 20.

11. *Shakespeare's Imagery and What It Tells Us* (New York, 1935), pp. 259–263.

12. See above, pp. 115–116. A recurrent feature of the type of pastoral which begins with something like "As I walked forth one morn in May" is a bank of flowers "for love to lie and play on," such as Perdita speaks of. This motif appears in the "bank where the wild thyme blows" where Titania sleeps "lull'd in these flowers by dances and delight." In such references there is a magical suggestion that love is infused with nature's vitality by contact.

13. See *Variorum*, p. 239, for Dr. Johnson's cogent note. Richmond Noble, in *Shakespeare's Use of Song* (Oxford, 1923), pp. 55–57), argues that the text as we have it is the text of the song, without, I think, meeting the arguments of Johnson and subsequent editors.

14. *Mediaeval Stage*, I, 165–166.

15. *Ibid.*, I, 122.

16. *Variorum*, p. 240.

17. *Characters of Shakespeare's Plays* (1817) in *The Complete Works*, ed. P. P. Howe (London, 1930), IV, 247–248; quoted *in Variorum*, pp. 299–300.

18. Sir Philip Sidney, *Astrophel and Stella*, No. V, in *Arcadia, 1593, and Astrophel and Stella*, ed. Albert Feuillerat (Cambridge, 1922), p. 244.

19. Coleridge, *Select Poetry and Prose*, ed. Stephen Potter (London, 1933), p. 342.

20. *The Elizabethan Fairies, The Fairies of Folklore and the Fairies of Shakespeare* (New York, 1930), Ch. V and passim. Professor Latham's excellent study points out in detail how Shakespeare, in keeping such features of popular superstition as, say, the taking of changelings, entirely alters the emphasis, so as to make the fairies either harmless or benign, as Titania is benign in rearing up the child of her dead vot'ress "for her sake." Dr. Latham develops and documents the distinction, recognized to a degree by some commentators from the time of Sir Walter Scott, between the fairies of popular belief and those of *Dream*. In particular she emphasizes that, in addition to being malicious, the fairies of common English belief were large enough to be menacing (Ch. II and passim). This difference in size fits with everything else—though it is not borne out by quite all of the evidence, especially if one considers, as Dr. Louis Wright has suggested to me in conversation, that Warwick is close enough to Wales to have possibly been influenced by Welsh traditions. (We have no direct knowledge, one way or the other, about Warwickshire lore in the Elizabethan period.)

Although Dr. Latham summarizes the appearances of fairies in entertainment pageantry, she does not consider the influence of this tradition, nor of the May game, in shaping what Shakespeare made of his fairies—or more accurately, in shaping what Shakespeare made of his play and so of the fairies in it. But her book made a decisive, cogent contribution to a subject that is often treated with coy vagueness. She surveys in Ch. VI the traditions current before Shakespeare about Robin Goodfellow, pointing out that he had not been a native of fairyland until Shakespeare made him so, but "occupied the unique position of the national practical joker" (p. 223).

21. Dr. Latham (*Fairies*, pp. 194–216) traces the way fairies derived from Shakespeare were perpetuated by Drayton and William Browne and others by elaborating conceits about their small size and their relationship to flowers. She develops the point that other writers had suggested earlier, that Shakespeare's influence soon altered popular conceptions of the fairies—and in the process of making them benign and tiny, made them purely literary creatures, without a hold on belief.

22. What Shakespeare exhibits in Bottom's dramatics by reduction to absurdity is expressed directly in the Prologues of *H.V.* There the dramatist is dealing with heroic events which cannot be presented "in their huge and proper life" (Pro. V, l. 5) and so appeals to his audience repeatedly to "eke out our performance with your minds," . . . "minding true things by what their mock'ries be" (Pro. III, l. 35, and Pro. IV, l. 53). The prologues insist continually on the mental process by which alone a play comes to life (Pro. I, ll. 23–25 and 28):

> Piece out our imperfections with your thoughts:
> Into a thousand parts divide one man
> And make imaginary puissance . . .
> For 'tis your thoughts that now must deck our kings . . .

In reference to the rapid shifting of his locale, Shakespeare uses an image which might describe Puck's powers to do what men can only conceive (Pro. III, ll. 1–3):

> Thus with imagin'd wing our swift scene flies,
> In motion of no less celerity
> Than that of thought . . .

Even in a play where, by contrast with *Dream*, Shakespeare is concerned to realize actual historical events, he insists that this realization must be by imaginative projection, not literal reproduction.

23. IV.ii.2. In their terrified response to Puck's intervention, Bottom's companions are like the man in the Hollywood ghost thriller. In showing the whites of his eyes and running without even an effort at courage, he is more credulous than the heroes are, and more than we are. For a moment we laugh at the fear of the uncanny which we ourselves have just experienced, and this comic relief prepares us for another spell of the creeps.

24. J. M. Manly, *Specimens of Pre-Shakespearean Drama* (Boston, 1897), I, 293, from *The Lutterworth Christmas Play*.

25. The familiar Ovidian story which Shakespeare elected to make into "very tragic mirth" is extremely similar, on the face of it, to the story of *Romeo*, which also hinges on surreptitious meetings and an accidental misunderstanding

leading to double suicide. The similarity seems to be underscored by allusions V.i.355–359):

> *Theseus.* Moonshine and Lion are left to bury the dead.
> *Demetrius.* Ay, and Wall too.
> *Bottom.* [starts up] No, I assure you; the wall is down that parted their fathers.

Perhaps there is another allusion to *Romeo* when, after Wall's earlier exit (V.i.210), Theseus makes the mock-sententious observation: "Now is the mural down between the two neighbours." There is nothing in Ovid about a reconciliation, but there is a great deal at the end of *Romeo*. Parts for Thisby's mother and father and Pyramus' father are assigned by Peter Quince in first mustering his actors (I.ii.62). Perhaps Shakespeare planned to make tragical mirth of their laments before he thought of Wall and Moonshine. Miss M. C. Bradbrook, in *Elizabethan Stage Conditions* (Cambridge, 1932), p. 39, notes that when Romeo, before the balcony scene, "ran this way and leap'd this orchard wall" to get away from his friends and into the Capulets' orchard, the staging of the wall presented an unusual problem. She adds that "it is amusing to note the parody of this same orchard wall" in *Dream*. Snout's "you can never bring in a wall" certainly seems a likely by-product of Shakespeare's having recent experience with the difficulty. The effect of the burlesque does not, of course, hinge on specifically recognizing *Romeo* as a prototype. An awareness of the connection adds a point; but the remarks about reconciliation are funny enough simply as comic versions of the *kind* of sentiment to be expected at the end of a tragedy.

The style of *Pyramus and Thisby* imitates with a shrewd eye for characteristic defects what Marlowe, in the Prologue to *Tamburlaine*, called the "jigging veins of rhyming mother wits." The most common devices used by inept early poets "to plump their verse withall" turn up in Shakespeare's parody. The leaden ring of the expletives "same" ("This *same* wall") and "certaine" ("This beauteous Lady, Thisby is *certaine*") recalls many pieces in Dodsley's *Old English Plays* and many passages in Golding's translation of Ovid. Golding's style may well have been Shakespeare's most immediate model. The comic possibilities of the story are very obvious indeed in the translation, whose fourteeners here are often incapable of carrying the elaborate rhetoric. One bit of this high-flown rhetoric is the apostrophizing of the wall, which appears in Golding thus (*Shakespeare's Ovid / Being Arthur Golding's Translation of the Metamorphoses*, ed. W. H. D. Rouse [London, 1904], pp. 83–84, Bk. IV, 11. 90–100):

> O thou envious wall (they sayd) why letst thou lovers thus?
> What matter were it if that thou permitted both of us
> In armes eche other to embrace? Or if that thou think this
> Were overmuch, yet mightest thou at least make roume to kisse.
> And yet thou shalt not finde us churles: we think
>   ourselves in det
> For this same piece of courtesie, in vouching safe to let
> Our sayings to our friendly ears thus freely to come and goe,
> Thus having where they stood in vaine complayned of their woe,
> When night drew nere, they bade adew and eche gave
>   kisses sweete
> Unto the parget on their side, the which did never meete.

In addition to the top-heavy personification which in Golding makes the wall into a sort of stubborn chaperon, Shakespeare's version exploits the fatuous effect of suddenly reversing the wall's attributes from envious to courteous, when the wall, after all, is perfectly consistent. Bottom at first wheedles a "courteous Wall" and then storms at a "wicked Wall." The would-be pathetic touch about kissing the parget (plaster) instead of each others' lips also reappears (V.i.204).

To fill out a line, or to make a rhyme as false as "Thisby . . . secretly," the mother wits often elaborate redundancies, so that technical ineptitude results in a most inappropriate and unpoetical factuality. Shakespeare exploits this effect repeatedly:

> My cherry lips have often kiss'd thy stones,
> Thy stones with lime and hair knit up in thee. (V.i.192–193)

There are also many redundant synonyms, like "Did scare away, or rather did affright." In imitating the use of such homemade stuffing, Shakespeare goes far back (or down) for his models, notably skipping an intermediate, more pretentious level of sophistication in bad Tudor poetry, where fustian classical allusions, "English Seneca read by Candlelight," replace bald redundancy as the characteristic means of plumping verse. Pistol's discharges are Shakespeare's burlesque of such bombast. Most of Bottom's rhetoric is a step down the ladder: the "Shafalus" and "Limander" of *Pyramus* are classical names as these appear in such pieces as *Thersites*.

Perhaps when Bottom starts up, very much alive despite his emphatic death, to correct the Duke in the matter of the wall, his comic resurrection owes something, directly or via the jig, to the folk play. When the St. George, or Fool, or whoever, starts up, alive again, after the miraculous cure, the reversal must have been played as a moment of comical triumph, an upset, more or less grotesque or absurd, no doubt, but still exhilarating—to come back alive is the ultimate turning of the tables on whatever is an enemy of life. The most popular of Elizabethan jigs, "The Jig of Rowland," involves a device of playing dead and pretending to come back to life which may well be a rationalized development of this primitive resurrection motif. Rowland wins back Margaret from the Sexton by getting into a grave and playing dead; she laments him and then starts to go off with his rival; but Rowland jumps up behind them, astonishes the Sexton, sends him packing and wins the wench. (Baskervill, *Jig*, pp. 220–222.) Such brief comic song and dance dramas as this were used as afterpieces following the regular play. *Pyramus and Thisby* almost amounts to a developed jig which has been brought into the framework of the play instead of being presented as an afterpiece, in the usual fashion. The dance element comes in when Bottom, after coming back alive, concludes by dancing a bergomasque.

1974—Alexander Leggatt. "*A Midsummer Night's Dream*," from *Shakespeare's Comedy of Love*

Alexander Leggatt has been a professor of English at University College, University of Toronto. He is the author of *King Lear* (2004), *Introduction* to *English Renaissance Comedy* (1999), *English Stage Comedy, 1490-1990: Five Centuries of a Genre* (1998), and *Shakespeare's Tragedies: Violation and Identity* (2005).

When Titania meets Bottom in the wood near Athens, we see a fairy confronting a mortal, and finding him more wonderful than he finds her. For Titania, Bottom—ass's head and all—is an object of rare grace and beauty; for Bottom, the queen of the fairies is a lady he has just met, who is behaving a bit strangely, but who can be engaged in ordinary, natural conversation:

> *Titania*: I pray thee, gentle mortal, sing again.
> Mine ear is much enamoured of thy note;
> So is mine eye enthralled to thy shape;
> And thy fair virtue's force perforce doth move me,
> On the first view, to say, to swear, I love thee.
> *Bottom*: Methinks, mistress, you should have little reason for that. And
> yet, to say the truth, reason and love keep little company together now-
> a-days. The more the pity that some honest neighbours will not make
> them friends. Nay, I can gleek upon occasion.
> *Titania*: Thou art as wise as thou art beautiful. (III. i. 125–35)

This is, by now, a familiar effect. Behind the sharply contrasted voices are two utterly different kinds of understanding, and each one comically dislocates the other. Titania's love is addressed to a hearer who uses it simply as the occasion for a bit of cheerful philosophizing. And the philosophy, in turn, is wasted on the listener. It is all very well for Bottom to chatter away about reason and love; he has the detachment of the totally immune. But Titania is caught up in the experience of which Bottom is only a detached observer, and, ironically, his cool philosophy only gives her one more reason for adoring him.

But while the essential technique is familiar, there is an important difference in the way it is used. When Speed and Launce commented on the loves of their masters, or when the ladies of France mocked the men who were courting them, we felt that the mockers had (temporarily, at least) a special authority, that they were sharing with the audience a more sophisticated awareness than that of their victims. In the confrontation of different understandings, we felt able to take sides. But in the confrontation of Bottom and Titania, the audience's judgement is delicately suspended between both parties. Each one's assessment of the other is amusingly wrong: Bottom is hardly an object of beauty and grace, nor is plain 'mistress' an adequate form of address for Titania. On reflection, there is something to be said for each of these mistaken views: for all his mortal grossness, Bottom *has* been touched by magic; and the fairy queen is in the grip of a passion we have already seen affecting mortals, and affecting them in a similar way. Yet this only compounds the joke, for while both have been transformed, shifted from their true natures, both are unaware of being anything but their normal selves. The special, sophisticated awareness of the ladies in *Love's Labour's Lost* made the dislocations of that play critical and satiric. But in *A Midsummer Night's Dream* no character has that kind of awareness: each is locked in his own private understanding, confident, self-enclosed and essentially innocent. The closest analogy, perhaps, is with *The Comedy of Errors*, where one brother thought he was subjected to enchantment, the other appeared to be going mad and only the audience knew the true state of affairs. But there at least the characters knew that something very strange was happening: Bottom and Titania, in a situation more genuinely fantastic than anything in *The Comedy of Errors*, accept it without bewilderment, Titania moving to gratify her love at once, and Bottom accepting his new role with cheerful equanimity. The keynote, again, is innocence.

Bottom and Titania present the play's most striking image, a pairing of disparate beings whose contact only emphasizes the difference between them. It looks for a moment as though the barrier between the mortal and immortal worlds has fallen; but on inspection, the barrier proves as secure as ever. Instead of a fusion of worlds we are given a series of neat comic contrasts. And throughout the play, we see four different groups of characters—the lovers, the clowns, the older Athenians and the fairies—each group preoccupied with its own limited problems, and largely unaware of the others. When they make contact, it is usually to emphasize the difference between them. All are to some degree innocent, though (as we shall see) the degree of innocence varies. But the play weaves them all together. Each group, so self-absorbed, is seen in a larger context, which provides comic perspective. Each in turn provides a similar context for the others, and if here and there we feel tempted to take sides, we can never do so for very long; for while each group has its own folly, it has its own integrity as well, and its own special, coherent view of life.

We are reminded throughout of the workings of perception, and in particular of the way we depend on perception—special and limited though it may be—for our awareness of the world. When Hermia finds Lysander, who has run away from her, her first words appear to be a digression:

> Dark night, that from the eye his function takes,
> The ear more quick of apprehension makes;
> Wherein it doth impair the seeing sense,
> It pays the hearing double recompense.
> Thou art not by mine eye, Lysander, found;
> Mine ear, I thank it, brought me to thy sound. (III. ii. 177–82)

The natural question—'But why unkindly didst thou leave me so?'—is asked only after she has discoursed in general terms on how the senses work. In the clown scenes, there is a recurring joke by which the senses are comically transposed (III. i. 81–2; IV. i. 206–9; V. i. 190–1).[1] For the most part, however, the general point is absorbed into the particular dramatic situations of the play. The conflict between Hermia and her father, for example, is seen as a difference of perception:

> *Hermia*: I would my father look'd but with my eyes.
> *Theseus*: Rather your eyes must with his judgment look. (I. i. 56–7)

When Hermia and Egeus look at Lysander, they see two different people, for she sees with the eyes of love, he with the eyes of cantankerous old age, obsessed with its own authority.

In the opening scene, the lovers are on the defensive, set against the hostility of Egeus and the more restrained, regretful opposition of Theseus. Egeus's lecture to Lysander presents love from an outsider's point of view, as trivial, deceitful and disruptive of good order:

> Thou hast by moonlight at her window sung,
> With feigning voice, verses of feigning love,
> And stol'n the impression of her fantasy
> With bracelets of thy hair, rings, gawds, conceits,
> Knacks, trifles, nosegays, sweetmeats, messengers
> Of strong prevailment in unhardened youth;
> With cunning hast thou filch'd my daughter's heart;
> Turn'd her obedience, which is due to me,
> To stubborn harshness. (I. i. 30–8)

Against this crabbed but concrete and detailed attack, Hermia's defence, though deeply felt, is inarticulate: 'I know not by what power I am made bold . . .' (I. i. 59). But it suggests that love is a force bearing down all normal authority, and arming the lover with strength to meet the hostility of the outside world. It gives Hermia the courage to defy her father and the Duke in open court, and to accept the pains and trials love must always bear:

> If then true lovers have been ever cross'd,
> It stands as an edict in destiny.
> Then let us teach our trial patience,
> Because it is a customary cross . . . (I. i. 150–3)

Love, to the outsider, appears foolish; but in accepting its demands the lovers acquire their own kind of integrity.

Their vision of the world is transformed. In Hermia's words,

> Before the time I did Lysander see,
> Seem'd Athens as a paradise to me.
> O, then, what graces in my love do dwell,
> That he hath turn'd a heaven into a hell! (I. i. 204–7)

And for Helena the forest is similarly transformed by the presence of Demetrius:

> It is not night when I do see your face,
> Therefore I think I am not in the night,
> Nor doth this wood lack worlds of company,
> For you, in my respect, are all the world. (II. i. 221–4)

But there is also something comically irrational in these transformations. In particular, the lover's perception of his beloved, and his judgement of her, are peculiar and inexplicable, so much so that even to the lovers themselves love seems blind. As Hermia says of Demetrius,

> And as he errs, doting on Hermia's eyes,
> So I, admiring of his qualities.
> Things base and vile, holding no quantity,
> Love can transpose to form and dignity.
> Love looks not with the eyes, but with the mind;
> And therefore is wing'd Cupid painted blind.
> Nor hath Love's mind of any judgment taste;
> Wings and no eyes figure unheedy haste;
> And therefore is Love said to be a child,
> Because in choice he is so oft beguil'd. (I. i. 230–9)

It is not Hermia's beauty that inspires Demetrius's love: 'Through Athens I am thought as fair as she' (I. i. 227). It is rather that love imposes its own peculiar kind of vision, which renders any other opinion—including that of common sense—irrelevant. How far Helena's own senses have been taken over by this vision may be judged by her decision to betray her friend to Demetrius:

> for this intelligence
> If I have thanks, it is a dear expense.

But herein mean I to enrich my pain,
To have his sight thither and back again. (I. i. 248–51)

In love, the mere sight of the beloved acquires an importance that by any normal standards would be absurd.

The lovers may find each other's choices inexplicable, but at least they share the same kind of experience: they are in the grip of a power that renders choice and will meaningless. One sign of that is that the lovers lack the conscious awareness of convention that distinguishes Berowne and the ladies in *Love's Labour's Lost*. They slip naturally into a stylized manner of speech:

> *Lysander*: Ay me! For aught that I could ever read,
> Could ever learn by tale or history,
> The course of true love never did run smooth;
> But either it was different in blood—
> *Hermia*: O cross! too high to be enthrall'd to low.
> *Lysander*: Or else ingraffed in respect of years—
> *Hermia*: O spite! too old to be engag'd to young.
> *Lysander*: Or else it stood upon the choice of friends—
> *Hermia*: O hell! to choose love by another's eyes. (I. i. 132–40)

There is something ceremonial about this passage, with its liturgical responses, and like all ceremonies it presents the individual experience as part of a larger and more general pattern. The individual can assert his independence of this process only by showing his awareness of it and standing partly outside it, as Berowne attempts to do. But Lysander and Hermia surrender to the ceremony, taking its patterned language as a normal mode of speech. Later in the same scene, Hermia falls into a playful, teasing style as she swears to meet Lysander:

> I swear to thee by Cupid's strongest bow,
> By his best arrow with the golden head,
> By the simplicity of Venus' doves,
> By that which knitteth souls and prospers loves,
> And by that fire which burn'd the Carthage Queen,
> When the false Troyan under sail was seen,
> By all the vows that ever men have broke,
> In number more than ever women spoke,
> In that same place thou hast appointed me,
> Tomorrow truly will I meet with thee. (I. i. 169–78)

There is, this time, a deliberate playfulness in the way the literary allusions pile up, as she teases her lover by comparing male infidelity and female faith. But the speech flows swiftly and easily, and the joking does no damage; she can afford to toy with her love because she is so sure of it. (There is a similar quality in their affectionate banter about sleeping arrangements in the forest—II. ii. 39–61.) The joking with love is not that of an outsider exposing its weakness, but that of an insider confident of its strength, and feeling that strength by subjecting it to a little harmless teasing. And once again, the character herself gives no indication that this manner of speech is anything other than perfectly natural.

The exchange on the course of true love is slow and brooding; Hermia's speech, swift and gay. The common factor is an air of literary artifice that sets the lovers' experience apart as something special; and throughout the play the range of expression achieved within this framework of artifice is remarkable. We see this, for example, when Lysander awakes to find himself in love with Helena:

> The will of man is by his reason sway'd,
> And reason says you are the worthier maid.
> Things growing are not ripe until their season;
> So I, being young, till now ripe not to reason;
> And touching now the point of human skill,
> Reason becomes the marshal to my will,
> And leads me to your eyes, where I o'erlook
> Love's stories, written in Love's richest book.
> *Helena*: Wherefore was I to this keen mockery born?
> When at your hands did I deserve this scorn?
> Is't not enough, is't not enough, young man,
> That I did never, no, nor never can,
> Deserve a sweet look from Demetrius' eye,
> But you must flout my insufficiency?
> Good troth, you do me wrong, good sooth, you do,
> In such disdainful manner me to woo. (II. ii. 115–30)

Lysander's speech is formal, solemn, sententious—and thoroughly dislocated by its context. He describes his love as natural and reasonable, but we know it is purely arbitrary. Here the character's unawareness of his own dependence on convention becomes sharply comic. Helena's irritable retort gives us, by contrast, the sound of a natural speaking voice; there is a striking difference in tone and pace. And yet it too is in rhyming couplets: her seemingly natural utterance is still contained within the framework of a convention; her anger, no less than his infatuation, is part of the larger, dance-like pattern in which all four lovers are unconsciously moving.

The lovers see their experiences in the forest as chaotic; but for the audience the disorder, like the disorder of a Feydeau farce, is neatly organized, giving us pleasure where it gives them pain.[2] When Hermia accuses Demetrius of killing

Lysander, the patterned language and the rhymed couplets cool the emotional impact the scene might have had (III. ii. 43–81). Over and over, the violence of the ideas is lightened by jingling rhythm and rhyme: 'I'll follow thee, and make a heaven of hell, / To die upon the hand I love so well' (II. i. 243–4). It is not so much that, as Enid Welsford suggests, 'the harmony and grace of the action would have been spoilt by convincing passion';[3] it is more that the manner of the action in itself ensures that the passion is convincing only to the characters. They lash out frantically at each other, but the audience is too far away to share in their feelings. Our detachment is aided by the presence of Puck and Oberon, acting as an onstage audience and providing a comic perspective. What is serious and painful to the lovers is simply a 'fond pageant' of mortal foolishness to the watchers (III. ii. 144). Puck in particular regards the whole affair as a show put on for his amusement (and incidentally if we can remember this in the final scene it adds a level of irony to the lovers' laughter as they watch Pyramus and Thisbe: they too, not so long ago, amused an audience with antics that they thought were serious).[4] The irony is compounded when the lovers indignantly accuse each other of playing games with serious feelings: 'Wink at each other; hold the sweet jest up; / This sport, well carried, shall be chronicled' (III. ii. 239–40). Helena's accusation is very close to the truth—except that it should be directed at the audience.

But our feelings are subtly managed here: there are two watchers—Puck, with his delight in chaos, and Oberon, who wishes to bring chaos to an end. We share in both these attitudes. When Helena recalls her childhood friendship with Hermia, the rhyme slips away and it becomes a little easier to take the characters' feelings seriously (III. ii. 195–219). From this point on, the formality breaks down into undignified, farcical squabbling, with physical knockabout and coarse insults—relieved, on one occasion, by a surprisingly quiet and dignified speech from Helena:

Good Hermia, do not be so bitter with me.
I evermore did love you, Hermia,
Did ever keep your counsel, never wrong'd you;
Save that, in love unto Demetrius,
I told him of your stealth unto this wood. . . .
And now, so you will let me quiet go,
To Athens I will bear my folly back,
And follow you no further. (III. ii. 306–16)

While still enjoying the confusion, we are beginning to feel that it had better stop soon. And Oberon and Puck see that it does.

But we are kept at a distance from the lovers' final union, no less than from their suffering. In the last stages of their ordeal, formality returns and is further heightened: a variety of rhymed verse forms accumulates as, one by one, the lovers enter and fall asleep. Their individuality is at a particularly low ebb, as Puck controls them more directly than ever, even to the point of assuming the men's voices (III. ii. 396–463). The final harmony he creates for them, like the earlier confusion, is seen as the working out of a dance pattern; and more than that, it is the fulfillment of a ritual sense of life embodied in homely clichés:

> And the country proverb known,
> That every man should take his own,
> In your waking shall be shown.
>> Jack shall have Jill;
>> Nought shall go ill;
> The man shall have his mare again, and all shall be well. (III. ii. 458–63)

Similarly, Theseus sees their coupling in terms of sport and pastime—'No doubt they rose up early to observe / The rite of May' (IV. i. 129–30)—and as a fulfilment of nature's most basic impulse: 'Good morrow, friends. Saint Valentine is past; / Begin these wood-birds but to couple now?' (IV. i. 136–7). The presence, and the comments, of other characters provide the awareness of convention that the lovers themselves lack, being too caught up in their own experiences. We see love's perceptions as special and limited, and the lovers themselves as lacking in full self-awareness. The magic flower is applied, significantly, to the eye; just as significantly, it is applied while the lover is asleep. And even the final harmony of love, when seen through the homely analogies of Puck and Theseus, is satisfying but nothing to get ecstatic about: 'The man shall have his mare again, and all shall be well' sounds like the voice of a parent comforting a child who has been making a great fuss about nothing. It is certainly not how the lovers themselves would have put it. At the same time, however, we recognize that the lovers *have* got what they want: the law of Athens, so formidable in the first scene, is swept away to accommodate them, and Egeus is reduced to spluttering impotence. In our final attitude to the lovers, there is respect as well as amused detachment.

We recognize, moreover, that they speak about love with some authority: they have been through it, with a vengeance. In this regard we can set them against Peter Quince's amateur dramatic society, who are trying to construct a tale of love and who are completely out of their depth. They belong, quite solidly, to the working-day world: 'Hard-handed men that work in Athens here, / Which never labour'd in their minds till now' (v. i. 72–3); 'A crew of patches, rude mechanicals, / That work for bread upon Athenian stalls' (III. ii. 9–10). Each one has a trade, by which he is identified, and they show a greater interest in the technical problems of placing walls and calculating moonshine than they do in working up convincing emotion (except of course for

Bottom, who will throw himself zealously into anything). They seem, in fact, too anxious about decorum to be dealing with anything so erotic as the story of Pyramus and Thisbe: 'You must say "paragon." A paramour is—God bless us!—a thing of naught' (IV. ii. 13–14). Like the characters of *Love's Labour's Lost*, they struggle with one of the most vital problems of expression— how to create a work of art. But if the lovers are so deeply embedded in the experience of love that they are unaware of convention, the mechanicals are so embroiled in the problems of convention that they are quite unconscious of the damage they are doing to the experience the convention should embody.

Yet there is a kind of logic in what they do. They are anxious not to give offence, and so they emphasize the illusory nature of their art—'we will do no harm with our swords' (III. i. 17). They are also anxious to make the technical side of their work as convincing as possible, to ensure that Wall and Moonshine are real to the audience. Once again, though this time inadvertently, the result is to emphasize the illusory nature of their play. It is easy for critics to lecture them on their failure to understand dramatic illusion;[5] but their stated intention is to give delight without giving offence—'And, most dear actors, eat no onions nor garlic, for we are to utter sweet breath; and I do not doubt but to hear them say it is a sweet comedy' (IV. ii. 37–9)—and on those terms, the play succeeds, though not in quite the way they planned. The effect on the onstage audience (not to mention the offstage one) is like the effect of the lovers' quarrel—it is so much fun to watch that the suffering of the characters does not communicate—except that here the gap between the lovers' feelings and the audience's reactions is more obvious, more broadly comic. Theseus can defend the actors by saying that 'The best in this kind are but shadows' (V. i. 210), but he can also say 'This palpable-gross play hath *well* beguil'd / The heavy gait of night' (V. i. 356–7: my italics). Despite Philostrate's misgivings, this proves to be the ideal entertainment for a nuptial: the dangers that threaten love are systematically destroyed by the way they are presented. The parents who stand in the way of the lovers, though they were originally cast (at I. ii. 50–6), do not appear at all; the wall is 'sweet', 'lovely' and 'courteous' (V. i. 174, 176)—not to mention co-operative, producing a chink on demand; the lion is 'A very gentle beast, and of a good conscience' (V. i. 224). The death of the hero is anything but final, for Pyramus-Bottom rises from the ground as easily as the indestructible hero of a mummers' St. George play, or Falstaff at the battle of Shrewsbury. The emotional effect of the play is summed up by Theseus: 'This passion, and the death of a dear friend, would go near to make a man look sad' (V. i. 280–1). And through all this, the actors maintain an unbroken confidence in the rightness of what they are doing: the nervous first-night mistakes so often seen in production are good fun, but have no warrant in the text. As Theseus says of the actors, 'If we imagine no worse of them than they of themselves, they may pass for excellent men' (V. i. 213–14). Far from being disconcerted by the audience's interruptions, Bottom meets them with condescending tolerance:

> *Theseus*: The wall, methinks, being sensible, should curse again.
> *Pyramus*: No, in truth, sir, he should not. *Deceiving me* is Thisby's cue.
> She is to enter now, and I am to spy her through the wall. You shall see
> it will fall out pat as I told you; yonder she comes. (V. i. 180–5)

The actors, like the lovers, inhabit a world of private satisfactions, and seem to a great extent oblivious of what the other characters think of them. But they have chosen an audience that has some experience of the crosses of love, and finds in their version of that experience nothing but a cause of hilarity.

The leading member of that audience is Theseus, and it may appear that he represents some kind of final, objective authority. But his cool daylight rationality is laced in a context that clearly shows its limits. His scepticism about the visions of 'the lunatic, the lover, and the poet' (V. i. 2–22) is offered with an air of conviction, and is easy to take seriously—until we reflect that in casting doubt on the lovers' story he is denying something we have seen with our own eyes only a few minutes before. More than that, he and Hippolyta have had dealings with the fairies in their younger and wilder days (II. i. 70–80).[6] Neither he—nor, more surprisingly, Hippolyta in her defence of the lovers—appears to recall this simple fact. It is as though, in growing up, they have simply forgotten what they once were, losing clarity of vision in one as they have gained it in another. At the end of the scene, the rational sceptic makes an interesting slip: 'Lovers, to bed; 'tis almost fairy time' (V. i. 353). It may be just a casual turn of phrase; or it may be an involuntary acknowledgement of a truth that in his more guarded moments Theseus would deny (like Chesterton's '"My God", said the atheist'). In any case, his words are borne out as soon as he leaves the stage, as the beings whose existence he has denied once more fill the scene. One final irony should be noticed: in scoffing at fantasy, he also scoffs at art, yet he himself is a figure in a work of art, owing his existence to a poet's imagination and an audience's willingness to suspend disbelief: as G. K. Hunter puts it, 'he himself is just another such "antique fable".'[7]

In his dealings with the lovers in the first scene, Theseus can also be seen as exerting an authority that has no final validity. In preparing to enforce the harsh Athenian law, and urging Hermia to recognize her father's power, he is counselling patience and submission of a kind that he himself finds difficult:

> but, O, methinks, how slow
> This old moon wanes! She lingers my desires,
> Like to a step-dame or a dowager,
> Long withering out a young man's revenue. (I. i. 3–6)

It seems ironic that as he himself is about to seal an 'everlasting bond of fellowship' (I. i. 85) he is prepared to allow a loveless match to take place. But to do him credit, he enforces the law with evident reluctance: he tactfully leaves the lovers together, and behind the mask of authority we can detect other feelings. In asking Demetrius and Egeus to go with him, he says 'I have some private schooling for you both' (I. i. 116), suggesting that he may want to talk them out of the match. And his words to Hippolyta, 'Come, my Hippolyta; what cheer, my love?' (I. i. 122), suggest a recognition that she too is upset by what is happening. Like the Duke of Ephesus he is trapped by a cruel law 'Which by no means we may extenuate' (I. i. 120); and like that other Duke he brushes the law aside with a wave of his hand once the action of the comedy has taken its course: 'Egeus, I will overbear your will' (IV. i. 176). It is part of the peculiar logic of comedy that rules which seem rigorously binding in the first act suddenly appear trivial when it is time to end the play. The mere sight of the lovers happily paired has become a force stronger than the law of Athens.

Theseus enforces the law with reluctance; Egeus insists on it with a grim fanaticism that makes him the only unsympathetic figure in the play; and a comparison between the two men helps us to see the value of Theseus's kind of authority. In the scene of the lovers' waking, the rich harmony of Theseus's speech on the hounds establishes an atmosphere in which Egeus's jerky, irritable style is utterly out of place:

> Enough, enough, my lord; you have enough;
> I beg the law, the law upon his head.
> They would have stol'n away, they would, Demetrius,
> Thereby to have defeated you and me:
> You of your wife, and me of my consent,
> Of my consent that she should be your wife. (IV. i. 151–6)

In the text as normally printed, Egeus does not appear in the last scene;[8] his fussy, sterile concern with his own power is the one kind of mentality the play's final harmony can find no room for. Theseus, on the other hand, is allowed considerable authority in the final scene. For all his limits as a commentator on art and love, he is not to be brushed aside as the representative of a worn-out order. His urbanity, common sense and good temper are necessary ingredients in society, as we see when he attempts to soften the conflict between generations, and when he accepts the lovers' union as a *fait accompli*. Throughout the final scene, Theseus and Hippolyta suggest not only mature love but a general principle of balance: he disbelieves the lovers, but she is more open-minded; conversely, he is the more tolerant with the players. Each corrects the other's excesses, but with tact and affection. They are not the play's final spokesmen for they have no means of comprehending what goes on in the woods; but their cool wisdom is as necessary to the play's total harmony as the desire of the lovers or the earnest good intentions of the clowns.

The fairies, on the other hand, seem to have the range of vision and the freedom of action that the other characters lack. At their first appearance, they are sharply juxtaposed with the plodding, prosaic minds of the mechanicals, and our initial impression is of lightness, speed and freedom

> *Puck*: How now, spirit! whither wander you?
> *Fairy*: Over hill, over dale,
> Thorough bush, thorough brier,
> Over park, over pale,
> Thorough flood, thorough fire,
> I do wander every where
> Swifter than the moon's sphere;
> And I serve the Fairy Queen,
> To dew her orbs upon the green. (II. i. 1–9)

At times, the whole created world seems to be their playground: they are, in Mark Van Doren's words, 'citizens of all the universe there is'.[9] But if they have all of space at their disposal, they have only half of time. The lovers and the clowns wander forth freely by day or night; the fairies are more circumscribed, and have to follow the night wherever it goes. They have freedom but no leisure: 'look thou meet me ere the first cock crow' (II. i. 267). If they seem more authoritative, less undermined by irony than the mortals, it may be because they are more conscious of their limits. There is a feeling of urgency as Puck and Oberon try to settle the affairs of the lovers, for they both sense that they are at the limits of their power:

> *Puck*: My fairy lord, this must be done with haste,
> For night's swift dragons cut the clouds full fast;
> And yonder shines Aurora's harbinger,
> At whose approach ghosts, wand'ring here and there,
> Troop home to churchyards. Damned spirits all,
> That in cross-ways and floods have burial,
> Already to their wormy beds are gone,
> For fear lest day should look their shames upon;
> They wilfully themselves exile from light,
> And must for aye consort with black-brow'd night.
> *Oberon*: But we are spirits of another sort:
> I with the morning's love have oft made sport;
> And, like a forester, the groves may tread
> Even till the eastern gate, all fiery red,

Opening on Neptune with fair blessed beams,
Turns into yellow gold his salt green streams.
But, notwithstanding, haste, make no delay;
We may effect this business yet ere day. (III. ii. 378–95)

Oberon's power takes him as far as sunrise but no further. This passage defines
as well as anything in the play the nature and the limits of the fairy kingdom.
They are spirits of the night, but they are not involved with its darkest and most
shameful secrets. They are not, like the ghosts of suicides, shut off forever from
normality. The flowers, insects, birds and animals of the normal world are theirs
also, though they see them with a special intimacy; they can touch the affairs of
men, and men know of them. They are spirits, not of the deepest night, but of
the border country between night and day, that part of the other world which
men too know about. But while Oberon exults in his power to go as far as the
sunrise, full daylight is as foreign to his nature as the deepest night. The passage
begins and ends with the urgency of time, the limits placed on the fairies by the
coming of day.

Even within their normal sphere of action, the fairies' power is not infallible:
Puck has no special knowledge, and has to go by appearances: 'Did not you
tell me I should know the man / By the Athenian garments he had on?' (III.
ii. 348–9). His eyesight, like that of the lovers, can play tricks on him. When
he exclaims 'Lord, what fools these mortals be!' (III. ii. 115), we recognize that
their folly is the product of his own mistakes, and the laughter is partly against
him. But he can fairly claim that Oberon's instructions were inadequate. While
the fairies exert an easy control over their own world, in dealing with mortals
they are a little out of their depth, and their touch is clumsy. Nor can they avoid
emotional problems of their own. When we first see Oberon and Titania the
fairy kingdom is in disarray, torn by a civil war over a small boy from the mortal
world. At the same time Theseus and Hippolyta, with their own more limited
power, have passed through their period of discord:

Hippolyta, I woo'd thee with my sword,
And won thy love doing thee injuries;
But I will wed thee in another key,
With pomp, with triumph, and with revelling. (I. i. 16–19)

Through much of the play the worlds of Theseus and Oberon—rulers,
respectively, of the day and night—are opposing and complementary.[10] While
other characters mingle, the two rulers never share the stage. In Theseus's city,
order and rationality are temporarily dominant, with suggestions of a period of
chaos in the past (and with some laws from the past that still need reforming:
Egeus invokes a barbaric 'ancient privilege'—I. i. 41). Though the point is not

stressed, this is consistent with the familiar legends of Theseus. In the fairy kingdom disorder is temporarily dominant: the mutual reproaches of Titania and Oberon suggest that this is hardly a normal state of affairs: 'Why should Titania cross her Oberon?' (II. i. 119) But while Shakespeare exploits this kind of contrast all through the play, he can also bring its various worlds together in more intimate and sympathetic contact. In the final scene, with the peace of his own kingdom restored, Oberon uses his blessing to forestall any approaching disorder in the mortal world:

> So shall all the couples three
> Ever true in loving be;
> And the blots of nature's hand
> Shall not in their issue stand. (V. i. 396–9)

The two worlds, though not intermingled, are finally brought to rest side by side.

The final scene also suggests that it is through the workings of nature that the mortal and immortal worlds come closest together. In love and procreation ('Begin these wood-birds but to couple now?') men become part of the larger harmony of nature, in which the fairies are also included, and over which they have some power. This harmony also touches other human activities: both in work and in social pleasure, man is a creature of the seasons and depends on nature; and just as nature is the medium for transmitting Oberon's final blessing ('With this field-dew consecrate . . .' V. i. 404), so it is the medium by which disorder in the fairy world passes into the human one, affecting both work and social pastime:

> The ox hath therefore stretch'd his yoke in vain,
> The ploughman lost his sweat, and the green corn
> Hath rotted ere his youth attain'd a beard;
> The fold stands empty in the drowned field,
> The crows are fatted with the murrion flock;
> The nine men's morris is fill'd up with mud,
> And the quaint mazes in the wanton green,
> For lack of tread are undistinguishable. (II. i. 93–100)

As in the final song of *Love's Labour's Lost*, the workings of nature provide a common ground of experience: the fairies discuss a world familiar to the audience, and for a moment they seem closer to us than any of the mortals have been. The flower struck by Cupid's dart has been part of a high, remote experience, which even Puck could not see (II. i. 155–68). But it is still a flower, something small and familiar from the world of nature. In a way, *Pyramus and*

Thisbe presents a world more fantastic than that of the fairies, a world where walls move and moons speak. But we laugh it off as an absurdity. The fantasy of the fairy world consists rather in viewing familiar things from a special angle: suddenly flowers, dewdrops and insects seem clearer and more formidable, and we find ourselves engulfed by a world we normally look down on from a height of five or six feet. Then, at the end, the fairies actually invade our world: the references to the 'wasted brands' and the 'dead and drowsy fire' (V. i. 364, 381) remind us of the dwellings of ordinary men. And when Oberon says 'To the best bride-bed will we, / Which by us shall blessed be' (V. i. 292–3) it may strike us that Theseus and Hippolyta will be there already: the two sets of rulers, kept apart throughout the play, are finally juxtaposed in the audience's imagination.

The play suggests that the mortal and immortal worlds are finally separate, and yet very close, divided by a line that is extremely thin but never gives way[11]—not even, as we have seen, when Bottom meets Titania. The mortals who have been affected by that other world feel a sense of deep strangeness, and have to grope to re-establish the normal certainties of life. Lysander, waking up in daylight, grasps the most simple facts only with an effort:

> But as yet, I swear,
> I cannot truly say how I came here,
> But, as I think—for truly would I speak,
> And now I do bethink me, so it is—
> I came with Hermia hither. (IV. i. 144–8)

The others are equally bewildered, poised between dream and waking:

> *Demetrius*: These things seem small and undistinguishable,
> Like far-off mountains turned into clouds.
> *Hermia*: Methinks I see these things with parted eye,
> When every thing seems double. (IV. i. 184.–7)

We are not sure whether by 'these things' they mean the experiences of the forest or the sight of Theseus and his huntsmen. But as they talk with each other the balance tilts, the immediate present is clearly seen as reality, and the social bonds of the daylight world are re-established. Bottom reverses the process: he wakes with the daylight world on his mind—'When my cue comes, call me, and I will answer' (IV. i. 197)—and gradually recovers the vision. In both cases, the characters are poised on the border between dream and reality, which is also the border between the fairy world and the mortal one. And while the two worlds are so radically different that each one challenges the reality of the other, turning it into a dream, they are also close enough for a single mind, with an effort, to sense them both at once.

Experiences from one world can even be absorbed into the other. One could say that Cupid's flower does nothing new to the lovers: what we hear of their behaviour in Athens in Act I suggests that there too they were subject to arbitrary and irrational changes of heart, leading to confusion and humiliation.[12] The flower simply provides a comic image of the normal operation of love, intensifying it and speeding it up. And while Demetrius, in one sense, will spend the rest of his life under an enchantment, in another sense what has happened to him is as normal as growing up:

> I wot not by what power—
> But by some power it is—my love to Hermia,
> Melted as the snow, seems to me now
> As the remembrance of an idle gaud
> Which in my childhood I did dote upon. (IV. i. 161–5)

Just as the passage as a whole is delicately poised between dream and reality, so there is a fine balance here between Demetrius's sense of wonder at what has happened, and his feeling that it is entirely natural. Bottom, of course, has his own way of absorbing the dream into his normal life:

> I will get Peter Quince to write a ballad of this dream. It shall be
> call'd 'Bottom's Dream,' because it hath no bottom; and I will sing it in
> the latter end of a play, before the Duke. (IV. i. 209–12)

The dream cannot be expounded: but it can be turned into material for a performance. One might even say that his transformation in the wood is a comic echo of the versatility he claims as an actor. When Puck, using Bottom's voice, shouts 'Sometime a horse I'll be, sometime a hound, / A hog, a headless bear, sometime a fire' (III. i. 98–9) we may recall Bottom's eagerness to be a lover, a tyrant, a lady and a lion. There are transformations and transformations; and perhaps it is not such a large step after all to go from changing beards to changing heads.

If much of the play's comic life depends on playing different groups of characters off against each other, much of its power to haunt the imagination comes from its suggestion of the ultimate unity of the various worlds it depicts. In a variety of small touches, echoes are set up between one scene and another. Immediately after Hermia awakes in panic from a dream of being attacked by a serpent, we find the mechanicals engaged in taking the terror out of their play, to avoid frightening the ladies. The music and dance of the fairies are followed by the more robust music of the daylight world, the hounds and horns of Theseus; and at the end of *Pyramus and Thisbe* the clowns, like the fairies, show that they too can dance, in their own way. In the final scene, Theseus's earthy jokes about the couples' impatience to get to bed introduce an idea that is picked up and transformed by Oberon's celebration of fertility; just as in Puck's opening words, 'Now the hungry lion roars' (V. i. 360), Snug's apologetic performance sets off an unexpected echo from a more serious world. The various worlds of the play mirror each other, and are ultimately seen as one world, moving in a single rhythm. This feeling is particularly strong from the later forest scenes to the end of the play, as references to time accumulate, and the characters all feel caught in a common rhythm, moving from night into day, and then back again.

Just as each group of characters is placed against the others, so the artistic world they all form together is seen in relation to other kinds of experience, outside the normal scope of comedy. Throughout the play we are made aware of the process of selection by which the comic world is created. The process begins, simply enough, with Theseus's words in the opening scene, 'Turn melancholy forth to funerals; / The pale companion is not for our pomp' (I. i. 14–15). Puck and Oberon are careful to draw a distinction between themselves and the 'damned spirits' of the night, but in so doing they remind us of the existence of those spirits (III. ii. 378–95; V. i. 360–79). Titania's lullaby invokes the slimy creeping things of the forest, telling them to keep their distance (II. ii. 9–24). Hermia's dream is frightening enough, but, as in other scenes with the lovers, the formal style with its rhyming couplets helps to cool the terror (II. ii. 145–56). Similarly, the suggestion of bestiality in Titania's affair with Bottom is kept under control by the cool, decorative poetry as she leads him off the stage:

Come, wait upon him; lead him to my bower.
The moon, methinks, looks with a wat'ry eye;
And when she weeps, weeps every little flower,
Lamenting some enforced chastity. (III. i. 182–5)

They are going off to bed, but there is nothing torrid about it. The forest might have been a place of unbridled eroticism, but it is not: Lysander and Hermia are very careful about their sleeping arrangements, and Demetrius warns Helena to keep away from him so as not to endanger her virginity (II. i. 214–19). Normally, couples going into the woods mean only one thing, but the lovers of this play are aware of the energies the forest might release, and determined to keep those energies under control. On the other hand the ideal of chastity, in Theseus's reference to Diana's nunnery and in Oberon's description of the imperial votaress who is immune to love, is set aside as something admirable but too high and remote for ordinary people. The play is aware of both extreme attitudes to sex, but steers a civilized middle course appropriate to comedy.

Other possible kinds of art are also referred to, and then banished. Theseus, selecting a play for his wedding night, rejects anything involving satire, eunuchs or the dismembering of poets (V. i. 44–55). Bottom and his crew try to perform a tragedy, and turn it into a glorious farce: the whole machinery of tragedy, Fates, Furies and all, disappears into laughter. More soberly, Oberon refers to some of the smaller miseries produced by the ordinary workings of nature, and banishes them:

> Never mole, hare-lip, nor scar,
> Nor mark prodigious, such as are
> Despised in nativity,
> Shall upon their children be. (V. i. 400–3)

Throughout the play, we seem to be witnessing a constant process of exorcism, as forces which could threaten the safety of the comic world are called up, only to be driven away. The play stakes out a special area of security in a world full of hostile forces: just as the mortal world is very close to the fairy world, yet finally separate from it, so the comic world of the play is very close to a darker world of passion, terror and chaos, yet the border between them, though thin, is never broken.

But despite the toughness of its defences, the play's world is fragile in another way:

> If we shadows have offended,
> Think but this, and all is mended,
> That you have but slumb'red here
> While these visions did appear.
> And this weak and idle theme,
> No more yielding but a dream,
> Gentles, do not reprehend.
> If you pardon, we will mend. (V. i. 4.12–19)

It is, finally, all an illusion, a dream. Not simply the fairies, or the amateur actors, but the entire company, are seen as 'shadows'.[13] The serpent, a standard image of fear throughout the play, is referred to for the last time: 'the serpent's tongue' (V. i. 422) is now the danger of being hissed by a hostile audience. But even this admission of fragility—the fragility of art itself—also contains an acknowledgement of strength. The dream metaphor is carefully chosen, for throughout the play characters have described as dreams experiences that the audience saw as real and solid. Titania's waking is a case in point:

> *Titania*: My Oberon! What visions have I seen!
> Methought I was enamour'd of an ass.
> *Oberon*: There lies your love. (IV. i. 73–5)

Oberon's demonstration of the reality of the dream is about as direct as it could be. The other dreams have the same reality for the audience, though they may fade in the characters' memories: quite simply, we saw it all happen. *The Taming of the Shrew* moves us into illusion and keeps us there; *Love's Labour's Lost* smashes several illusions and ends before the pieces can be picked up; but *A Midsummer Night's Dream* moves us freely in and out of illusion, giving us a clear sense of both its fragility and its integrity.

How, finally, do we react to this dream? Bottom's warning is clear: 'Man is but an ass if he go about to expound this dream' (V. i. 202–3). There is no point in rooting through the play for morals or allegories. But Puck's final emphasis on the play's fragility reminds us that we as an audience have some responsibility, and within the play there is a hint of what that responsibility might be:

> *Theseus*: The best in this kind are but shadows; and the worst are no worse, if imagination amend them.
> *Hippolyta*: It must be your imagination then, and not theirs.
> (V. i. 210–12)

The performers of *Pyramus and Thisbe* are severely heckled, but all the same they get a gentler reception than the performers of the Nine Worthies: for one thing, they are allowed to play out their play to the end. For another, their adoption of their parts is accepted, if only for the sake of the joke:

> *Demetrius*: Well roar'd, Lion.
> *Theseus*: Well run, Thisby.
> *Hippolyta*: Well shone, Moon. Truly, the moon shines with a good grace. (V. i. 257–60)

The Princess of France was prepared to take her pleasure from the incompetence of the show: 'Their form confounded makes most form in mirth, / When great things labouring perish in their birth' (V. ii. 517–18). Theseus takes a more kindly pleasure in looking behind the performers' incompetence to their good intentions, and if it all amounts to nothing, then

> The kinder we, to give them thanks for nothing.
> Our sport shall be to take what they mistake;
> And what poor duty cannot do, noble respect
> Takes it in might, not merit. (V. i. 89–92)

The audience has the most important role of all. It must, by its own response, give value to things that might otherwise be trivial. If it is to take the illusions of art as a kind of reality, then its perceptions must be, like those of a lover, generous to the point of irrationality: 'Things base and vile, holding no quantity, / Love can transpose to form and dignity' (I. i. 232–3).

Each kind of existence the play shows—the passion of the lovers, the well-meaning bungling of the clowns, the cool order of Theseus and the fantastic disorder of the fairies—is valued for its own sake. Its uniqueness is clearly seen in relation to everything else in the play, and emphasized by the usual comic dislocations. But each element in the play's world, being unique, is also precious, for only by its uniqueness can it contribute to the overall harmony—just as each hound in Theseus's pack, by baying a different note, contributes to the total effect: they are

> Slow in pursuit, but match'd in mouth like bells,
> Each under each. A cry more tuneable
> Was never holla'd to, nor cheer'd with horn,
> In Crete, in Sparta, nor in Thessaly. (IV. i. 120–3)

As in other plays, an important image is drawn from sport: but this time, we should notice, Theseus values the harmonious chiming of his hounds more than their swiftness in the hunt. And it is, finally, the harmony of the play's vision that gives us most delight.[14]

But the artistic vision itself, which draws these disparate experiences together, is also limited. The epilogue's urbane apology for the triviality of the play picks up other suggestions about art that can be detected throughout. Bottom the actor is the play's greatest fool, yet in a sense he is the character with the most comprehensive vision, who not only sees fairies but greets them with easy familiarity. His versatility as an actor who can play any role (and will, if given half a chance) is a comic image of the dramatist's own power of creation,[15] and when he promises to 'roar you as gently as any sucking dove' (I. ii. 73) he shows the artist's prerogative of rearranging reality. Puck, on the other hand, suggests the artist's manipulative craft, arranging the mechanics of the plot. He too is a figure of small authority in his own world, a licensed jester and runner of errands who has to have the higher mysteries explained to him. But just as Bottom is the only mortal to speak to the fairies, Puck is the only character to speak to the audience; and this gives him, like Bottom, some identification with the dramatist. Bottom with his innocent egotism and power of fantasy, and Puck with his love of mischief, are both like children;[16] Theseus is the responsible adult. Without him as patron and audience, there would be no performance; but without the artist, for all his childishness, there would be no play.

The understanding of art is necessarily limited; it cuts out a lot of reality in order to create an ordered work. Shakespeare deals with this charge by admitting it, by (paradoxically) suggesting within the play some of the things that have been left out, so that we see the process of selection at work. Art, like love, is a limited and special vision; but like love it has by its very limits a transforming power, creating a small area of order in the vast chaos of the world. The technique of comic dislocation, developed so skilfully in earlier plays, here becomes an instrument of celebration as well as of mockery, and the two are so closely bound together that we can hardly tell which is which. The very qualities we value in Bottom are the ones we find most amusing; and in seeing, and laughing at, the limits of each character's vision, we get a clearer sense of the importance of each. This applies to the work of art itself: at the moment when the play most clearly declares itself to be trivial, we have the strongest appeal to our sympathy for it, and, along with this, the clearest recognition that our own responsiveness is a vital factor in the total harmony:

Give me your hands, if we be friends,
And Robin shall restore amends. (V. i. 426–7)

It is an offer any normal audience is glad to take.

NOTES

1. This appears to have been a standard comic routine. In *Mucedorus* the clown Mouse declares, 'I can keepe my tongue from picking and stealing, and my handes from lying and slaundring, I warrant you, as wel as euer you had man in all your life' (I. iv. 128–31)—*The Shakespeare Apocrypha*, ed. C. F. Tucker Brooke (Oxford, 1967). But in *A Midsummer Night's Dream*—as in Costard's 'mistaking words' in *Love's Labour's Lost* (I. i. 292–4)—the stock device is used to serve the play's special comic vision.

2. There are similar effects in *The Comedy of Errors* and *Love's Labour's Lost*, in which the scenes of most intense confusion—such as Antipholus of Ephesus's vain attempt to break into his own house, and the Russian masque in which the men court the wrong ladies—contain some of the most patterned writing in their respective plays.

3. *The Court Masque* (New York, 1962), p. 332.

4. See G. K. Hunter, *William Shakespeare: The Late Comedies* (London, 1962), p. 14; and Bertrand Evans, *Shakespeare's Comedies* (London, 1967), p. 40.

5. See, for example, R. W. Dent, 'Imagination in *A Midsummer Night's Dream*', *Shakespeare Quarterly*, XV (spring 1964), pp. 123–6; and David P. Young, *Something of Great Constancy* (New Haven, 1966), p. 150.

6. See Young, *Something of Great Constancy*, p. 139.

7. *John Lyly: The Humanist as Courtier* (London, 1962), p. 328. See also Philip Edwards, *Shakespeare and the Confines of Art* (London, 1968), p. 56.

8. Egeus is omitted from this scene in the Quarto; the Folio gives Philostrate's part to him, but the Quarto arrangement seems more sensible and is normally adopted by editors. Directors often relent and invite him to the party; but the only time I have seen his presence there used creatively was in John Hirsch's production at Stratford, Ontario in 1968, in which Egeus, puffing on a cigar, grunted with crusty approval at Theseus's lecture on the imagination.

9. *Shakespeare* (New York, 1939), p. 77.

10. Paul A. Olson reminds us that, traditionally, Athens is a city of philosophers and woods are places of unreason. See 'A Midsummer Night's Dream and the meaning of court marriage', *ELH*, XXIV (March 1957), pp. 106–7.

11. In two other comedies of the period, *Wily Beguiled* and *Grim the Collier of Croydon*, Robin Goodfellow not only appears to mortals, but is on neighbourly terms with them. Shakespeare's Puck, for all his mischief, is far more detached than this, appearing to mortals—when he appears at all—in an assumed shape.

12. See Larry S. Champion, *The Evolution of Shakespeare's Comedy* (Cambridge, Mass., 1970), p. 48.

13. Something like this was suggested at the end of Peter Brook's production for the Royal Shakespeare Company in 1970: the performers took off the cloaks which had distinguished their characters, and faced the audience in a uniform white garb, suggesting that they were all fairies, or (which amounted to the same thing) all actors.

14. Stanley Wells has drawn the connection between Theseus's speech on his hounds and the total harmony of the play: see his introduction to the New Penguin edition of *A Midsummer Night's Dream* (Harmondsworth, 1967), p. 36.

15. See John Palmer, *Political and Comic Characters of Shakespeare* (London, 1964), p. 45.

16. On the childlike qualities of Bottom and the fairies, see, respectively, C. L. Barber, *Shakespeare's Festive Comedy* (Cleveland, 1967), p. 151; and E. K. Chambers, *Shakespeare: A Survey* (Harmondsworth, 1964), p. 69.

—◄◊◊►— —◄◊◊►— —◄◊◊►—

1980—Ruth Nevo. "Fancy's Images," from *Comic Transformations in Shakespeare*

Ruth Nevo is professor emeritus at the Hebrew University of Jerusalem. She is the author of *Tragic Form in Shakespeare* (1972); *Shakespeare's Other Language* (1988), and *The Dial of Virtue: A Study of Poems on Affairs of State in the Seventeenth Century* (1963).

"*A Midsummer Night's Dream* is best seen," says G. K. Hunter, "as a lyric divertissement . . . Shakespeare has lavished his art on the separate excellencies of the different parts, but has not sought to show them growing out of one another in a process analogous to that of symphonic 'development.'"[1] I would claim, on the contrary, symphonic development of a particularly subtle kind; both itself an impressive achievement in the unifying of complexities, and a distinct conquest in the zig-zag progress towards Shakespeare's comic paradigm. This is a highly intellectual, highly speculative comedy, like *Love's Labour's Lost* not the refashioning of a previously-treated story or play but an original invention. Through his basic comic structure of initial privation or perversity, comic device both deceptive and remedial, knots of errors and final recognitions,

Shakespeare has achieved not only a benign resolution to the dialectic of folly and wisdom, but a complex and witty exploration of the infirmities and frailties and deficiencies and possibilities of the imaginative faculty itself.

The problem presented to Theseus four days before his wedding is a knotty one. From the point of view of the father, what is required is that his daughter yield to his bidding and accept the suitor he has approved. But this would please no one but himself (and Demetrius). Theseus adopts the patriarchal view, naturally enough. But suppose (in another age and another clime) the young people had been left to choose their own mates? This procedure would not have solved the problem any more satisfactorily than the first, since the predicament we are asked to take in consists precisely of the asymmetry in the feelings of these four young people. The father's peremptoriness and the Duke's supportive edict lend urgency to their problem, but do not create it. The initial presentation of the situation invites us to perceive that while the tyrannical *senex* provides the outward and immediate obstacle to be surmounted, the root of the problem is elsewhere and within. The initiating recalcitrancy is the fact that two young men are competing with each other for one girl, when there is another available, and willing, to turn a triangle into a suitable set of couples. Two of both kinds makes up four, as Puck succinctly expresses it. And, it seems, some such arrangement had once been contemplated by these young Athenians themselves. Lysander (and later Helena) tells us that Demetrius made love to Helena before obtaining Egeus's consent to a match with Hermia. He deserted her then, it seems, for Hermia. But why? And when? "This man," says Egeus (of Demetrius) "hath my consent to marry her" (Hermia). "This man" (of Lysander), "hath bewitch'd the bosom of my child." But it is impossible to determine the sequence of tenses. Did the bewitching occur before the consent, or since, or simultaneously? Was it perhaps some sudden new interest in Hermia on the part of Demetrius that stimulated Lysander's desire for her? Or could it possibly be a case of the other foot? Did Lysander's interest in Hermia deflect Demetrius's previous affection for Helena and draw it with magnetic attraction towards the object of Lysander's love?

The square-dance view of these proceedings is less helpful than it seems, mainly because it takes no account of the girls. "The lovers are like dancers," says G. K. Hunter, "who change partners in the middle of a figure; the point at which partners are exchanged is determined by the dance, the pattern, and not by the psychological state of the dancers." But we are asked to attend quite closely to "the psychological state of the dancers,"[2] to the "fierce vexations" of their dream. The girls, in point of fact, do not change partners at all. They are subjected to drastic changes in their lovers' attitudes, to which they bewilderedly respond, but their own attachments do not waver. Moreover, the play's peripeteia is a comic reversal which leaves in effect everything exactly where it was: Puck's mistake with the magic juice—designed by Oberon to rectify unrequited love—in fact compounds error and disturbance by causing the two young men to continue to be both in love with the same love object, though this time in the shape of the other girl. It is thus not a question of mistaken identity, or of disguise, those time-honoured sources of identity confusion in New Comedy plots. Nor is it quite true to say, though it is often said, that the lovers simply don't know what they want, are fickle, capricious and unreasonable, creatures of the senses, of the eye merely. It is worth attending to Helena's observations at the play's outset:

> How happy some o'er other some can be!
> Through Athens I am thought as fair as she.
> But what of that? Demetrius thinks not so;
> He will not know what all but he do know;
> And as he errs, doting on Hermia's eyes,
> So I, admiring of his qualities.
> Things base and vile, holding no quantity,
> Love can transpose to form and dignity.
> Love looks not with the eyes but with the mind;
> And therefore is wing'd Cupid painted blind.
> Nor hath Love's mind of any judgment taste;
> Wings, and no eyes, figure unheedy haste;
> And therefore is Love said to be a child,
> Because in choice he is so oft beguil'd.
> As waggish boys in game themselves forswear,
> So the boy Love is perjur'd every where;
> For ere Demetrius look'd on Hermia's eyne,
> He hail'd down oaths that he was only mine;
> And when this hail some heat from Hermia felt,
> So he dissolv'd, and show'rs of oaths did melt. (1.1.226–45)

If only Demetrius would use his eyes she says in effect, he would see that I am as fair as Hermia. If Demetrius' infected will did not betray him he would recognize this open and palpable truth. But if Helena and Hermia are identical in this cardinal matter of their beauty, then there are no visual grounds for preference either way, and therefore there can be no question of errors in choice. Helena intelligently perceives this catch and she also perceives that what is sauce for the goose is sauce for the gander. "So I" (err), she says, "admiring in *his* qualities." Helena announces with bitterness this insight concerning the total and wayward non-dependence of erotic preference upon visual perception: "Love looks not with the eyes but with the mind; / And therefore is wing'd Cupid painted blind."[3] The comedy of the speech lies, of course, in Helena's assumption that "eyes" offer a more objective basis for judgment in love than mind. Eyes don't indeed provide any security for love, nor any true representation of reality, as the woods prove; but then neither does (rational) mind. Later the bewitched Lysander's assertion that "the will of man is by his reason sway'd; / And reason says you are the worthier maid" will be sufficient evidence of that. Helena's "mind" is Desdemona's: "I saw Othello's visage in his mind" (1.3.252) and Othello's: "I therefore beg it not . . . But to be free and bounteous to her mind" (1.3.265). Only there (tragically) and here (comically) the mind, that subjective source of value, of form and of dignity, is subject to all kinds of disabilities and derangements. Mind, in its aspect as the image-making and image-perceiving faculty, is an errant faculty indeed, unstable, uncertain, wavering, and seeking anchorage among a welter of rival images and self-images. It is to these, I believe, that the opening of the play draws our attention.

What we are invited to perceive is a falling out among rivals, and what we are invited to infer is that, at a deeper psychic level than they are aware of, they do indeed know what they want: each wants what his brother-at-arms or rival has. We have the case of Proteus and Valentine for confirmation of Shakespeare's interest in the phenomenon. Says Proteus, with admirable candour:

> Even as one heat another heat expels,
> Or as one nail by strength drives out another,
> So the remembrance of my former love
> Is by a newer object quite forgotten.
> [Is it] mine [eye], or Valentinus' praise,
> Her true perfection, or my false transgression,
> That makes me, reasonless, to reason thus? (2.4.192–98)

Consider the extremely provoking nature of Lysander's remark to Demetrius:

> You have her father's love, Demetrius,
> Let me have Hermia's; do you marry *him*
>   (my italics; 1.1.93–94)

Consider too the amplitude and intensity with which the sisterly affection between the two girls is treated:

> all the counsel that we two have shar'd,
> The sister's vows, the hours that we have spent
> All school-day's friendship, childhood innocence
> Both on one sampler, sitting on one cushion,
> Both warbling of one song, both in one key
>   So we grew together,
> Like to a double cherry.
>   (3.2.198–209 passim)

It furthermore transpires, as the play winds deeper into its conflicts in Act 2, that Oberon and Titania are also at odds over a love object they both want. The competitive marital duel of this couple features antecedent jealousies, but at the moment in time the play dramatizes they are quarrelling over possession of the changeling child. We find immediate parodic confirmation of the incidence of this malady as early as Act 1, scene 2, where the good Bottom, magnifier of folly, wants to play all the parts Peter Quince distributes to his cast—tyrants, lovers, ladies and lions—and is in his comic hubris convinced that he can do better at them all than any of his fellows.

Rivalry, then, fraternal or quasi-sibling, or marital is the comic disposition which the comic device exposes and exacerbates. It is also worth noting that the story of the night is set within a frame of *concordia discors* between erstwhile military rivals. Theseus wooed Hippolyta, we learn, with his sword, and won her love doing her injuries. This reconciliatory *concordia discors* is symbolized in the description of the hunt in Act 4, scene 1, just before the royal pair discovers the one time "rival enemies" now "new in amity." Theseus invites his Queen to the mountain top to

> mark the musical confusion
> Of hounds and echo in conjunction (4.1.110–11)

and she, remembering the hounds of Sparta, transforms his notion of dissonant confusion into the perception of a higher harmony:

> Never did I hear
> Such gallant chiding; for besides the groves,
> The skies, the fountains, every region near
> Seem all one mutual cry. I never heard
> So musical a discord, such sweet thunder. (4.1.114–18)

Hippolyta is consistently Theseus's informant in the play and indeed Egeus might have done well to appeal to her judgment rather than his at the beginning. Fortunately, however, for what the play enables us to discover about rivalries, he did not. Rivalry is benign when it leads to differentiation, since concord requires distinct entities between which to exist; and harmful when it leads to the blurring of boundaries, to "unnatural" imitative, or confusing conjunctions. Hippolyta is no longer playing the role of a man-woman Amazon by this time. The play explores the comedy of mimicry in four different and complementary perspectives—that of the quasi-fraternal lovers, the quasi-sibling "sisters," the Fairy Queen and her votaress, and the amateur comedians, the artisans of Athens, with the putative arch-mimic Bottom, who is never anything but himself, at their head.

Sibling rivalry takes the form of unconscious mimicry, an identification with the brother who must therefore be outdone in *his* sphere. I am as good as he. I am better than he. I must have what he has. "I am, my lord as well deriv'd as he, / As well possess'd," says Lysander, and what is more, beloved of beauteous Hermia. And Demetrius later: "I love thee more than he can do." From the girls' side of the picture we have Helena: "Through Athens I am thought as fair as she." Sensible siblings fight their way into maturity by seeking, finding, exploiting, inventing if necessary, precisely those differences and distinctions between them which establish their individual identities, on the basis of which they can freely choose their mates. This is no doubt why identical twins are such a problem, and so disturbing we are told, to the primitive mind encountering sameness where difference is not only in order, is not only expected, but is indispensable to individuation. But identical twins are an accident of nature which the comic artist may exploit for errors, if he wishes. What we have in *Midsummer Night's Dream* is imagined identical twinship. It is just such an idealized childhood twinship that Helena invokes in her remonstrance to Hermia over the latter's treacherous confederacy (as she believes) with the men, both now in pursuit of her to mock her:

> Is all the counsel that we two have shar'd,
> The sisters' vows, the hours that we have spent,
> When we have chid the hasty-footed time
> For parting us—O, is all forgot?
> All school-days' friendship, childhood innocence?
> We, Hermia, like two artificial gods,
> Have with our needles created both one flower,
> Both on one sampler, sitting on one cushion,
> Both warbling of one song, both in one key,
> As if our hands, our sides, voices, and minds
> Had been incorporate. So we grew together,
> Like to a double cherry, seeming parted,
> But yet an union in partition,
> Two lovely berries moulded on one stem;
> So, with two seeming bodies, but one heart,
>
> And will you rent our ancient love asunder,
> To join with men in scorning your poor friend? (3.2.198–212; 215–16)

A replica of such an "incorporation" at a later and more complex stage of a woman's life is Titania's relationship with her favourite votaress. Titania's account of her friendship with the boy's mother contains a wonderfully articulated image of imaginative mimicry:

> His mother was a vot'ress of my order.
> And in the spiced Indian air, by night,
> Full often hath she gossip'd by my side,

> And sat with me on Neptune's yellow sands,
> Marking th' embarked traders on the flood;
> When we have laugh'd to see the sails conceive
> And grow big-bellied with the wanton wind;
> Which she, with pretty and with swimming gait,
> Following (her womb then rich with my young squire)
> Would imitate, and sail upon the land
> To fetch me trifles, and return again,
> As from a voyage, rich with merchandise. (2.1.123–34)

Peter Quince's troupe literalize metaphors, too, but here the Indian maid's imitation of the big-bellied sails has a function other than *reductio ad absurdum*. The friends share the playful vision of the billowing sails as pregnant, which the expectant mother then playfully mimes, for the amusement and gratification of her companion. What is rendered here, we are invited to infer, is a vividly empathetic, imaginative sharing of the experience of pregnancy; and therefore when the mother dies it is no wonder that Titania's attachment to the child is more than the charitable rearing of an orphan. "And for her sake do I rear up her boy: / And for her sake I will not part with him" has the ring of self-justification—she is claiming nothing for this adoption but an act of conventional piety—but what we see is that she has so identified herself with her votaress that the child has become her own. Oberon, furiously observing his exclusion from this relationship, wants to possess himself of the love object she is so wrapped up in, and, failing, will punish her by caricaturing her defection. She is to dote upon the first living creature she sees:

> (Be it on lion, bear, or wolf, or bull,
> On meddling monkey, or on busy ape), (2.1.180–81)

The animus, however, of

> Set your heart at rest;
> The fairy land buys not the child of me. (2.1.121–22)

invites us to infer (especially if we remember "childing" autumn in her description of the disordered and distemperatured seasons) that Oberon might mend his marriage more effectively by getting Titania with child than by trying to get Titania without child. But rivalry and revenge (for previous peccadilloes real or imagined, with Theseus and Hippolyta)[4] is the order of the day at this stage—a midsummer madness—of the battle of the sexes, and at this stage of the comic development, which is the laying bare of the particular comic disposition dominant in the play.

The double plotting of *A Midsummer Night's Dream* is superb because it is so subtly related. Marital rivalry is more complex because double-decked: marriage partners must maintain their distinctive personalities, recognize each other's and enter into a new corporate personality, or transaction of personalities. But in this marriage on the rocks, with Titania playing the part of imagined twin to her votaress, and Oberon competing with her for possession of the Indian boy, rivalry has taken the place of reciprocity, competition of co-operation, and a riotous mimicry of clearly differentiated sexual roles.

We begin to perceive the nature of the comic infirmity in *A Midsummer Night's Dream*. It is that fluidity and instability of imagination which causes an individual to be either too identified or not identified enough; to resemble when to discriminate would be more politic and more appropriate; to represent reality in images generated by the desires of the mind.

Nature spirits that they are, these fairies, nature perfectly reflects their marital dissensions:

Therefore the winds . . .
As in revenge, have suck'd up from the sea
Contagious fogs; which, falling in the land,
Hath every pelting river made so proud
That they have overborne their continents . . .
        and the green corn
Hath rotted ere his youth attain'd a beard . . .
The nine men's morris is fill'd up with mud,
And the quaint mazes in the wanton green,
For lack of tread, are undistinguishable . . .
        hoary-headed frosts
Fall in the fresh lap of the crimson rose,
And on old Hiems' [thin] and icy crown
An odorous chaplet of sweet summer buds
Is, as in mockery, set; the spring, the summer,
The childing autumn, angry winter, change
Their wonted liveries; and the mazed world,
By their increase, now knows not which is which. (2.1.88–114 passim)[5]

"Undistinguishability" and the wilder follies of not knowing which is which receive their richest comic gloss from the good artisans of Athens in their entanglement with the problems of dramatic representation—when a wall is a wall for example, or a lion Snug the Joiner; but the message of this *paysage moralisé* is quite clear: confusion, disorder, disarray, mock mimicry reign in the woods, and with all distinction gone, all relations are perverse or fruitless or unnatural. Puck's mischievous translation of Bottom literally embodies asininity.

But it also reflects Titania's wrong-headed "incorporation" of the Indian boy. It is a bonus for Oberon's punitive plan (he did not envisage monsters), while the metamorphosis and the coupling of Titania with this comic monster inflates the folly of misconceived images *ad absurdum*, revealing (but not to the victims) truth in motley.

The strategy of comedy is to maximalize error before matters will mend; the maximalizing indeed generates the mending. To Helena there does come a glimmer of liberating wisdom in the woods when she says: "What wicked and dissembling glass of mine / Made me compare with Hermia's sphery eyne?" (2.2.98–99). This anticipates remedy but is as yet in too self-abasing a form.[6] The *processus turbarum*, with its cumulative and preposterous turbulence brings about for the lovers an intensification of folly to the point of giddying exhaustion; and discernment—the wisdom of discrimination, of getting images right—will emerge from the chaos, or decomposition of topsy-turvydom.

There should be no expounding of dreams, as Bottom knows, but the magic juice applied to sleeping eyes—the comic device—reveals in this play its fully Shakespearean iridescence. It is both delusive and applied in error and so causes the knot of errors and perturbations; but it is also the cause of ultimate reclamation and recognition. The magic at work operates therapeutically, cathartically, like dreams indeed.[7] It discovers, enlarging as in a distorting mirror, the shadowy wishes and fears of the mind, and by so doing enables the victims to enfranchize themselves from their obsessions. Shakespeare's moonlit wood, alive with trolls, grotesques and ambivalence is a potent symbol for the creative subconscious. And Puck, conveyor of dreams and potions, impish homogenizer, can be seen as a genius of comedy itself, mimicking (in the likeness of a filly foal, or a roasted crab), mocking, de-creating as he gives all nature's ingredients a great stir. As does Bottom, counterpoint Buffoon to Puck's Eiron (and unwitting Impostor as Titania's lover), giving all the theatre's ingredients a great stir:

> Nay; you must name his name, and half his face must be seen through
> the lion's neck, and he himself must speak through, saying thus, or to
> the same defect: . . . my life for yours. If you think I come hither as a
> lion, it were pity of my life. (3.1.36–43)

Puck's error—to him all Athenians are alike—is homeopathic. It reflects the comic disposition of the play, exposes it, and is exactly what is required to exacerbate and exorcise it.

Thus, so far from the warblings of one song in one key, the fierce vexations of misprision in Act 3 bring about a positively inflamed consciousness of difference: "'Little' again? Nothing but 'low' and 'little'?" Abuse and vilification are not lacking on all sides: "Thou cat, thou bur! Vile thing . . . tawny Tartar . . . loathed medicine" are a string of epithets from a sometime lover sufficient to draw from

Hermia (to Helena) "You juggler! You canker-blossom! You thief of love!" For which she gets as good as she gives with Helena's "Fie, fie, you counterfeit, you puppet, you!" "'Puppet'?" shouts Hermia at this point:

> Ay, that way goes the game.
> Now I perceive that she hath made compare
> Between our statures: she hath urg'd her height,
> And with her personage, her tall personage,
> Her height, forsooth, she hath prevail'd with him.
> And are you grown so high in his esteem,
> Because I am so dwarfish and so low?
> How low am I, thou painted maypole? Speak!
> How low am I? I am not yet so low
> But that my nails can reach unto thine eyes. (3.2.289–98)

"O, when she is angry," retorts a onetime part of an incorporate double cherry,

> she is keen and shrewd!
> She was a vixen when she went to school;
> And though she be but little, she is fierce. (3.2.323–35)

This knot of errors is the world upside down, and Helena's idyllic and lost childhood "incorporation" is well and truly mocked, as are Lysander's protestations of love to Hermia when transposed to

> Get you gone, you dwarf;
> You minimus, of hind'ring knot-grass made;
> You bead, you acorn. (3.2.328–30)

At the same time these frenetic hyperboles are the fulfilment and the acting out of everyone's deepest anxieties, misgivings and obsessions. Hermia foresaw all and foresuffered all when she dreamt of Lysander watching a serpent eating her heart away, and Helena's masochism—her seeking to "enrich her pain"—to cause the pain she dreads and loves—has progressed from her embracing of the role of fawning and beaten spaniel (1.1.246–51) to a paroxysm of self-abasement: "No, no; I am as ugly as a bear" (2.2.94). And this even before she becomes convinced of her victimization at the hand of all.

The *processus turbarum* of Act 3, by intensifying aberration and detonating hidden psychic dynamite discomposes, disorients and disintegrates. They all collapse in the end, exhausted by these traumas and by the hectic pursuit through the woods, and when they awake they are tranquil and clear-seeing. Now that vision is improved they are able to look back upon their "dream" experience as upon something distant and blurred. Hermia says: "Methinks I see these things with parted eye, / When every thing seems double," and Helena concurs: "So methinks; / And I have found Demetrius like a jewel, / Mine own, and not mine own" (4.1.189–92). These are pregnant sayings, these musings of the wondering and half-enlightened lovers. Perception and self-perception have passed through the alembic of dream and have been catalyzed. Demetrius, now seeing his love for Hermia as a childhood gaud and Helena as once again "the object and the pleasure of (his) eye" speaks for all four when he says:

> These things seem small and undistinguishable,
> Like far-off mountains turned into clouds. (4.1.187–88)

It is an interesting word "undistinguishable." And it occurs only once again in Shakespeare: in Titania's description of confusion and disorder in nature already quoted.

The formal remedy, as Puck himself calls it, of the play is purely ophthalmic. Oberon's corrective juice causes the lovers when they awake from their sleep to sort themselves out into suitable couples—Jacks and Jills, as Puck puts it with benign contempt—and Titania to be released from her unsuitable coupling with sweet bully Bottom. But the whole question of corrected vision, of the tutored imagination, goes beyond the merely technical exigencies of plot. It is the essential mediator of the benign, non-disjunctive dialectic which conjures rejoicing out of mockery, and wisdom out of folly.

In the lovers' case errors of "vision" are removed so that true relations can be re-discerned.[8] The lovers recuperate, literally, from their "trip." Lysander, it is now clear, fell into an infatuation with Helena when he was really in love with Hermia, and Demetrius fell into an infatuation with Hermia when he was really in love with Helena. But in the fairies' case, Titania, chastened by the onslaughts of the tender passion, relinquishes the child; and this yielding to Oberon's will produces in him the impulse of compassion required to melt hard-heartedness, soften anger and renounce retaliation. The passage is worth particular attention:

> Her dotage now I do begin to pity.
> For meeting her of late behind the wood,
> Seeking sweet favors for this hateful fool,
> I did upbraid her, and fall out with her.
> For she his hairy temples then had rounded
> With coronet of fresh and fragrant flowers;
> And that same dew which sometime on the buds
> Was wont to swell like round and orient pearls,

Stood now within the pretty flouriets' eyes,
Like tears that did their own disgrace bewail.
When I had at my pleasure taunted her,
And she in mild terms begg'd my patience,
I then did ask of her her changeling child;
Which straight she gave me, and her fairy sent
To bear him to my bower in fairy land.
And now I have the boy, I will undo
This hateful imperfection of her eyes. (4.1.47–63)

In this recognition scene Oberon sees her, perhaps for the first time, certainly for the first time since "Ill met by moonlight, proud Titania" in Act 2, with detachment and tenderness.

Eyes are organs of visions; eyes (especially when starry) are beautiful objects of vision. But eyes are also vessels for tears. Titania's amorous fantasy as she orders Bottom led away to her bower will be recalled:

The moon methinks looks with a wat'ry eye;
And when she weeps, weeps every little flower,
Lamenting some enforced chastity. (3.1.198–200)

Drugs, potions, condiments alter vision and visibility, but the true transfigurations are those which take place invisibly at the heart. Bottom himself makes this point, as modestly as ever. When told by Peter Quince that Pyramus had been a lover "that kills himself most gallant for love," "That," remarks the sage Bottom, "will ask some tears in the true performing of it. If I do it, let the audience look to their eyes."

A Midsummer Night's Dream juggles conspicuously with multiple levels of representation, with plays-within-plays and visions within dreams. What is performed, what is meant, what is seen are often, as Theseus said of Peter Quince's prologue "like a tangled chain; nothing impair'd, but all disorder'd" (5.1.125–26). The Athenian lovers, Lysander and Hermia, fall asleep and dream (in Act 2), fall asleep and wake (in Act 4), and what happens to them is ambiguously dream/reality, just as Oberon king of shadows, is ambiguously real/not real, visible to the audience but not to the lovers; and the "angel" that wakes Titania "from her flow'ry bed" (3.1.129) is visible to her but not to the audience, who perceive only Nick Bottom assified. Puck stage-manages these "transfigurations" for Oberon's delectation just as Peter Quince does for Theseus' and Shakespeare for ours.[9] And the audience is more than once pointedly invited to conflate these frames. When Theseus says "The best in this kind are but shadows," his remark applies with equal validity to the artisans of Athens and the Lord Chamberlain's Men. By the same token Puck's "shadows" in the epilogue ("if we shadows have offended") refers, intentionally, both to the fairies and the actors—the visible and the invisible.

Act 5 dazzlingly catches up and re-focuses the issues of the play, recapitulating its schooling of the imagination. When Theseus tempers Hippolyta's impatience with the mechanicals' efforts: "This is the silliest stuff that ever I heard" (5.1.210) with "The best in this kind are but shadows; and the worst are no worse, if imagination amend them" (5.1.211–12) he is retracting his previous repudiation of the imagination as the faculty which "sees more devils than vast hell can hold," or "Helen's beauty in a brow of Egypt," or some bringer of what is a merely "apprehended" joy, or a bear in a bush on a dark night. The rationalistic and empirically minded duke has been more than cautious about the seething tricks of that fertile and moonstruck faculty; and it is in reply to his dismissal of the lovers' story as so much irrational and illusory dream stuff that Hippolyta enters her caveat concerning the story of the night:

> But all the story of the night told over,
> And all their minds transfigur'd so together,
> More witnesseth than fancy's images,
> And grows to something of great constancy . . . (5.1.23–26)

The ducal pair, as we have seen, are a model of *concordia discors* ("How shall we find the concord of this discord?" Theseus asks of the "very tragical mirth" about to be presented by the artisans) and so it is fitting that they should conduct the dialectic of real and imaginary, meant and performed, visible and invisible towards a resolution for theatre-goers and lovers alike. When Hippolyta reflects upon the story of the night, she is inviting not only Theseus but the theatre audience as well to further reflection. She is inviting a retrospective reappraisal of all that has been enacted in the moonlit woods. Hippolyta's organic metaphor is interesting; cognition, it says, or recognition, grows in the mind in the process of recounting, re-telling. What the play celebrates as remedial, beneficient, recuperative it will have discovered by working its way through the fantastic follies the initial deficiencies or infirmities generated. These follies, reduced (or expanded) to absurdity, will prove to have been homeopathically therapeutic, if imagination amend them by making them intelligible. "It must be your imagination then, not theirs," says wise Hippolyta, knowing that to stout bully Bottom nothing is invisible, not even a voice from behind a wall. So far as that parodic literalist of the imagination is concerned, moonlight cannot be better represented than by moonlight, shining in at the casement in all its factual actuality. And when a person is a wall, he must be well and truly plastered and roughcast. No fancy Brechtian placards will do for him, any more than he can conceive that anyone (of any size) called Mustardseed should not be instantly applied to roast beef.

Pyramus and Thisbe presents a tragedy of lovers' misprisions, and neutralizes disaster with its ludicrous comicality. It is irresistibly amusing in itself and needs no amending, by imagination or any other means; and it is also the vehicle of Shakespeare's most ironic private joke to *his* audience over the heads, so to speak, of Peter Quince and his. The latter possess the capacity to distinguish between walls and witty partitions, between run-on and end-stopped pentameters, between a lion and a goose and between a man and a moon. But they haven't always been so good at distinguishing. Their own follies have been, in their own way, no less de-constructive; but also no less recreative.

"Your play needs no excuse," says Theseus, amused, ironic and kind. "Marry, if he that writ it had play'd Pyramus, and hang'd himself in Thisby's garter, it would have been a fine tragedy; and so it is truly, and very notably discharg'd" (5.1.357–61). A great deal, and of great constancy, has been "discharged" in this play. And not only Hippolyta, it has been suggested, has had an inkling that the fantasy of folly may grow into the wisdom of the imagination.

This resonant insight marks, at the level of overt theme, the dramatic growth in *A Midsummer Night's Dream* of the dramatist's capacity to conceive and render the interlacing of sexual and individual roles. Further growth will issue, in due course, in the achievement of a comic form completely adequate for the dialectical battle of sex and self, a form which will resolve the ambivalencies of that warfare's tamings and matings. Here the idea is still inchoate, for it lacks as yet the crystallizing force of the heroine protagonist in all the fullness of her virtuosity and her autonomy. Shakespeare's next comedy appears to present us, in Portia, with exactly such a missing link.

NOTES

1. G. K. Hunter, *The Later Comedies* (London: Longman Green, 1962), p. 4.

2. ibid., p. 5. A similar view is taken by Alexander Leggatt, *Shakespeare's Comedy of Love* (London: Methuen, 1974), p. 96.

3. Helena's exegesis of the blind Cupid commonplace does not merely repeat the platitudes of a received iconology. The medieval Cupid was blind because love was taken by medieval Christianity to be irrational, not seeing with the eyes of reason and judgment. The Renaissance Cupid was blind because love was taken by Florentine neo-Platonism to be intellectual, not seeing with a merely sensible organ. See Edgar Wind, *Pagan Mysteries of the Renaissance* (New Haven: Yale University Press, 1958), and Erwin Panovsky, *Studies in Iconology* (New York: Oxford University Press, 1939). ch. IV, pp. 95–9. We can make no sense of the logic of Helena's 'Nor hath' unless we see that it precludes a neo-Platonic 'mind,' for it cannot be said of intellect that it 'hath not of any judgment taste.' Nor, however, can the denigratory medieval view of love as sensual appetite, a lust of the eyes, be made to sort with Helena's conception of love's capacity to transpose to form and dignity. Cf. also Sonnet CXIII: 'Since I left you, mine eye is in my mind . . .'

4. See David P. Young, *Something of Great Constancy* (New Haven: Yale University Press, 1966), p. 139.

5. Thomas McFarland, *Shakespeare's Pastoral Comedy* (Chapel Hill: University of North Carolina Press, 1972), is misled by his determination to find an idealized pastoralism in Shakespeare's comedies to read this speech as an affirmation of 'the overwhelmingly ideal setting of *Midsummer Night's Dream*. Nothing could be less evil than the "progeny of evil" catalogued; it is in fact an account of paradise itself' (p. 84).

6. 'The erotic instincts' as Freud said drily, in *Contributions to the Psychology of Love* (1910) 'are hard to mould; training of them achieves now too much, now too little.' The statement could serve as an epigraph to Shakespeare's collected comic works.

7. A similar view of dream in Shakespeare has been developed by Marjorie B. Garber, *Dreams in Shakespeare: From Metaphor to Metamorphosis* (New Haven: Yale University Press, 1974).

8. It is surely not true, as Larry Champion claims, in *The Evolution of Shakespeare's Comedy* (Cambridge, Massachusetts: Harvard University Press, 1970) that 'their victimisation by whimsical passion is no less at the conclusion of the play than at the beginning' (p. 99).

9 See Anne Righter (Barton), *Shakespeare and the Idea of the Play* (Harmondsworth: Penguin, 1967), Philip Edwards, *Shakespeare and the Confines of Art* (London: Methuen, 1968), p. 46, and Leo Salingar, *Shakespeare and the Traditions of Comedy* (Cambridge: Cambridge University Press, 1974), pp. 277–82 passim, for suggestive comments on self-reflexive plays-within-plays.

⥈⥇⥆ ⥈⥇⥆ ⥈⥇⥆

1986—Northrop Frye. "The Bottomless Dream," from *Northrop Frye on Shakespeare*

The Canadian scholar Northrop Frye (1912–1991) was one of the most influential literary critics of the twentieth century. Harold Bloom has called him "the largest and most crucial literary critic in the English language" since Walter Pater and Oscar Wilde. One of Frye's most famous books is *The Anatomy of Criticism*.

Elizabethan literature began as a provincial development of a Continent-centred literature, and it's full of imitations and translations from French, Italian and Latin. But the dramatists practically had to rediscover drama, as soon as, early in Elizabeth's reign, theatres with regular performances of plays on a thrust stage began to evolve out of temporary constructions in dining halls and courtyards. There was some influence from Italian theatre, and some of the devices in *Twelfth Night* reminded one spectator, who kept a diary, of Italian sources. There was also the influence of the half-improvised *commedia dell'arte*, which I'll speak of later. Behind these Italian influences were the Classical plays from which the Italian ones partly derived.

For tragedy there were not many precedents, apart from the Latin plays of Seneca, whose tragedies may not have been actually intended for the stage. Seneca is a powerful influence behind Shakespeare's earliest tragedy, *Titus Andronicus*, and there are many traces of him elsewhere. In comedy, though, there were about two dozen Latin plays available, six by Terence, the rest by Plautus. These had been adapted from the Greek writers of what we call New Comedy, to distinguish it from the Old Comedy of Aristophanes, which was full of personal attacks and allusions to actual people and events. The best known of these Greek New Comedy writers was Menander, whose work, except for one complete play recently discovered, has come down to us only in fragments. Menander was a sententious, aphoristic writer, and one of his aphorisms ("evil communications corrupt good manners") was quoted by Paul in the New Testament. Terence carried on this sententious style, and we find some famous proverbs in him, such as "I am a man, and nothing human is alien to me." When we hear a line like "The course of true love never did run smooth" in *A Midsummer Night's Dream*, familiar to many people who don't know the play, we can see that the same tradition is still going strong. And later on, when we hear Bottom mangling references to Paul's epistles, we may feel that we're going around in a circle.

New Comedy, in Plautus, and Terence, usually sets up a situation that's the opposite of the one that the audience would recognize as the "right" one. Let's say a young man loves a young woman, and vice versa, but their love is blocked by parents who want suitors or brides with more money. That's the first part. The second part consists of the complications that follow, and in a third and last part the opening situation is turned inside out, usually through some gimmick in the plot, such as the discovery that the heroine was kidnapped in infancy by pirates, or that she was exposed on a hillside and rescued by a shepherd, but that her social origin is quite respectable enough for her to marry the hero. The typical characters in such a story are the young man (*adulescens*), a heavy father (sometimes called *senex iratus*, because he often goes into terrible rages when he's thwarted), and a "tricky slave" (*dolosus servus*), who helps out the young man with some clever scheme. If you look at the plays of Molière, you'll see these characters over and over again, and the tricky servant is still there in the Figaro operas of Rossini and Mozart—and in Wodehouse's Jeeves. Often the roles of young man and young woman are doubled: in a play of Plautus, adapted by Shakespeare in *The Comedy of Errors*, the young men are twin brothers, and Shakespeare adds a pair of twin servants.

In Shakespeare's comedies we often get two heroines as well: we have Rosalind and Celia in *As You Like It*, Hero and Beatrice in *Much Ado about Nothing*, Olivia and Viola in *Twelfth Night*, Julia and Silvia in *The Two Gentlemen of Verona*, Helena and Hermia in this play. It's a natural inference that there were two boys in Shakespeare's company who were particularly good at female roles. If so, one seems to have been noticeably taller than the other. In *As You Like It* we're not sure which was the taller one—the indications are contradictory—but here they're an almost comic-strip contrast, Helena being long and drizzly and Hermia short and spitty.

Shakespeare's comedies are far more complex than the Roman ones, but the standard New Comedy structure usually forms part of their actions. To use Puck's line, the Jacks generally get their Jills in the end (or the Jills get their Jacks, which in fact happens more often). But he makes certain modifications in the standard plot, and makes them fairly consistently. He doesn't seem to like plots that turn on tricky-servant schemes. He does have smart or cheeky servants often enough, like Lancelot Gobbo in *The Merchant of Venice*, and they make the complacent soliloquies that are common in the role, but they seldom affect the action. Puck and Ariel come nearest, and we notice that neither is a human being and neither acts on his own. Then again, Shakespeare generally plays down the outwitting and baffling of age by youth: the kind of action suggested by the title of a play of Middleton's, *A Trick to Catch the Old-One*, is rare in Shakespeare. The most prominent example is the ganging up on Shylock in *The Merchant of Venice* that lets his daughter Jessica marry Lorenzo. Even that leaves a rather sour taste in our mouths, and the sour taste is part of the play, not just part of our different feelings about stage Jews. In the late romances, especially *Pericles* and *The Winter's Tale*, the main comic resolution concerns older people, who are united or reconciled after a long separation. Even in this play, while we start out with a standard New Comedy situation in which lovers are forbidden to marry but succeed in doing so all the same, it's the older people, Theseus and Hippolyta, who are at the centre of the action, and we could add to this the reconciling of Oberon and Titania.

In the Roman plays there's a general uniformity of social rank: the characters are usually ordinary middle-class people with their servants. The settings are also uniform and consistent: they're not "realistic," but the action is normally urban, taking place on the street in front of the houses of the main characters, and there certainly isn't much of mystery, romance, fairies, magic or mythology (except for farcical treatments of it like Plautus's *Amphitryon*). I've spoken [elsewhere] of the highbrows in Shakespeare's time who thought that Classical precedents were models to be imitated, and that you weren't writing according to the proper rules if you introduced kings or princes or dukes into comedies, as Shakespeare is constantly doing, or if you introduced the incredible or mysterious, such as fairies or magic. Some of Shakespeare's younger contemporaries, notably Ben Jonson, keep more closely to Classical precedent, and Jonson tells us that he regularly follows nature, and that some other people like Shakespeare don't. Shakespeare never fails to introduce something mysterious or hard to believe into his comedies, and in doing so he's following the precedents set, not by the Classical writers, but by his immediate predecessors.

These predecessors included in particular three writers of comedy, Peele, Greene and Lyly. Peele's *Old Wives' Tale* is full of themes from folk tales; in

Greene's *Friar Bacon and Friar Bungay* the central character is a magician, and in his *James IV*, while there's not much about the Scottish king of that name, there's a chorus character called Oberon, the king of the fairies; in Lyly's *Endimion* the main story retells the Classical myth of Endymion, the youth beloved by the goddess of the moon. These are examples of the type of romance-comedy that Shakespeare followed. Shakespeare keeps the three-part structure of the Roman plays, but immensely expands the second part, and makes it a prolonged episode of confused identity. Sometimes the heroine disguises herself as a boy; sometimes the action moves into a charmed area, often a magic wood like the one in this play, where the ordinary laws of nature don't quite apply.

If we ask why this type of early Elizabethan comedy should have been the type Shakespeare used, there are many answers, but one relates to the audience. *A Midsummer Night's Dream* has the general appearance of a play designed for a special festive occasion, when the Queen herself might well be present. In such a play one would expect an occasional flattering allusion to her, and it looks as though we have one when Oberon refers to an "imperial votaress" in a speech to Puck. The Queen was also normally very tolerant about the often bungling attempts to entertain her when she made her progressions through the country, and so the emphasis placed on Theseus's courtesy to the Quince company may also refer to her, even if he is male. But if there were an allusion to her, it would have to be nothing more than that.

Even today novelists have to put statements into their books that no real people are being alluded to, and in Shakespeare's day anything that even looked like such an allusion, beyond the conventional compliments, could be dangerous. Three of Shakespeare's contemporaries did time in jail for putting into a play a couple of sentences that sounded like satire on the Scotsmen coming to England in the train of James I, and worse things, like cutting off ears and noses, could be threatened. I make this point because every so often some director or critic gets the notion that this play is really all about Queen Elizabeth, or that certain characters, such as Titania, refer to her. The consequences to Shakespeare's dramatic career if the Queen had believed that she was being publicly represented as having a love affair with a jackass are something we fortunately don't have to think about.

An upper-class audience is inclined to favour romance and fantasy in its entertainment, because the idealizing element in such romance confirms its own image of itself. And whatever an upper-class audience likes is probably going to be what a middle-class audience will like too. If this play was adapted to, or commissioned for, a special court performance, it would be the kind of thing Theseus is looking for at the very beginning of the play, when he tells his master of revels, Philostrate, to draw up a list of possible entertainments. One gets an impression of sparseness about what Philostrate has collected, even if Theseus doesn't read the whole list; but however that may be, the Peter Quince play has something of the relation to the nuptials of Theseus that Shakespeare's play would have had to whatever occasion it was used for. We notice that the reason for some of the absurdities in the Quince play come from the actors' belief that court ladies are unimaginably fragile and delicate: they will swoon at the sight of Snug the joiner as a lion unless it is carefully explained that he isn't really a lion. The court ladies belong to the Quince players' fairyland: Shakespeare knew far more about court ladies than they did, but he also realized that court ladies and gentlemen had some affinity, as an audience, with fairyland.

This play retains the three parts of a normal comedy that I mentioned earlier: a first part in which an absurd, unpleasant or irrational situation is set up; a second part of confused identity and personal complications; a third part in which the plot gives a shake and twist and everything comes right in the end. In the opening of this play we meet an irrational law, of a type we often do meet at the beginning of a Shakespeare comedy: the law of Athens that decrees death or perpetual imprisonment in a convent for any young woman who marries without her father's consent. Here the young woman is Hermia, who loves Lysander, and the law is invoked by her father, Egeus, who prefers Demetrius. Egeus is a senile old fool who clearly doesn't love his daughter, and is quite reconciled to seeing her executed or imprisoned. What he loves is his own possession of his daughter, which carries the right to bestow her on a man of his choice as a proxy for himself. He makes his priorities clear in a speech later in the play:

> They would have stol'n away, they would, Demetrius,
> Thereby to have defeated you and me:
> You of your wife, and me of my consent,
> Of my consent that she should be your wife. (4.1.155–58)

Nevertheless Theseus admits that the law is what Egeus says it is, and also emphatically says that the law must be enforced, and that he himself has no power to abrogate it. We meet this situation elsewhere in Shakespeare: at the beginning of *The Comedy of Errors*, with its law that in Ephesus all visitors from Syracuse are to be beheaded, and in *The Merchant of Venice*, with the law that upholds Shylock's bond. In all three cases the person in authority declares that he has no power to alter the law, and in all three cases he eventually does. As it turns out that Theseus is a fairly decent sort, we may like to rationalize this scene by assuming that he is probably going to talk privately with Egeus and Demetrius (as in fact he says he is) and work out a more humane solution. But he gives Hermia no loophole: he merely repeats the threats to her life and freedom. Then he adjourns the session:

> Come, my Hippolyta—what cheer, my love? (1.1.122)

which seems a clear indication that Hippolyta, portrayed throughout the play as a person of great common sense, doesn't like the set-up at all.

We realize that sooner or later Lysander and Hermia will get out from under this law and be united in spite of Egeus. Demetrius and Helena, who are the doubling figures, are in an unresolved situation: Helena loves Demetrius, but Demetrius has only, in the Victorian phrase, trifled with her affections. In the second part we're in the fairy wood at night, where identities become, as we think, hopelessly confused. At dawn Theseus and Hippolyta, accompanied by Egeus, enter the wood to hunt. By that time the Demetrius–Helena situation has cleared up, and because of that Theseus feels able to overrule Egeus and allow the two marriages to go ahead. At the beginning Lysander remarks to Hermia that the authority of Athenian law doesn't extend as far as the wood, but apparently it does; Theseus is there, in full charge, and it is in the wood that he makes the decision that heads the play toward its happy ending. At the same time the solidifying of the Demetrius–Helena relationship was the work of Oberon. We can hardly avoid the feeling not only that Theseus is overruling Egeus's will, but that his own will has been overruled too, by fairies of whom he knows nothing and in whose existence he doesn't believe.

If we look at the grouping of characters in each of the three parts, this feeling becomes still stronger. In the opening scene we have Theseus, Egeus and an unwilling Hippolyta in the centre, symbolizing parental authority and the inflexibility of law, with three of the four young people standing before them. Before long we meet the fourth, Helena. In the second part the characters are grouped in different places within the wood, for the most part separated from one another. In one part of the wood are the lovers; in another are the processions of the quarrelling king and queen of the fairies; in still another Peter Quince and his company are rehearsing their play. Finally the remaining group, Theseus, Hippolyta and Egeus, appear with the sunrise. In the first part no one doubts that Theseus is the supreme ruler over the court of Athens; in the second part no one doubts that Oberon is king of the fairies and directs what goes on in the magic wood.

In the third and final part the characters, no longer separated from one another, are very symmetrically arranged. Peter Quince and his company are in the most unlikely spot, in the middle, and the centre of attention; around them sit Theseus and Hippolyta and the four now reconciled lovers. The play ends; Theseus calls for a retreat to bed, and then the fairies come in for the final blessing of the house, forming a circumference around all the others. They are there for the sake of Theseus and Hippolyta, but their presence suggests that Theseus is not as supremely the ruler of his own world as he seemed to be at first.

A Midsummer Night's Dream seems to be one of the relatively few plays that Shakespeare made up himself, without much help from sources. Two sources he did use were tragic stories that are turned into farce here. One was the story of Pyramus and Thisbe from Ovid, which the Quince company is attempting to tell, and which is used for more than just the Quince play. The other was Chaucer's *Knight's Tale*, from which Shakespeare evidently took the names of Theseus, Hippolyta and Philostrate, and which is a gorgeous but very sombre story of the fatal rivalry of two men over a woman. So far as this theme appears in the play, it is in the floundering of Lysander and Demetrius after first Hermia and then Helena, bemused with darkness and Puck's love drugs. I spoke [elsewhere] of the relation of the original Pyramus and Thisbe story to *Romeo and Juliet*, and the theme of the *Knight's Tale* appears vestigially in that play too, in the fatal duel of Romeo and Paris. I spoke also of the role of the oxymoron as a figure of speech in *Romeo and Juliet*, the self-contradictory figure that's appropriate to a tragedy of love and death. That too appears as farce in this play, when Theseus reads the announcement of the Quince play:

> Merry and tragical? Tedious and brief?
> That is hot ice, and wondrous strange snow!
> How shall we find the concord of this discord? (5.1.58–60)

Why is this play called *A Midsummer Night's Dream*? Apparently the main action in the fairy wood takes place on the eve of May Day; at any rate, when Theseus and Hippolyta enter with the rising sun, they discover the four lovers, and Theseus says:

> No doubt they rose up early to observe
> The rite of May. (4.1.131–32)

We call the time of the summer solstice, in the third week of June, "midsummer," although in our calendars it's the beginning of summer. That's because originally there were only three seasons, summer, autumn and winter: summer then included spring and began in March. A thirteenth-century song begins "sumer is i-cumen in," generally modernized, to keep the metre, as "summer is a-coming in," but it doesn't mean that: it means "spring is here." The Christian calendar finally established the celebration of the birth of Christ at the winter solstice, and made a summer solstice date (June 24) the feast day of John the Baptist. This arrangement, according to the Fathers, symbolized John's remark in the Gospels on beholding Christ: "He must increase, but I must decrease." Christmas Eve was a beneficent time, when evil spirits had no power; St. John's Eve was perhaps more ambiguous, and there was a common phrase, "midsummer madness," used by Olivia in *Twelfth Night*, a play named after the opposite end of the year. Still, it was a time when spirits of nature, whether benevolent or malignant, might be supposed to be abroad.

There were also two other haunted "eves," of the first of November and of the first of May. These take us back to a still earlier time, when animals were brought in from the pasture at the beginning of winter, with a slaughter of those that couldn't be kept to feed, and when they were let out again at the beginning of spring. The first of these survives in our Hallowe'en, but May Day eve is no longer thought of much as a spooky time, although in Germany, where it was called "Walpurgis night," the tradition that witches held an assembly on a mountain at that time lasted much longer, and comes into Goethe's *Faust*. In *Faust* the scene with the witches is followed by something called "The Golden Wedding of Oberon and Titania," which has nothing to do with Shakespeare's play, but perhaps indicates a connection in Goethe's mind between it and the first of May.

In Shakespeare's time, as Theseus's remark indicates, the main emphasis on the first of May fell on a sunrise service greeting the day with songs. All the emphasis was on hope and cheerfulness. Shakespeare evidently doesn't want to force a specific date on us: it may be May Day eve, but all we can be sure of is that it's later than St. Valentine's Day in mid-February, the day when traditionally the birds start copulating, and we could have guessed that anyway. The general idea is that we have gone through the kind of night when spirits are powerful but not necessarily malevolent. Evil spirits, as we learn from the opening scene of *Hamlet*, are forced to disappear at dawn, and the fact that this is also true of the Ghost of Hamlet's father sows a terrible doubt in Hamlet's mind. Here we have Puck, or more accurately Robin Goodfellow *the* puck. Pucks were a category of spirits who were often sinister, and the Puck of this play is clearly mischievous. But we are expressly told by Oberon that the fairies of whom he's the king are "spirits of another sort," not evil and not restricted to darkness.

So the title of the play simply emphasizes the difference between the two worlds of the action, the waking world of Theseus's court and the fairy world of Oberon. Let's go back to the three parts of the comic action: the opening situation hostile to true love, the middle part of dissolving identities and the final resolution. The first part contains a threat of possible death to Hermia. Similar threats are found in other Shakespeare comedies: in *The Comedy of Errors* a death sentence hangs over a central character until nearly the end of the play. This comic structure fits inside a pattern of death, disappearance and return that's far wider in scope than theatrical comedy. We find it even in the central story of Christianity, with its Friday of death, Saturday of disappearance and Sunday of return. Scholars who have studied this pattern in religion, mythology and legend think it derives from observing the moon waning, then disappearing, then reappearing as a new moon.

At the opening Theseus and Hippolyta have agreed to hold their wedding at the next new moon, now four days off. They speak of four days, although the rhetorical structure runs in threes: Hippolyta is wooed, won and wed

"With pomp, with triumph and with revelling." (This reading depends also on a reasonable, if not certain, emendation: "new" for "now" in the tenth line.) Theseus compares his impatience to the comedy situation of a young man waiting for someone older to die and leave him money. The Quince company discover from an almanac that there will be moonshine on the night that they will be performing, but apparently there is not enough, and so they introduce a character called Moonshine. His appearance touches off a very curious reprise of the opening dialogue. Hippolyta says "I am aweary of this moon: would he would change!" and Theseus answers that he seems to be on the wane, "but yet, in courtesy . . . we must stay the time." It's as though this ghastly play contains in miniature, and caricature, the themes of separation, postponement, and confusions of reality and fantasy that have organized the play surrounding it.

According to the indications in the text, the night in the wood should be a moonless night, but in fact there are so many references to the moon that it seems to be still there, even though obscured by clouds. It seems that this wood is a fairyland with its own laws of time and space, a world where Oberon has just blown in from India and where Puck can put a girdle round the earth in forty minutes. So it's not hard to accept such a world as an antipodal one, like the world of dreams itself, which, although we make it fit into our waking-time schedules, still keeps to its own quite different rhythms. A curious image of Hermia's involving the moon has echoes of this; she's protesting that she will never believe Lysander unfaithful:

> I'll believe as soon
> This whole earth may be bored, and that the moon
> May through the centre creep, and so displease
> Her brother's noontide with th' Antipodes. (3.2.52–55)

A modern reader might think of the opening of "The Walrus and the Carpenter." The moon, in any case, seems to have a good deal to do with both worlds. In the opening scene Lysander speaks of Demetrius as "this spotted and inconstant man," using two common epithets for the moon, and in the last act Theseus speaks of "the lunatic, the lover and the poet," where "lunatic" has its full Elizabethan force of "moonstruck."

The inhabitants of the wood-world are the creatures of legend and folk tale and mythology and abandoned belief. Theseus regards them as projections of the human imagination, and as having a purely subjective existence. The trouble is that we don't know the extent of our own minds, or what's in that mental world that we half create and half perceive, in Wordsworth's phrase. The tiny fairies that wait on Bottom—Mustardseed and Peaseblossom and the rest—come from Celtic fairy lore, as does the Queen Mab of Mercutio's speech, who also had tiny fairies in her train. Robin Goodfellow is more Anglo-Saxon and Teutonic. His propitiatory name, "Goodfellow," indicates that he could be dangerous, and his fairy friend says that one of his amusements is to "Mislead night-wanderers, laughing at their harm." A famous book a little later than Shakespeare, Robert Burton's *Anatomy of Melancholy*, mentions fire spirits who mislead travellers with illusions, and says "We commonly call them pucks." The fairy world clearly would not do as a democracy: there has to be a king in charge like Oberon, who will see that Puck's rather primitive sense of humour doesn't get too far out of line.

The gods and other beings of Classical mythology belong in the same half-subjective, half-autonomous world. I've spoken of the popularity of Ovid's *Metamorphoses* for poets: this, in Ovid's opening words, is a collection of stories of "bodies changed to new forms." Another famous Classical metamorphosis is the story of Apuleius about a man turned into an ass by enchantment, and of course this theme enters the present play when Bottom is, as Quince says, "translated." In Classical mythology one central figure was the goddess that Robert Graves, whose book I'll mention [elsewhere], calls the "white goddess" or the "triple will." This goddess had three forms: one in heaven, where she was the goddess of the moon and was called Phoebe or Cynthia or Luna; one on earth, where she was Diana, the virgin huntress of the forest, called Titania once in Ovid; and one below the earth, where she was the witch-goddess Hecate. Puck speaks of "Hecate's triple team" at the end of the play. References to Diana and Cynthia by the poets of the time usually involved some allusion to the virgin queen Elizabeth (they always ignored Hecate in such contexts). As I said, the Queen seems to be alluded to here, but in a way that kicks her upstairs, so to speak: she's on a level far above all the "lunatic" goings-on below.

Titania in this play is not Diana: Diana and her moon are in Theseus's world, and stand for the sterility that awaits Hermia if she disobeys her father, when she will have to become Diana's nun, "Chanting faint hymns to the cold fruitless moon." The wood of this play is erotic, not virginal: Puck is contemptuous of Lysander's lying so far away from Hermia, not realizing that this was just Hermia being maidenly. According to Oberon, Cupid was an inhabitant of this wood, and had shot his erotic arrow at the "imperial votaress," but it glanced off her and fell on a white flower, turning it red. The parabola taken by this arrow outlines the play's world, so to speak: the action takes place under this red and white arch. One common type of Classical myth deals with a "dying god," as he's called now, a male figure who is killed when still a youth, and whose blood stains a white flower and turns it red or purple. Shakespeare had written the story of one of these gods in his narrative poem *Venus and Adonis*, where he makes a good deal of the stained flower:

No flower was nigh, no grass, herb, leaf, or weed,
But stole his blood and seem'd with him to bleed.

The story of Pyramus and Thisbe is another such story: Pyramus's blood stains the mulberry and turns it red. In Ovid's account, when Pyramus stabs himself the blood spurts out in an arc on the flower. This may be where Shakespeare got the image that he puts to such very different use.

Early in the play we come upon Oberon and Titania quarrelling over the custody of a human boy, and we are told that because of their quarrel the weather has been unusually foul. The implication is that the fairies are spirits of the elements, and that nature and human life are related in many ways that are hidden from ordinary consciousness. But it seems clear that Titania does not have the authority that she thinks she has: Oberon puts her under the spell of having to fall in love with Bottom with his ass's head, and rescues the boy for his own male entourage. There are other signs that Titania is a possessive and entangling spirit—she says to Bottom:

> Out of this wood do not desire to go
> Thou shalt remain here, whether thou wilt or no. (3.1.143–44)

The relationship of Oberon and Titania forms a counterpoint with that of Theseus and Hippolyta in the other world. It appears that Titania has been a kind of guardian spirit to Hippolyta and Oberon to Theseus. Theseus gives every sign of settling down into a solidly married man, now that he has subdued the most formidable woman in the world, the Queen of the Amazons. But his record before that was a very bad one, with rapes and desertions in it: even as late as T. S. Eliot we read about his "perjured sails." Oberon blames his waywardness on Titania's influence, and Titania's denial does not sound very convincing. Oberon's ascendancy over Titania, and Theseus's over Hippolyta, seem to symbolize some aspect of the emerging comic resolution.

Each world has a kind of music, or perhaps rather "harmony," that is characteristic of it. That of the fairy wood is represented by the song of the mermaid described by Oberon to Puck. This is a music that commands the elements of the "sublunary" world below the moon; it quiets the sea, but there is a hint of a lurking danger in it, a siren's magic call that draws some of the stars out of their proper spheres in heaven, as witches according to tradition can call down the moon. There is danger everywhere in that world for mortals who stay there too long and listen to too much of its music. When the sun rises and Theseus and Hippolyta enter the wood, they talk about the noise of hounds in this and other huntings. Hippolyta says:

> ˙ never did I hear
> Such gallant chiding; for, besides the groves,
> The Skies, the fountains, every region near

Seem'd all one mutual cry; I never heard
So musical a discord, such sweet thunder. (4.1.113–17)

It would not occur to us to describe a cry of hounds as a kind of symphony orchestra, but then we do not have the mystique of a Renaissance prince about hunting. Both forms of music fall far short of the supreme harmony of the spheres described in the fifth act of *The Merchant of Venice*: Oberon might know something about that, but not Puck, who can't see the "imperial votaress." Neither, probably, could Theseus.

So the wood-world has affinities with what we call the unconscious or subconscious part of the mind: a part below the reason's encounter with objective reality, and yet connected with the hidden creative powers of the mind. Left to Puck or even Titania, it's a world of illusion, random desires and shifting identities. With Oberon in charge, it becomes the world in which those profound choices are made that decide the course of life, and also (we pick this up later) the world from which inspiration comes to the poet. The lovers wake up still dazed with metamorphosis; as Demetrius says:

These things seem small and undistinguishable
Like far-off mountains turnèd into clouds. (4.1.186–87)

But the comic crystallization has taken place, and for the fifth act we go back to Theseus's court to sort out the various things that have come out of the wood.

Theseus takes a very rational and common-sense view of the lovers' story, but he makes it clear that the world of the wood is the world of the poet as well as the lover and the lunatic. His very remarkable speech uses the words "apprehend" and "comprehend" each twice. In the ordinary world we apprehend with our senses and comprehend with our reason; what the poet apprehends are moods or emotions, like joy, and what he uses for comprehension is some story or character to account for the emotion:

Such tricks hath strong imagination
That if it would but apprehend some joy,
It comprehends some bringer of that joy (5.1.18–20)

Theseus is here using the word "imagination" in its common Elizabethan meaning, which we express by the word "imaginary," something alleged to be that isn't. In spite of himself, though, the word is taking on the more positive sense of our "imaginative," the sense of the creative power developed centuries later by Blake and Coleridge. So far as I can make out from the *OED*, this more positive sense of the word in English practically begins here. Hippolyta

is shrewder and less defensive than Theseus, and what she says takes us a great
deal further:

> But all the story of the night, told over
> And all their minds transfigur'd so together,
> More witnesseth than fancy's images,
> And grows to something of great constancy;
> But howsoever, strange and admirable. (5.1.23–27)

Theseus doesn't believe their story, but Hippolyta sees that something has
happened to them, whatever their story. The word "transfigured" means that
there can be metamorphosis upward as well as downward, a creative transforming
into a higher consciousness as well as the reduction from the conscious to the
unconscious that we read about in Ovid. Besides, the story has a consistency to it
that doesn't sound like the disjointed snatches of incoherent minds. If you want
disjointing and incoherence, just listen to the play that's coming up. And yet the
Quince play is a triumph of sanity in its way: it tells you that the roaring lion is
only Snug the joiner, for example. It's practically a parody of Theseus's view of
reality, with its "imagination" that takes a bush for a bear in the dark. There's a later
exchange when Hippolyta complains that the play is silly, and Theseus says:

> The best in this kind are but shadows; and the
> worst are no worse, if imagination amend them (5.1.209–10)

Hippolyta retorts: "It must be your imagination, then, and not theirs." Here
"imagination" has definitely swung over to meaning something positive and
creative. What Hippolyta says implies that the audience has a creative role in
every play; that's one reason why Puck, coming out for the Epilogue when the
audience is supposed to applaud, repeats two of Theseus's words:

> If we shadows have offended
> Think but this, and all is mended. (5.1.412–13)

Theseus's imagination has "amended" the Quince play by accepting it, listening
to it, and not making fun of the actors to their faces. Its merit as a play consists in
dramatizing his own social position and improving what we'd now call his "image"
as a gracious prince. In itself the play has no merit, except in being unintentionally
funny. And if it has no merit, it has no authority. A play that did have authority,
and depended on a poet's imagination as well, would raise the question that
Theseus's remark seems to deny: the question of the difference between plays by
Peter Quince and plays by William Shakespeare. Theseus would recognize the
difference, of course, but in its social context, as an offering for his attention and

applause, a Shakespeare play would be in the same position as the Quince play. That indicates how limited Theseus's world is, in the long run, a fact symbolized by his not knowing how much of his behavior is guided by Oberon.

Which brings me to Bottom, the only mortal in the play who actually sees any of the fairies. One of the last things Bottom says in the play is rather puzzling: "the wall is down that parted their fathers." Apparently he means the wall separating the hostile families of Pyramus and Thisbe. This wall seems to have attracted attention: after Snout the tinker, taking the part of Wall, leaves the stage, Theseus says, according to the Folio: "Now is the morall downe between the two neighbours." The New Arden editor reads "mural down," and other editors simply change to "wall down." The Quarto, just to be helpful, reads "moon used." Wall and Moonshine between them certainly confuse an already confused play. One wonders if the wall between the two worlds of Theseus and Oberon, the wall that Theseus is so sure is firmly in place, doesn't throw a shadow on these remarks.

Anyway, Bottom wakes up along with the lovers and makes one of the most extraordinary speeches in Shakespeare, which includes a very scrambled but still recognizable echo from the New Testament, and finally says he will get Peter Quince to write a ballad of his dream, and "it shall be called Bottom's Dream, because it hath no bottom." Like most of what Bottom says, this is absurd; like many absurdities in Shakespeare, it makes a lot of sense. Bottom does not know that he is anticipating by three centuries a remark of Freud: "every dream has a point at which it is unfathomable; a link, as it were, with the unknown." When we come to *King Lear*, we shall suspect that it takes a madman to see into the heart of tragedy, and perhaps it takes a fool or clown, who habitually breathes the atmosphere of absurdity and paradox, to see into the heart of comedy. "Man," says Bottom, "is but an ass, if he go about to expound this dream." But it was Bottom the ass who had the dream, not Bottom the weaver, who is already forgetting it. He will never see his Titania again, nor even remember that she had once loved him, or doted on him, to use Friar Laurence's distinction. But he has been closer to the centre of this wonderful and mysterious play than any other of its characters, and it no longer matters that Puck thinks him a fool or that Titania loathes his asinine face.

———

1987—Harold Bloom. "Introduction," from *A Midsummer Night's Dream* (Bloom's Modern Critical Interpretations)

Harold Bloom (1930–) is Sterling Professor of the Humanities at Yale University. He has edited many anthologies of literature and literary criticism and is the author of more than 30 books, including *The Western Canon* and *Shakespeare: The Invention of the Human.*

A Midsummer Night's Dream
On the loftiest of the world's thrones we still are sitting only on our own Bottom.
—MONTAIGNE, "Of Experience"
I will get Peter Quince to write a ballet of this dream. It shall be call'd "Bottom's Dream," because it hath no bottom.

I wish Shakespeare had given us Peter Quince's ballet (ballad), but he may have been too wise to attempt the poem. *A Midsummer Night's Dream*, for me, is Puck and Bottom, and I prefer Bottom. Perhaps we reduce to Puckish individuals or Bottoms. Pucks are more charming, but Bottoms are rather more amiable. Shakespeare's Bottom is surpassingly amiable, and I agree with Northrop Frye that Bottom is the only mortal with experience of the visionary center of the play. As the possible lover (however briefly) of the Fairy Queen, Bottom remains a lasting reproach to our contemporary fashion of importing sacred violence, bestiality, and all manner of sexual antics into Shakespeare's most fragile of visionary dramas. For who could be more mild mannered, better natured, or sweetly humorous than the unfailingly gentle Bottom? Titania ends up despising him, but he is simply too good for her!

Bottom, when we first encounter him, is already a Malaprop, inaccurate at the circumference, as it were, but sound at the core, which is what his name means, the center of the skein upon which a weaver's wool is wound. And surely that is his function in the play; he is its core, and also he is the most original figure in *A Midsummer Night's Dream*. Self-assertive, silly, ignorant, he remains a personage of absolute good will, a kind of remote ancestor to Joyce's amiable Poldy. Transformed into an outward monstrosity by Puck, he yet retains his courage, kindness, and humor, and goes through his uncanny experience totally unchanged within. His initial dialogue with Titania is deliciously ironic, and he himself is in full control of the irony:

TITANIA: I pray thee, gentle mortal, sing again.
Mine ear is much enamored of thy note;
So is mine eye enthralled to thy shape;
And thy fair virtue's force (perforce) doth move me
On the first view to say, to swear, I love thee.
BOTTOM: Methinks, mistress, you should have little reason for that.
And yet, to say the truth, reason and love keep little company together
now-a-days. The more the pity that some honest neighbors will not
make them friends. Nay, I can gleek upon occasion.

TITANIA: Thou art as wise as thou art beautiful.
BOTTOM: Not so, neither; but if I had wit enough to get out of this wood, I have enough to serve mine own turn.

Knowing that he lacks both beauty and wisdom, Bottom is realistic enough to see that the faery queen is beautiful but not wise. Charmed by (and charming to) the elven foursome of Peaseblossom, Cobweb, Moth, and Mustardseed, Bottom makes us aware that they mean no more and no less to him than Titania does. Whether or not he has made love to Titania, a subject of some nasty debate among our critical contemporaries, seems to me quite irrelevant. What does matter is that he is sublimely unchanged, for worse or for better, when he wakes up from his bottomless dream:

BOTTOM: [*Awaking.*] When my cue comes, call me, and I will answer. My next is, "Most fair Pyramus." Heigh-ho! Peter Quince! Flute the bellowsmender! Snout the tinker! Starveling! God's my life, stol'n hence, and left me asleep! I have had a most rare vision. I have had a dream, past the wit of man to say what dream it was. Man is but an ass, if he go about [t'] expound this dream. Methought I was—there is no man can tell what. Methought I was, and methought I had— but man is but [a patch'd] fool, if he will offer to say what methought I had. The eye of man hath not heard, the ear of man hath not seen, man's hand is not able to taste, his tongue to conceive, nor his heart to report, what my dream was. I will get Peter Quince to write a ballet of this dream. It shall be ca-l'd "Bottom's Dream," because it hath no bottom; and I will sing it in the latter end of a play, before the Duke. Peradventure, to make it the more gracious, I shall sing it at her death.

Bottom's revision of 1 Corinthians 2:9–10 is the heart of the matter:

Eye hath not seen, nor ear heard, neither have entered into the heart of man, the things which God hath prepared for them that love him.
But God hath revealed them unto us by his Spirit.
(ST. PAUL)
The eye of man hath not heard, the ear of man hath not seen, man's hand is not able to taste, his tongue to conceive, nor his heart to report, what my dream was.
(BOTTOM)

Bottom's scrambling of the senses refuses St. Paul's easy supernaturalism, with its dualistic split between flesh and spirit. Our prophet Bottom is a monist, and so his dream urges upon us a synesthetic reality, fusing flesh and spirit. That

Bottom is one for whom God has prepared the things revealed by his Spirit is made wonderfully clear in the closing dialogue between the benign weaver and Theseus:

> BOTTOM: [*Staring up.*] No, I assure you, the wall is down that
> parted their fathers. Will it please you to see the epilogue, or to hear a
> Bergomask dance between two of our company?
> THESEUS: No epilogue, I pray you; for your play needs no excuse.

Only Bottom could assure us that the wall is down that parted all our fathers. The weaver's common sense and natural goodness bestow upon him an aesthetic dignity, homely and humane, that is the necessary counterpoise to the world of Puck that otherwise would ravish reality away in Shakespeare's visionary drama.

Puck, being the spirit of mischief, is both a hobgoblin and "sweet Puck," not so much by turns but all at once. *A Midsummer Night's Dream* is more Puck's play than Bottom's, I would reluctantly agree, even as *The Tempest* is more Ariel's drama than it is poor Caliban's. If Puck, rather than Oberon, were in charge, then Bottom never would resume human shape and the four young lovers would continue their misadventures forever. Most of what fascinates our contemporaries about *A Midsummer Night's Dream* belongs to Puck's vision rather than to Bottom's. Amidst so much of the Sublime, it is difficult to prefer any single passage, but I find most unforgettable Puck's penultimate chant:

> Now the hungry [lion] roars,
> And the wolf [behowls] the moon;
> Whilst the heavy ploughman snores,
> All with weary task foredone.
> Now the wasted brands do glow,
> Whilst the screech-owl, screeching loud,
> Puts the wretch that lies in woe
> In remembrance of a shroud.
> Now it is the time of night
> That the graves, all gaping wide,
> Every one lets forth his sprite,
> In the church-way paths to glide.
> And we fairies, that do run
> By the triple Hecat's team
> From the presence of the sun,
> Following darkness like a dream,
> Now are frolic. Not a mouse
> Shall disturb this hallowed house.

I am sent with broom before,
To sweep the dust behind the door.

Everything problematic about Puck is summed up there; a domestic, work-a-
day spirit, yet always uncannily *between*, between men and women, faeries and
humans, nobles and mechanicals, nature and art, space and time. Puck is a spirit
cheerfully amoral, free because never in love, and always more amused even than
amusing. The triple Hecate—heavenly moon maiden, earthly Artemis, and ruler
of Hades—is more especially Puck's deity than she is the goddess worshipped
by the other faeries. Hazlitt wisely contrasted Puck to Ariel by reminding us
that "Ariel is a minister of retribution, who is touched with the sense of pity
at the woes he inflicts," while Puck "laughs at those whom he misleads." Puck
just does not care; he has nothing to gain and little to lose. Only Oberon could
call him "gentle," but then Oberon could see Cupid flying between moon and
earth, and Puck constitutionally could not. Puck says that things please him
best "that befall preposterously," where I think the last word takes on the force
of the later coming earlier and the earlier later. As a kind of flying metalepsis or
trope of transumption, Puck is indeed what the rhetorician Puttenham called a
far-fetcher.

The midsummer night's dream, Puck tells us in his final chant, is ours,
since we "but slumb'red here, / While these visions did appear." What are we
dreaming when we dream Puck? "Shadows" would be his reply, in a familiar
Shakespearean trope, yet Puck is no more a shadow than Bottom is. Free of love,
Puck becomes an agent of the irrational element in love, its tendency to over-
value the object, as Freud grimly phrased it. A man or woman who incarnates
Puck is sexually very dangerous, because he or she is endlessly mobile, invariably
capable of transforming object-libido back into ego-libido again. Puckish
freedom is overwhelmingly attractive, but the blow it strikes you will cause it
no pain. Falling in love with a Puck is rather like turning life into the game of
hockey.

Theseus, in the play's most famous speech, associates the lover with the poet
and the lunatic in a perfectly Freudian conglomerate, since all forsake the reality
principle, all assert the omnipotence of thought, and all thus yield themselves up
to an ultimate narcissism. If Theseus is a Freudian, Bottom is not, but represents
an older wisdom, the amiable sapience, mixed with silliness, of the all-too-
natural man. Puck, quicksilver and uncaring, defines the limits of the human by
being so far apart from the human.

How can one play contain both Bottom and Puck? Ariel and Caliban both
care, though they care on different sides and in different modes. Puck has
no human feelings, and so no human meaning; Bottom is one of the prime
Shakespearean instances of how human meaning gets started, by a kind of
immanent overflow, an ontological excess of being in excess of language. Only

a dream, we might think, could contain both Bottom and Puck, but the play, however fantastic, is no fantasy, but an imitation that startles the reality principle and makes it tremble, rather like a guilty thing surprised.

—*∿∿*— —*∿∿*— —*∿∿*—

1998—David Wiles. "The Carnivalesque in *A Midsummer Night's Dream*," from *Shakespeare and Carnival: After Bakhtin*

David Wiles is a professor of theatre in the Department of Drama and Theatre at Royal Holloway, University of London. He is the author of *A Short History of Western Performance Space* (2003), *Greek Theatre Performance: An Introduction* (2000), *Tragedy in Athens: Performance Space and Theatrical Meaning* (1997), and *Shakespeare's Almanac: A Midsummer Night's Dream, Marriage and the Elizabethan Calendar* (1993).

Carnival theory did not begin with Bakhtin, and we shall understand Bakhtin's position more clearly if we set it against classical theories of carnival.[1] From the Greek world the most important theoretical statement is to be found in Plato:

> The gods took pity on the human race, born to suffer as it was, and gave it relief in the form of religious festivals to serve as periods of rest from its labours. They gave us as fellow revellers the Muses, with Apollo their leader, and Dionysus, so that men might restore their way of life by sharing feasts with gods.[2]

This is first a *utopian* theory, maintaining that carnival restores human beings to an earlier state of being when humans were closer to the divine. And second, it associates carnival with communal *order*. Plato argues that festive dancing creates bodily order, and thus bodily and spiritual well-being. He clarifies his orderly view of carnival by dissenting from an alternative view, relating specifically to the worship of Dionysus, which maintains that Hera caused Dionysus to lose his reason, and Dionysus inflicts his revenge upon mortals, making them drunk and wild in their dancing.[3] Plato thus dissents from an *anarchic* view comparable to the later Christian idea that carnival is an expression of the Devil.

Aristotle's most relevant discussion concerns the music of the pipes, which troubles him because of its effect upon the emotions of player and listener. He cites the myth that Athena invented the pipes, but being rational threw them away. Orgiastic music, and implicitly the festivals associated with such music, placed Aristotle in a dilemma. He refused to let upper-class youth meddle with the pipes, but allowed the lower classes with their disordered minds and bodies to indulge; nevertheless he accepted some usage by the elite on the grounds of 'catharsis', observing that 'enthusiasm' (i.e. possession by the god)

> affects some people very strongly . . . They are, as it were, set on their feet, as if they had undergone a curative and purifying treatment . . . Cathartic music brings men an elation which is not at all harmful.[4]

Aristotle introduces two important notions to the debate about festive practice. One is *popular culture*, a debilitating or demoralizing form of recreation which the upper class must avoid. The other is catharsis, normally termed in discussions of carnival as *'safety-valve* theory'.[5] It is an important aspect of Aristotelian 'safety-valve' theory that it analyses the individual rather than the social process. Where Plato was concerned with the way choral dance binds the community together, Aristotle's analytic approach is concerned with the breeding of individual leaders.

In the Roman republic the Dionysia was suppressed and in the course of the imperial period the Saturnalia emerged as the major festival. The festive focus shifted from the spring equinox to the winter solstice. Macrobius cites two major theories of the Saturnalia.[6] The dominant theory is *utopian*, locating Saturn as the god who brought fertility to Italy in the golden age, teaching Janus the art of agriculture. There was no war in the age of Saturn, and most importantly no class distinction. The inversion of master and slave at the Saturnalia is seen as a means of honouring the god who symbolizes this uncorrupted, egalitarian past. The theme of class inversion becomes dominant in Roman rather than Greek carnival because Roman society at all levels was rigidly stratified. We should also take note in Macrobius of the explicit calendrical symbolism, for Saturn suddenly vanishes leaving two-faced Janus (January) to face forwards towards the new year. Saturn is associated with the Greek C[h]ronos, who symbolizes time and the *orderly* progress of the seasons. The main competing theory, which Macrobius attributed to Varro at the end of the Republican period, is *propitiatory*, and relates to the Greek settlement of Sicily. Masks and lights are a symbolic substitute for human sacrifice, and Saturn is linked to the god of Death. Varro's theory is rationalistic and historicizing, and presumes that the human condition is advancing rather than declining. But it points up a negative aspect of Saturn, whose sickle is used to castrate the father as well as to reap the harvest.

In the medieval period the Saturnalia, in its new guise as the 12 days of Christmas, remained important, but the focus of communal celebration in continental Europe shifted to *Mardi gras*, 'carnival' in the strict sense of 'farewell to flesh', flesh in the dual form of sexual intercourse and eating meat. Medieval education was steeped in Aristotle, and Aristotelian 'safety-valve' theory provided an obvious means of theorizing carnival. Udall in the preface to *Ralph Roister*

Doister speaks of how 'mirth prolongeth life, and causeth health; mirth recreates our spirits and voideth pensiveness.'[7] The explanation turns on the Aristotelian and Hippocratic theory of the four humours. Celebration evacuates melancholy and thus restores the body to equilibrium. Similar thinking underlies the famous Parisian apologia of 1444:

> We do these things in jest and not in earnest, as the ancient custom
> is, so that once a year the foolishness innate in us can come out and
> evaporate. Don't wine skins and barrels burst very often if the air-hole is
> not opened from time to time?[8]

The humoral conception is here linked to a Christian conception, for the jest/earnest dichotomy relates to the Manichaean division of Devil and God within the human individual. If the Devil is innate, then by definition it cannot be overcome and must be rendered harmless in other ways.

For scholars of the Enlightenment and Romantic periods, carnivalesque phenomena were either distasteful, or symbols of an idealized past. Whereupon, enter Bakhtin, with the impetus of Marxism behind him. In his study of Rabelais, Bakhtin identified 'carnival' as the basis of an autonomous and historically progressive popular culture. The 'carnivalesque' is for Bakhtin a genre synonymous with 'grotesque realism', but becomes also a sociological category. In the ancient world Bakhtin seems to have envisaged a homogeneous community with no distinctive 'popular' culture. The satyr play is cited as an example of how each genre has 'its own parodying and travestying double, its own comic-ironic *contre-partie*'.[9] In the ancient world, Bakhtin declares, 'there could be no sharp distinction between official and folk culture, as later appeared in the Middle Ages.'[10] In the seventh, eighth and ninth centuries feudalism had yet to take root, and the homogeneous classical tradition was still strong,[11] and Bakhtin's folk culture seems to have appeared somewhere in the early Middle Ages. Rabelais is interpreted as a historically progressive figure, whose use of a residual popular culture supported monarchy against feudalism.[12] Bakhtin sees this historically-specific popular culture as the means whereby people overcame their fears and freely expressed their views about authority. Bakhtin's theory of carnival is not a 'safety-valve' theory, and he extrapolates from the 1444 text cited above the alternative principle that human beings have two separate natures.[13] Bakhtin's theory is, in the tradition of Plato and Macrobius, a *utopian* theory, positing a primal wholeness to which fallen humanity, ruined in this case by the devil of class, is temporarily restored.

Bakhtin's most influential contribution to subsequent discussion of carnival is his semiotics of the body. The carnivalesque body with its orifices, protuberances and excretions is related to the flux of the self-renewing cosmos, whilst the hermetic classical body is individualized and sterile.[14] One of the difficulties in using this theory is Bakhtin's tendency to lump all festivals together, slipping from carnival in the narrow sense of *carnevale* or *mardi gras* to the wide sense of popular celebration. 'Carnival' in the narrow sense is specifically concerned with the body, which has to be mortified during Lent, and its most potent symbol is the fat man who bloats his body to the point of expiry. The symbol of the classical Dionysia was the erect phallus, appropriate to the spring season and the renewal of life. The ithyphallic satyr of the Dionysia was sexually rampant, but not bloated, and his grotesqueness was specifically goat-like. The Saturnalia focused on structures of authority, and the ugliness of an inversionary Christmas king was in the first instance a symbol of class, not eating. Midsummer giants were grotesque in a very specific way, being occasions for setting a fire high above the ground on the night of the solstice.[15] Bakhtin's generalizing tendency encourages us to see popular culture and the carnival grotesque as a more uniform entity than it is.

The assumption that we can usefully separate out popular culture from official culture in the Middle Ages cannot pass unchallenged. Peter Burke, drawing his terminology from Redfield, allows a binary model of society, but argues that:

> There were two cultural traditions in early modern Europe, but they did not correspond symmetrically to the two main social groups, the elite and the common people. The elite participated in the little tradition, but the common people did not participate in the great tradition.[16]

The educated elite had access to a language and tradition from which the many were excluded, but the many had no autonomous cultural tradition of their own. Ladurie's analysis of carnival practices in Romans in the Shakespearean period demonstrates that all the different social factions in the town had their independent carnival traditions which served to emblematize local solidarities. It was members of the elite who constituted the jocular 'Abbey of Misrule', erected the annual maypole, and policed marriage within the community.[17] Bercé's wide-ranging analysis of French festival and rebellion in the period concludes that festival only thrives in a town where there is social solidarity. When solidarity breaks down, festive symbolism can be used temporarily to express dissidence, but the framework for such symbolism rapidly evaporates.[18] Bercé emphasizes the discontinuities in festive traditions, which are for ever being renewed and reinvented, and he sees timeless ritual practice as a utopian myth.[19] The work of Burke, Ladurie and Bercé obliges us to view with scepticism Bakhtin's overarching notion of an on-going autonomous popular culture.

The situation in England in the Shakespearean period is in many specific respects hard to accommodate with the Bakhtinian paradigm. In Marxist terms one cannot see festivals as historically 'progressive', for the land-owning aristocracy began to use rites associated with the land to lay claim to authentic

Englishness in opposition to the urban and bourgeois Puritan movement.[20] King James' *Book of Sports* (1618) is the most blatant example of such ideological manipulation of carnival, but Elizabeth engaged in the same strategy. At court Shakespeare's plays were performed according to the rhythm of the festive calendar, whilst in the city his plays were performed according to the sabbatarian rhythm of the Reformation. When we look at the plays in their performance context, the festive or carnivalesque dimension relates to the experience of the aristocratic audience much more closely than it does to the experience of the 'popular' audience.

'Carnival' is a troublesome term because in its narrow sense the English festival bears the penitential term 'Shrovetide'. The festival was not the occasion for public processions as on the continent,[21] and the 'King of Christmas' is the dominant celebratory figure, not the continental 'Carnival' who engages in mortal combat with Lent. Bakhtin's generalized view of carnival renders him blind to the highly specific way in which festivals organize and give meaning to the passage of time. He does not explore, for example, how the pattern of early modern festivals relates both to the narrative of Christ's life-cycle and to the major points of transition in the life-cycle of Everyman and Everywoman. Bakhtin's concern is with epochs, not with chronological minutiae, and he is content to identify a general festive merging of death with birth apparent in images of the harvest or the marriage bed. His concern as a critic is with genre rather than performance, and so for example the life/death nexus that he discerns in Aristophanes finds a 'significant kinship' in the Shakespearean clown.[22] He is also preoccupied with the novel rather than drama, which, perhaps because of the dominance of naturalism at the time when he wrote, seemed to him a relatively monologic medium.[23] The carnivalesque is experienced as a textual artefact belonging to a given historical moment rather than as a performance belonging to a specific calendrical moment.

Michael Bristol, a critic sympathetic to Bakhtin, offers a reading of *A Midsummer Night's Dream* along broadly Bakhtinian lines. He criticizes C. L. Barber's 'saturnalian' approach to Shakespearean comedy as a version of 'safety-valve' theory. For Barber, 'release' is followed by a 'clarification' that Bristol rightly interprets as a reaffirmation of the status quo.[24] For Barber, the maying in which Theseus engages is the dominant festive motif, the single critical key that unlocks the whole. Bristol attempts to effect a dialogic reading, contrasting the official discourse of the aristocracy with the heteroglossia of the mechanicals, so that the latter provides a critique of the former and the text becomes an open one. In the mechanicals he sees an emphasis on the body, and a denial of individual subjectivity.[25] Bristol's reading offers us a more radical and progressive Shakespeare than before, but seems in some ways to force the play to fit the theory. Bristol emphasizes the aristocratic/popular binary in a play that is more obviously trinary, with its three layers of commoners, aristocracy and fairies.

The activities of the fairies provide a more obvious critique of marriage than the activities of the mechanicals. It seems to be the unspoken assumption of a materialist modern age that the fairy couple are the superegos of Theseus and Hippolyta, and thus no more than psychoanalytic projections. The binaries of youth/age and male/female remain subordinate in Bristol's reading to the overarching Bakhtinian paradigm of them-and-us, officialdom and the folk. Another critic who has attempted a Bakhtinian reading of Shakespeare is Manfred Pfister, who adopts a position much closer to Barber, finding that the multiple inversions of the early comedies are safely contained 'within an over-ruling framework of a benign and flexible order'. Pfister dismisses these inversionary plot structures as 'instances of saturnalian revelling rather than subversive carnivalesque revelling'.[26] A Bakhtinian reading leads Bristol and Pfister to focus on an apparently straightforward question: Are the texts univocal or dialogic? Are they ordered classical structures or open-ended carnivalesque structures?

Posed in these terms, the question, I would suggest, is an unsatisfactory one because it implies that the text has immanent properties. The text under investigation has been extracted from its historical context of performance, and defined as a self-contained and complete entity. To bind the text between the covers of a book is already to impose an over-ruling framework, and to define its level of discourse. The alternative, however, is not easy, for in addition to the literal heteroglossia provided by the multiple voices of the actors, and the more subtle heteroglossia provided by the different linguistic registers in the dialogue, we also have the language of gesture which may speak against the words. The twentieth-century director will often seek to create dialogism by playing against the text, and we may wonder whether Elizabethan performers did not also have critical attitudes to the texts they were given. More important still we have the voice of the audience. Through laughing, clapping, hissing and by their visible socially structured presence, the Elizabethan audience were necessarily an integral part of the performance event, interacting with the players far more than a modern audience would do.

The starting point for my own analysis will be the proposition that although we encounter *A Midsummer Night's Dream* as a text, it was historically part of an aristocratic carnival. It was written for a wedding, and part of the festive structure of the wedding night. The audience who saw the play in the public theatre in the months that followed became vicarious participants in an aristocratic festival from which they were physically excluded. My purpose will be to demonstrate how closely the play is integrated with a historically specific upper-class celebration.

I have argued at length elsewhere[27] that the play was written for the marriage of Elizabeth Carey, daughter of George Carey, who became patron of Shakespeare's company of actors and later commissioned *The Merry Wives of Windsor*. The argument, in brief, is that aristocratic weddings customarily took place on significant calendrical dates. The Careys eschewed Saint Valentine's Day in favour of 19 February 1596, because that day saw the planetary conjunction of the new moon and Venus, the most favourable conditions an astrologer could imagine, and both parties to the wedding took astrology very seriously. The parents of the bride and groom must have consulted an almanac, just as Bottom tells Quince to do. The moon changed (whilst remaining occluded) on 18 February and thus the fictitious setting of the action announced in the first lines of the play when 'four happy days bring in another moon' became Saint Valentine's Day, 1596. Lest the audience miss the point, Hippolyta repeats that

> Four days will quickly steep themselves in night:
> Four nights will quickly dream away the time:
> And then [on the fifth night] the Moon, like to a silver bow,
> Now bent in heaven, shall behold the night
> Of our solemnities. (1.1.7–11)[28]

The central action of the play inhabits a liminal, dream-like space characterized by the inversion of real conditions, being set out-of-doors, in the country, in summer and under a full moon.

Saint Valentine's Day is only mentioned once, at the moment when the lovers return from the liminal world of their dream to the courtly world of Theseus. Within the closed system of the text, Theseus' jest on May Day seems inconsequential: 'Saint Valentine is past: Begin these wood-birds but to couple now?' (4.1.138–9). The importance of Saint Valentine's Day rites in structuring the narrative of the play has long been overlooked, because critics viewing the play as a purely textual entity have been fixated by the overt verbal references to May. Let us spend a while investigating those forgotten rites.

If we step back to the world of John Paston, we can see how the Saint Valentine tradition shaped medieval courtship. Financial negotiations were under way, the girl was getting impatient, and the romantic interview had yet to take place when John Paston's prospective mother-in-law wrote inviting him to visit on Saint Valentine's eve:

> Cousin, upon Friday is Saint Valentine's Day, and every bird chooseth
> him a mate. And if it like you to come on Thursday at night, and so
> purvey you that ye may abide there till Monday, ye shall so speak to my
> husband.

Soon afterwards, the prospective bride wrote a love-letter to Paston, her 'right well-beloved Valentine', lamenting that her father would not increase her portion. Her next letter, written in mounting distress, urged her 'good, true and loving Valentine' not to pursue the matter of marriage if he could not accept her father's terms. She signed herself 'your Valentine'.[29] We discern from these letters the important part which Saint Valentine rituals played in shaping the emotional aspect of relationships within a system of arranged marriages.

Like Paston's mother-in-law, Theseus alludes to the proverbial notion that birds choose their mates on this day when he asks: 'Begin these wood-birds but to couple now?' The major medieval poets—Chaucer, Gower, Lydgate—all made play with this tradition, and it continued to flourish in Surrey and Herrick.[30] The tradition is strictly literary, for birds do not pair off at this time of year in the English climate.[31] The poet normally seeks to develop a contrast between the natural behaviour of birds and unnatural behaviour amongst human beings. George Wither, in his epithalamium written for the marriage of James I's daughter on Saint Valentine's Day, reverses the motif, and suggests that the blackbird and thrush have learned from the human couple.[32] Lydgate lists numerous wood-birds, while Chaucer and Gower both use the image of a 'parliament' of birds. John Donne, in his epithalamium for James' daughter, produces a similar listing of birds, both common birds like the robin and blackbird, and aristocrats like the goldfinch and kingfisher; at the head of this unparliamentary hierarchy, the marrying couple are likened to phoenixes.[33]

The tradition of a parliament of courting birds establishes a generic context for Bottom's musical catalogue of wood-birds: the ousel cock, the thrush, the wren, the finch, the sparrow, the lark and the cuckoo (3.1.120ff.). Bottom's song evokes the different musical qualities of the different birds. The birds in the first stanza are explicitly masculine, and implicitly phallic:

The ousel cock, so black of hue,
With orange-tawny bill,
The throstle, with his note so true,
The wren with little quill—

While Donne's poem ends gloriously with the phoenix, Bottom ends with bathos. No man can deny that he is a cuckoo/cuckold:

The finch, the sparrow, and the lark,
The plain-song cuckoo grey,
Whose note full many a man doth mark,
And dares not answer nay.

Bottom's mating-song, which identifies the singer as the sexually inadequate cuckoo, culminates in the emergence of Titania the dominant female from her flowery bed, enraptured by what she hears. Perhaps the bed resembled a nest as in Brook's production, we do not know. Certainly, Bottom's bird-song contrasts grotesquely with the lullaby which laid Titania to rest in her bed, where the sounds are supposedly uttered by Philomel the nightingale (2.2.13). The bird motif ties the love of Bottom and Titania to the important Saint Valentine tradition, which likes to contrast the natural coupling found in the greenwood with the constraints which society imposes on human beings.

Two other aspects of Saint Valentine's day relate closely to the plot structure of *A Midsummer Night's Dream*. First is the tradition of drawing lots on the night before Saint Valentine's day. This custom derives from the Roman Lupercalia on February 15th, when men drew lots with the names of women. One medieval poet describes how

> Of custom year by year
> Men have an usaunce in this region
> To look and search Cupid's calendar
> And choose their choice by great affection—
> Such as been moved with Cupid's motion
> Taking their choice as their sort doth fall . . .[34]

'Sort' is of course the French word for 'lot'. The drawing of lots on Saint Valentine's eve is documented at Jesus College, Cambridge in 1608: a man was expected to give a pair of gloves to the girl whose name he drew.[35] The custom is described in some detail by the Frenchman, Henri Misson, at the end of the seventeenth century:

> An equal number of maids and bachelors get together, each writes their true or some feigned name upon separate billets, which they roll up, and draw by way of lots, the maids taking the men's billets, and the men the maids'; so that each of the young men lights upon a girl that he calls his Valentine, and each of the girls upon a young man which she calls hers. By this means each has two Valentines; but the man sticks faster to the Valentine that is fallen to him, than to the Valentine to whom he is fallen. Fortune having thus divided the company into so many couples, the Valentines give balls and treats to their mistresses, wear their billets several days upon their bosoms or sleeves, and this little sport often ends in love.[36]

From an anthropological perspective, the drawing of lots is functional in relation to village life. Couples are not formed on the basis of individual inclinations (though force of personality must play a part in determining whether the boy finishes up with the girl who chases him or the girl whom he chases), nor are pairings going to reflect economic and political power blocs, as they must do in any system where marriages are arranged according to parental choice. The Saint Valentine's lottery was profoundly egalitarian.

Ben Jonson's nostalgic Caroline reconstruction of Elizabethan life, *A Tale of a Tub*, was written soon after the reissue of James I's *Book of Sports*,[37] and the play has a Saint Valentine's Day setting. The main plot centres on the attempt by the constable to marry his daughter, Audrey Turf, to a bridegroom called Clay. Squire Tub (i.e. a tub of fertilizer) is a rival, as is young Justice Bramble. The constable has chosen Clay because

> Mistress Audrey Turf
> Last night did draw him for her Valentine:
> Which chance it hath so taken her father and mother,
> Because themselves drew so on Valentine's Eve
> Was thirty year, as they will have her married
> Today by any means. (1.1.45–50)

Another character reminisces in similar vein that 'Sin' Valentine

> had a place, in last King Harry's time,
> Of sorting all the young couples, joining 'em,
> And putting 'em together; which is yet
> P'rformed as on his day . . . (1.2.22–5)

Jonson goes on to give his plot the structure of a Saint Valentine's lottery. The audience have no idea whom the heroine will marry, and it is pure chance that leads her at the last into the arms of a stranger, 'Pol Marten'. Apparently a bird (and thus an appropriate hero for Saint Valentine's Day), it transpires that the groom is really 'Martin Polecat', and knows how to burrow into the 'turf'.

The game played on Saint Valentine's day whereby boy A chases girl B who chases boy C who chases girl D is startlingly analogous to the plot structure of *A Midsummer Night's Dream*. A random principle seems to govern the pairing of the young couples, and Shakespeare provides no clues to character which might suggest that the choices made by Hermia and Helena are anything other than arbitrary. Despite all odds, the two women pursue the men whom fate seems to have allotted them. Puck views the proceedings as a 'fond pageant' and a 'sport', and functions as a master of ceremonies by manipulating his magic potion (3.2.114, 119). Initially, Helena → Demetrius → Hermia → Lysander. The circle is complete when, thanks to the potion, Lysander → Helena. Oberon begins to move the game to a conclusion when Demetrius → Helena, and the final resolution is achieved when Lysander's eyes are re-anointed.

The second custom which characterizes Saint Valentine's Day is the custom whereby one's 'Valentine' is the first person whom one sees when one wakes in the morning. For a full picture of this ritual, we can turn to Pepys' entries for 14 February. In 1666, the early morning ritual is associated with the lot-drawing of the night before. Pepys records that he was

> called up by Mr Hill, who my wife thought had come to be her Valentine, she it seems having drawn him last night, but it proved not; however, calling him up to our bedside, my wife challenged him.

Mrs Pepys subsequently went off with her Valentine to an all-night party. The next day a lady who had drawn Pepys' name in a lottery appeared 'with my name in her bosom, which will cost me money'. Young people frequently present themselves at the Pepys' bedside, motivated by the fact that the wealthy older person will have to provide a present of money or gloves. There is a colourful entry for 1665, when Pepys was visited by the young wife of a ship's carpenter. Three weeks previously, his wife being incapacitated with period pains, Pepys had dined and had his pleasure with this lady, who wanted him to find work for her husband, and he subsequently swore an oath to let women go, in order to concentrate on business. He now complains on 14 February that this woman

> had the confidence to say she came in time enough to be my Valentine, and so indeed she did—but my oath preserved me from losing any time with her.

There was always the risk that one might clap eyes upon a wholly inappropriate Valentine. When he went visiting in 1661, Pepys had to ask whether the servant about to open the door was male or female, and the servant, a negro male, teased him by answering 'a woman'. The next year, his wife had to cover her eyes with her hands all morning in order not to see the painters who were gilding the plasterwork.[38]

These early morning visitations, resurrected at the Restoration, were common practice in the Elizabethan period. In *Hamlet*, Ophelia's ballad describes the tragic plight of a girl who goes out early in the morning to seek her Valentine:

> Tomorrow is Saint Valentine's day,
> All in the morning betime,
> And I a maid at your window,
> To be your Valentine.
> Then up he rose, and donned his clothes,
> And dupped the chamber door—
> Let in the maid, that out a maid
> Never departed more. (4.5.48–55)

Nashe, in a rather different vein, also drains Saint Valentine's day of all idealism. His poem 'The Choice of Valentines' describes how young men rise before day-break in order to seek Valentines whom they will accompany dancing, eating cream and cakes, or watching a play. The girl whom the poet is seeking turns out to be a prostitute, who has been driven from her home and now works in a brothel.[39]

The sub-plot of *Tale of a Tub* centres on the middle-aged mother of Squire Tub, who decides to set off across the frosty fields to find a Valentine for herself. She wants her son for company, but he is said to be asleep, so she takes her serving-woman, Wispe. Since both are women, this causes complications. When they knock at the constable's house, the servant Hannibal Puppy comes to the door, and both women claim him:

> *Lady*: Come hither, I must kiss thee, Valentine Puppy.
> Wispe, ha' you got you a Valentine?
> *Wispe*. None, Madam.
> He's the first stranger that I saw.
> *Lady*: To me
> He is so, and such. Let's share him equally. (3.4.23–6)

Puppy calls for help as the two women set upon him in order to claim him with a kiss. The women resolve that they will divide him in half: the right-hand side will belong to one, the left-hand side to the other. Lady Tub passes money to her servant in order that both can complete the ritual by giving a gift to the Valentine whom both have claimed. At the end of the play, courtship leads to marriage, and Wispe and Puppy marry.

Lots were drawn on the eve of Saint Valentine's Day, and the game was thus a nocturnal one. We saw in Pepys that if one drew a name in the lottery, one might well choose to accost that person the next morning—or attempt to do so. Oberon's love juice, derived from Cupid's arrow, 'Will make or man or woman madly dote / Upon the next live creature that it sees' (2.1.171–2), in a way that is precisely analogous to the rules which ritual prescribed for the morning of Saint Valentine's Day. When Theseus greets the lovers with the words: 'Good-morrow friends. Saint Valentine is past: Begin these wood-birds but to couple now?' the stage direction which immediately precedes his words in the Quarto text reads: 'Shout within: they all start up. Wind horns.'[40] To the sound of horns, the ritual of 14 February is accomplished. The lovers transmit the kisses which secure their Valentines and bring the game to an end. Hermia confirms her choice via a socially prescribed ritual designed precisely to override parental efforts at match-making.

The custom that one could claim as one's Valentine the first stranger of the opposite sex whom one saw could result in embarrassment for the gentry.

We have seen Mrs Pepys' fear of being accosted by a workman, and Samuel Pepys' anxiety on account of a negro, and in a fictional context we have seen how a young male servant benefited from the largesse of Lady Tub. Titania's awakening to the sight of an ass represents an extreme version of a common occurrence, a temporary liaison between people of divergent status. When Titania plies Bottom with gifts and goes about the wood 'Seeking sweet favours for this hateful fool' (4.1.48) she behaves precisely as a Valentine ought towards a social inferior. As permitted by the ritual, the liaison ends as abruptly as it begins.

The rituals of Saint Valentine's Day imply a considerable degree of sexual equality. While in ordinary life the male always initiated courtship, on Saint Valentine's Day women seem to have been free to approach men. A writer at the start of the eighteenth century commented that according to the rules of the lottery system 'the obligations are equal, and therefore it was formerly the custom mutually to present [gifts], but now it is customary only for gentlemen.'[41] Helena and Hermia are forced in the play to pursue their respective men, and Helena complains that Daphne now has to chase Apollo:

> Your wrongs do set a scandal on my sex.
> We cannot fight for love, as men may do;
> We should be woo'd, and were not made to woo. (2.1.240–2)

The difference between the women's role in the greenwood, governed by festive laws, and the women's role at court, governed by social norms, becomes striking when the young women sit in respectful silence through 'Pyramus and Thisbe'.

The rites of May, though more overt in the play, are no less pertinent to the narrative structure of *A Midsummer Night's Dream* than the rites of February. Although the journey into the greenwood before dawn is normally associated with May Day, we should remember that on Saint Valentine's Day likewise the young rose very early—though the weather did not encourage expeditions into the greenwood. It was not difficult for Shakespeare to draw the two festive contexts together. The literary tradition, whereby the poet on Saint Valentine's Day goes out into the greenwood into a surprisingly summery landscape to look at the pairing of the birds, helped to make the link an easy one. We find this linkage in one of Shakespeare's source texts, Chaucer's *Legend of Good Women*, where the poet goes out into the meadows on the morning of May Day and hears the birds singing of Saint Valentine's Day.

I shall not dwell on the rites of May because Barber, Young and others have sufficiently signalled their importance.[42] The expedition into the greenwood, the gathering of dew and the importance of the hawthorn bush all complement the scene in which Theseus and Hippolyta enter wearing (as we must assume) the garlands of hawthorn which were the main visual emblem of the ceremony.

Perhaps less obvious is the relationship between the play and a 'midsummer night', for there is no trace of the corporate processions and bonfires that marked the solstitial ceremony.

Shakespeare's title is in the first instance a homage to Spenser, whose 'Epithalamion' was published in 1595, and has been identified as a Shakespearean source.[43] The poem celebrates Spenser's own wedding on the day of the summer solstice in 1594, and develops tight parallels between the internal structure of the poem, the hours of the day, the days of the year, and the bride's rite of passage.[44] The transition of the year from its waxing to its waning correlates with the bride's transition from virgin to woman. It is relevant that maidens on midsummer night were supposed to dream of the man they were to love.[45] Young women who had missed out on the annual cycle of renewal in one year positioned themselves for the next. Shakespeare creates an important image of midsummer night through the medium of stage iconography. While Hermia is short and dark—a 'minimus', an 'Ethiope'—Helena is tall and fair like a 'painted maypole'. As a pair, Hermia and Helena constitute an emblem of midsummer when the bright day is very long and the dark night is very short. The conflict between them reflects the battle of day and night, a battle which reaches its turning point at midsummer.

The three festivals of Saint Valentine's day, May Day and Midsummer are interwoven in the central, liminal portion of *A Midsummer Night's Dream*, framed by the scenes at court. They are not selected at random for they reflect symbolically three phases in the life cycle of a young person: mate selection, courtship and marriage. And this is the process through which the young aristocrats pass in the liminal, greenwood section of the play. Calendar festivals provided Shakespeare and his audience(s) with a symbolic vocabulary which allowed them to relate the phases of an individual life to laws of nature inscribed in the cosmos. The three festivals thrived in the relatively stable social structure of rural early modern England, and were cherished by an Elizabethan aristocracy that wanted to preserve social stability.

And so we return to the question of theorizing the carnivalesque. One of my favourite images of *A Midsummer Night's Dream* is a fresco at Buscot House in Oxfordshire, evidently of the 1930s. The image is part of a diptych, located under an arch that leads aristocratic bathers from their swimming pool to a view of the estate. One half of the diptych shows the local Faringdon Communist Party marching in the background, whilst in the foreground Lord Faringdon, the lord of the house, stands on a hay cart as if at the hustings, and is evidently warning his employees (who were doubtless fortunate to be employed during the depression) not to follow the red flag. On the other side Titania in her bower embraces the ass. The bower is constituted by a white valance at head height supported by four spears and embroidered with Tudor roses. The fairies who look on are evidently young women of the family. Oberon's green costume and position link him as a nature spirit to the estate that lies behind. The vista in the painting leads down a long avenue to an artificial lake, and precisely replicates the real landscape that belongs to Lord Faringdon and confronts him as he passes through the arch. The play is thus conceived as an idyll justifying in symbolic terms the appropriation of nature as property. Its political message is overt.

On what grounds can we claim that the artist of the 1930s subverted Shakespeare's play? Or was he rather in a position that allowed him to share the viewpoint of the aristocrats who commissioned? It may be that the fairies were played by choristers in a wedding performance, and that those roles were taken over by adults in the public playhouse,[46] introducing a new element of the grotesque to the public performance. It is, however, not upon the fairies but upon the slim and melancholy ass that we must focus if we are to mount a serious challenge to Lord Faringdon's painting and salvage some elements of the Bakhtinian carnival grotesque for a wedding performance in 1596. The ass-head has always pushed productions of the play towards sentimentality, and Peter Brook substituted a simple black rubber nose in his production which sought to emphasize the rampant sexuality of Bottom, following Jan Kott's vision of the play. The time-honoured ass-mask has long helped to obscure in performance the symbolism of the bird song which is so important to the Saint Valentine motif. It seems to me far more likely that a fool's cap with ass ears was used to create Bottom's 'transformed scalp' (4.1.63). The ears could have been held up as a cuckold's horns when Bottom at the end of the song becomes the 'cuckoo'. The figure of Bottom/clown/Kemp seems to refer back to this fool's attire when he recalls

> Man is but an ass if he go about to expound this dream. Methought I
> was—there is no man can tell what. Methought I was—and methought
> I had—but man is but a patched fool if he will offer to say what
> methought I had. (4.1.205–8)

The wooing of the fool seems more appropriate to the recurrent festive motif than the wooing of the ass.[47] It is in the figure of Bottom the clown, the lower-class male locked in the arms of a queen, that we must seek the elusive Bakhtinian grotesque, the dimension of ugliness not proffered to the elegant bathers at Buscot.

Bottom is part of a company of players. These players are a metaphor for Shakespeare's own company who, by performing *A Midsummer Night's Dream* at a wedding, intruded upon an elite gathering to which they would not normally have been admitted. Their 'Pyramus and Thisbe' is, as has long been recognized, a parody of the company's recent *Romeo and Juliet*. To present the players of 'Pyramus and Thisbe' as grotesques may thus be construed, in the context of a wedding performance, as a sign of deference, a humorous apology for the fact that the entertainment on such an important night is provided not by illustrious aristocratic masquers but by common players.[48] The case becomes rather more complex in the public playhouse, where the audience are simultaneously positioned (a) as fellow spectators with Theseus, laughing at the folly of the players, and (b) as fellow commoners alongside the players, granted through their visit to the playhouse vicarious access to an elite private gathering.

In the context of a wedding performance we may see Bottom's copulation with Titania as a kind of preparation for the real bedding ceremony. The 'grotesque realism' of Bottom would be a means of preparing the bride and groom for the intimidating and embarrassing rite of passage that social custom required of them. There is a clear correlation between Bottom's low social station and a low carnal aspect of human identity. Within the frame of an aristocratic wedding night, however, there is no cause to see the scene as a critique of marriage, or as a celebration that belongs in any way to the folk. There is nothing inherently subversive in the proposition that aristocrats have bodies just as estates have workers, and that these indispensable bodies/workers need to be controlled. In the context of a public performance the scene works rather differently, of course. The clown, representative of the commons, gains temporary access to the forbidden body of the aristocratic lady.

To summarize: I have located Bakhtin's theory of carnival within a classical tradition which locates festival as the return to a lost Utopia. While 'safety-valve' theories stress how individuals adapt to the status quo, 'utopian' theories show how carnival envisages a better way for society to be organized—and they thus offer a more dynamic and positive view of popular culture. Bakhtin's theory is a blunt critical instrument, however, because the concept of 'carnival' is effectively monologic, postulating a single model and obscuring the differences which allowed festivals to function as a complex semiotic system—as we see in the interplay of festivals in *A Midsummer Night's Dream*. Dionysia, Saturnalia, Mardi Gras and English summer festivals are molten by Bakhtin into a single entity. The assumption that this entity dubbed 'carnival' is the property of the folk as distinct from the elite seriously obscures the mechanisms by which power was validated and maintained in the early modern period. Bakhtin's logocentric methodology is not easily adapted to the phenomenon of performance. In the analysis of theatre, the time and place of the performance, the placing and status of the audience all have to be considered before we can effect a satisfactory analysis of festive or carnivalesque elements.

NOTES

1. By permission of the publisher, this essay reproduces some passages from chapter 6 of my *Shakespeare's Almanac: A Midsummer Night's Dream, Marriage and the Elizabethan Calendar* (Woodbridge: D. S. Brewer, 1993).

2. Plato, *Laws*, 654: translation adapted from that of T. J. Saunders in *The Laws* (Harmondsworth: Penguin, 1970), p. 86. The untranslatable phrase *epanorthontai tas ge trophas* could be literally rendered 'set straight again their upbringings'.

3. *Laws*, 672, Penguin edn., pp. 113–14.

4. *Politics*, viii.5–7, *The Politics* trans. T. A. Sinclair (Harmondsworth: Penguin, 1962), pp. 307–14.

5. Important discussions include Peter Burke, *Popular Culture in Early Modern Europe* (London: Temple Smith, 1978), pp. 202–5; and Michael D. Bristol, *Carnival and Theater: Plebeian Culture and the Structure of Authority in Renaissance England* (New York & London: Routledge, 1989), pp. 27–32.

6. A. T. Macrobius, *The Saturnalia*, i.7–8, trans. P. V. Davies (New York & London: Columbia University Press, 1969), pp. 55–65.

7. *Dramatic Writings of Nicholas Udall*, ed. J. S. Farmer (London: Early English Text Society, 1906), prologue.

8. Cited in Burke, p. 202.

9. 'From the prehistory of novelistic discourse' in *The Dialogic Imagination*, pp. 53–4. Contrast Tony Harrison's vision of the satyr play as popular culture in his play *Trackers*.

10. *Rabelais and His World*, trans. by Hélène Iswolsky (Bloomington: Indiana University Press, 1984), p. 121.

11. *Ibid.*, p. 76.

12. *Ibid.*, pp. 97, 452.

13. *Ibid.*, p. 75.

14. *Ibid.*, p. 312ff.

15. For examples, see François Laroque, *Shakespeare's Festive World*, trans. J. Lloyd (Cambridge: Cambridge University Press, 1991), p. 141, with note p. 242.

16. Burke, p. 28.

17. Emmanuel Le Roy Ladurie, *Carnival in Romans: A People's Uprising at Romans 1579–1580*, trans. M. Feeney (Harmondsworth: Penguin, 1981), pp. 274–6.

18. Yves-Marie Bercé, *Fête et révolte* (Paris: Hachette, 1976), p. 88.

19. *Ibid.*, pp. 9ff., p. 189.

20. See especially Leah S. Marcus, *The Politics of Mirth. Jonson, Herrick, Milton, Marvell and the Defense of Old Holiday Customs* (Chicago: University of Chicago Press, 1986); Peter Stallybrass, '"We feaste in our Defense": Patrician carnival in early modern England and Robert Herrick's "Hesperides"', *English Literary Renaissance* 16 (1986), pp. 234–252; also Laroque, *Shakespeare's Festive World*, p. 70.

21. Laroque, pp. 96–7. Bristol makes the most he can of the festival in *Carnival and Theater*, pp. 72–87. I have examined the festival in London in '"That day are you free": *The Shoemaker's Holiday*', *Cahiers Élisabéthains* 38 (1990), pp. 49–60.

22. 'Forms of Time and Chronotope in the Novel', in *The Dialogic Imagination*, pp. 216–19.

23. See Marvin Carlson, 'Theater and Dialogism', in *Critical Theory and Performance*, ed. J. G. Reinelt and J. R. Roach (Ann Arbor: University of Michigan Press, 1992), pp. 313–23.

24. Bristol, pp. 30–2; C. L. Barber, *Shakespeare's Festive Comedy* (Princeton, NJ: Princeton University Press, 1959), p. 9.

25. *Ibid.*, pp. 172–8, following the discussion of Bakhtin on pp. 19–25.

26. Manfred Pfister, 'Comic Subversion: a Bakhtinian view of the comic in Shakespeare', *Deutsche Shakespeare Gesellschaft West Jahrbuch* (1987), pp. 27–43: p. 39.

27. Wiles, *Shakespeare's Almanac*, chapter 10.

28. Whilst 'Now bent' is the Quarto and Folio reading, modern editors prefer 'New bent'. All quotations are from Harold F. Brooks' Arden edition.

29. *The Paston Letters*, ed. J. Gairdner (London: Chatto & Windus, 1904), v. 266–9.

30. See Chaucer, *Parliament of Fowls, The Complaint of Mars, Complaint d'amours*; Gower, *Balades*, xxxiiii, xxxv; Lydgate, 'The Flower of Courtesy' in *Minor Poems* Vol. II (London: Early English Text Society, 1934); Clanvowe, *The Cuckoo and the Nightingale*; Herrick, 'To his Valentine, on S. Valentine's day', in *Poetical Works*, ed. L.C. Martin (Oxford: Oxford University Press, 1956), p. 149; Surrey, *Poems*, ed. E. Jones (Oxford: Oxford University Press, 1964), no. 15.

31. Note that 14 February in the Julian calendar is equivalent to 4 February on the modern calendar.

32. *Juvenilia* (Manchester: Spenser Society, 1871), ii.474.

33. *Complete Poetry and Selected Prose*, ed. J. Hayward (London: Nonesuch Press, 1946), pp. 103–6.

34. First printed by Joseph Strutt in *Horda Angel-Cynna* (London, 1776), iii.179, and attributed to Lydgate. R.T. Hampson, in *Medii Aevi Kalendarium* (London, 1841), i.162, cites the manuscript reference as Harl. MSS Cod.v.2251 fo.268b. The origins of St Valentine's Day were explored by Francis Douce, in *Illustrations of Shakespeare* (London, 1807).

35. William Boswell, cited in John Brand and W.C. Hazlitt, *Popular Antiquities of Great Britain* (London: J. R. Smith, 1870), i.32.

36. *Misson's Memoirs and Observations in his travels over England*, trans. J. Ozell (London, 1719), pp. 330–1.

37. For the ideological context, see Marcus, *The Politics of Mirth*, pp. 133–5.

38. *Pepys' Diary*, ed. R.C. Latham and W. Matthews (London: G. Bell & Sons, 1970–83), vii.42-4, vi.35, 20, ii.36, iii.29, etc.

39. Nashe, *Works*, ed. R. B. McKerrow (Oxford: Oxford University Press, 1958), iii.403.

40. The stage direction in the Folio reads: 'Horns and they wake. Shout within, they all start up.' With the separation of music and ritual action, the festive context seems to have become lost. Perhaps Jacobean performers no longer associated the play with Saint Valentine's Day.

41. *British Apollo* (1709), cited in Brand and Hazlitt, *Popular Antiquities of Great Britain*, i.33.

42. Barber, *Shakespeare's Festive Comedy*; David P. Young, *Something of Great Constancy* (New Haven, Conn.: Yale University Press, 1966).

43. See the Arden edition, ed. Harold F. Brooks (London: Methuen, 1979), pp. xxxv–xxxvi.

44. See A. Kent Hieatt, *Short Time's Endless Monument* (New York: Columbia University Press, 1960); also Wiles, *Shakespeare's Almanac*, pp. 67–9.

45. Young explores some of these links in *Something of Great Constancy*.

46. William A. Ringler 'The Number of Actors in Shakespeare's Early Plays', in G. E. Bentley (ed.), *The Seventeenth Century Stage* (Chicago: Chicago

University Press, 1968), pp. 110–34. For the suggestion that choir boys were used, see E. K. Chambers, *William Shakespeare* (Oxford: Oxford University Press, 1931), ii.86. T. J. King, in *Casting Shakespeare's Plays* (Cambridge: Cambridge University Press, 1992), opposes Ringler's view of the doubling.

47. See Laroque's documentation of the morris dance, in *Shakespeare's Festive World*, pp. 121–36. On Kemp as Bottom, see David Wiles, *Shakespeare's Clown* (Cambridge: Cambridge University Press, 1987), pp. 74–5 and passim.

48. It is sometimes falsely asserted that plays were not performed at Elizabethan weddings, only masques. Players did perform at the marriage of the Earl of Northumberland in 1594 for a fee of ten pounds: Wiles, *Shakespeare's Almanac*, p. 44.

A MIDSUMMER NIGHT'S DREAM
IN THE TWENTY-FIRST CENTURY
❧

Critics in the twenty-first century continue to present new insights and explore ambiguities within the text. The issues of the play's portrayal of female power and Elizabethan politics have both been prominent topics in recent years, but scholars have also increasingly examined Shakespeare's classical and mythological sources. A. B. Taylor's essay begins by discussing Quince the carpenter, the "other playwright" of *A Midsummer Night's Dream*. As Taylor points out, Quince knows some Latin, something not unusual in Elizabethan England, where it was often taught in free grammar schools. More importantly, he is apparently writing his play "with a copy of Ovid's *Metamorphoses* open before him," as demonstrated by what seem to be his literal translations from Ovid's Latin. However, Quince makes frequent and obvious mistakes of both translation and understanding. Taylor notes that Quince, like Shakespeare, is an actor-playwright who appears to have an imperfect grasp of Latin, which suggests that Quince is in fact an elaborate Shakespearean self-parody.

2003—A.B. Taylor. "'When Everything Seems Double': Peter Quince, the Other Playwright in *A Midsummer Night's Dream*," from *Shakespeare Survey*, vol. 56

A. B. Taylor is retired dean of faculty at The Swansea Institute. He is the editor of *Shakespeare's Ovid: The Metamorphoses in the Plays and Poems* (2000) and co-editor, with Charles Martindale, of *Shakespeare and the Classics* (2004).

The final version of 'Pyramus and Thisbe', the play-within-a-play in *A Midsummer Night's Dream*, is arrived at only after a series of last minute, rather frenetic changes. At the first meeting of the tradesmen in the city, their play is apparently complete; parts are assigned, and each player given his lines to learn for the rehearsal next night in the forest. However, by the time the play is performed half of the original six parts, Thisbe's mother and father, and

Pyramus's father (see 1.2.56–9),[1] have disappeared without a trace. When the 'company' meet in the forest, in the discussion before rehearsal begins, two new parts, 'Wall' and 'Moonshine', are added; a prologue, to be spoken by Pyramus telling the audience he 'is not killed indeed' (3.1.18), promised but never written; and curiously, the scene they rehearse never performed. At one level, this makes sense, but it also adds to the impression that the emergence of 'Pyramus and Thisbe' is somewhat chaotic. And in the middle of all this, either directly suggesting changes himself or responding to suggestions by members of the 'company', is *A Midsummer Night's Dream*'s other playwright, Peter Quince the carpenter. As his play undergoes deletion and revision which will mean his adding fifty-three new lines to the final script, itself only 133 lines in total,[2] he is remarkable for his genial tolerance and enthusiasm.

For a 'hard-handed' man, Quince is also remarkable for another thing: knowing Latin. There is ample evidence of this in his basic method in writing the play which is discussed below, but it is also obvious in incidentals like the pun on the Latin for 'left' (*sinister*) in the reference to the hole in the wall through which the young lovers communicate as 'right and *sinister*' (5.1.162 [my italics]), and the unusual reference to Pyramus as a 'juvenal' (3.1.89) from '*juvenalis*' (youthful). An Elizabethan audience would have found a carpenter knowing Latin less surprising than might be imagined. It has been calculated that, after learning the basics in the petty school, half the boys in England went on to attend free grammar schools.[3] Regardless of academic ability, then, half the boys in England would have embarked on the prescribed and rigorous study of Latin writers. Woe betide the unacademic brethren in a rigid, monolithic educational system where corporal punishment was the order of the day. When one considers the lower ability range in Elizabethan grammar schools, Jacques's picture of 'the whining schoolboy with his satchel / And shining morning face, creeping like snail / Unwillingly to school' (*As You Like It* 2.1.145–7) might also serve as an emblem of the educational inhumanity of the age. With what relief such boys must have escaped school to serve an apprenticeship in the kind of trades followed by the 'rude mechanicals'; during that time they would live in their master's household and be taught not only their trade and allied subjects but also a wider, general curriculum, all, of course, in their own language.[4] The fact that their masters were legally bound to provide such instruction[5] explains why tradesmen, whether they had attended grammar schools or not, were literate. So much is evident by those in *A Midsummer Night's Dream*; Snug may be 'slow of study' (1.2.63) but he is referring to learning his part—there is no question of his not being able to read. Of course, there were also 'hard-handed' tradesmen who were gifted classical scholars and who, through circumstances, had had to discontinue their education, the most eminent example being 'the learned Ben' who began his working life as a bricklayer. But although not in that league, Quince clearly has a grammar school background.

Quince's knowing Latin explains what has surprisingly passed unremarked about his basic method: he is clearly composing his play with a copy of Ovid's *Metamorphoses* open before him at the story of Pyramus and Thisbe (IV.51–166).[6] His closeness to the Latin text is reflected in a stream of phrases translated from it word-for-word: *Dumque fugit . . . velamina lapsa reliquit* (101) becomes 'as she fled her mantle she did fall' (5.1.141); *Conveniant ad busta Nini* (88) his lovers agreeing 'to meet at Ninus' tomb' (137); *vestem . . . sanguine tinctam* (107) Thisbe's 'mantle . . . / . . . stained with blood' (272); *Ore cruentato* (104) the lion's tearing it 'with bloody mouth' (142); and *questi* (84) becomes the lovers 'make moan' (322). In addition, there is the moment ruined by Nick Bottom's Pyramus having misread the script when lions *'devouring'* one of the lovers (*consumite viscera . . . / O . . . leones* 113–14; 'o lions devour me entirely') becomes 'Since lion vile hath here *delfower'd* my dear' (286 [my italics]). Moreover, the suggestion that has been made from time to time that the problematic 'most lovely *Jew*' (3.1.89) should read 'most lovely *Juv*' [my italics][7] has viability as Quince half translating, half picking up the Latin with which Ovid introduces Pyramus, *iuvenum pulcherrimus* (55; 'the most lovely of youths' [my emphasis]).

Its closeness to Latin also explains another curious feature of Quince's play: occasionally it slips into Latin syntax. In the grammar school, boys would have been taught that this was of two kinds: 'naturall or Grammaticall order', and the more elevated 'artificiall or Rhetoricall order' (also known as 'the Order of Tully').[8] The most notable rule of 'Grammaticall order' was that adjectives followed nouns as in *puella pulcherrima*: when transposed to English, the practice sounded unnatural, for as George Gascoigne observed, 'if we should say in English a woman fayre, a house high, etc., it would have small grace, for we say a good man, not a man good'.[9] Nonetheless, although unidiomatic in English, this feature of 'Grammaticall order' occasionally appeared in Elizabethan poetry; but it is heavy in Quince's play where we find 'savours sweet' (3.1.77), 'lion rough' (5.1.217), 'lion fell' (219), 'lions vile' (281), 'mantle good' (271), 'furies fell' (273), 'sisters three' (323). 'Rhetoricall order' had a small cluster of 'precepts', the first and most conspicuous of which was the location of the verb at the end of the clause or sentence; an example in Latin is *Munitissimam hostium civitatem Caesar occupavit* ('Caesar *took* the very heavily fortified town of the enemy').[10] When imposed on English, however, 'Rhetoricall order' appeared so eccentric that it does not feature elsewhere, with the exception of one group of Elizabethan writers. Led by Thomas Phaer, the early Elizabethan translators of the classics misguidedly embraced both kinds of Latin syntax in the mistaken belief that it added an epic tone to their work.[11] In this respect, where Phaer led, the others followed.[12] He occasionally but not invariably uses 'Grammaticall order' yet sometimes his taste for it can be pronounced; in the opening twenty lines of Book 3, for example, we find 'kingdome stout' (1), 'fortresse proude' (3), 'navy great' (8), 'freendship old' (19). And he is very fond of 'Rhetoricall Order'; verbs

are regularly placed at the end of sentences and clauses, notwithstanding the
strain on intelligibility, as in these examples from the middle of Book 3:

These tokens I thee *tell*, . . . (405)

But whan approching Sicil coast the winde thee foorth *doth blow* (430)

Epirus and Italia lond, whose founder both of name King Dardan *is*, . . .
(528–9)

. . . and at Ceraunia neere our selfs we *put* (533 [my italics])

Like 'Grammaticall order', 'Rhetoricall order' also features in Quince's play;
some examples are,

And by and by I will to thee *appear* (3.1.82)

And this the cranny *is*, . . . (5.1.162)

. . . her mantle she *did fall* (141)

. . . till fates me *kill* (194 [my italics])

Readers might mistake Quince's tortured syntax as part of a desperate struggle
to meet the demands of metre or rhyme-scheme but, while it would be unwise
to discount entirely the convenience factor, like the early Elizabethan translators,
he is basically mangling English syntax in a misguided effort to elevate his verse
to epic heights.

But for all his closeness to the *Metamorphoses* and quirky syntax, Quince's
Latin itself is very thin. For example, there is no lion in Ovid's story of Pyramus
and Thisbe. Snug's part of 'Lion' is the result of Quince not knowing the
meaning of *leaena* (IV.97, 102); as Chaucer and translators like Golding and
Sandys knew, the animal that causes the tragedy in Ovid is a 'lioness'.[13] Quince
was aware of the thinness of his Latin vocabulary. Translating key words in
Ovid's text, he notably keeps to the beaten track, using words that had long
been drilled into schoolboys such as 'chink' (5.1.175) and 'cranny' (162) for the
hole in the wall through which the lovers communicate (*rima* IV.65).[14] Other
slight variations on the Latin are to be accounted for by his use of the standard
dictionary of the day, Cooper's *Thesaurus*. Where Ovid writes that Thisbe 'sits
beneath the tree' (*sub arbore sedit* 95), Quince has her *'tarrying'* beneath it
(147), for Cooper, besides defining *'sedere'* as 'to sit', also has it as 'to *tarie* or
abyde' [my italics].[15] Indeed, Quince seems to have worked with Cooper at his

elbow—and he comes unstuck by doing so when in a serene and magnanimous mood, his Pyramus nonsensically declares 'Sweet moon, I thank thee for *thy sunny beams*' (261 [my italics]). In Ovid, Quince had found the lovers' meeting took place 'by the rays of the moon' (*ad Lunae radios* 99), but nervous about his Latin and hurriedly consulting his dictionary, he had found only the stock definition of *radius* as 'A beame of the sunne'. The howler he consequently produces stems from two factors. When under pressure—an example is opening his play by ludicrously misreading his own prologue,—he gets flummoxed and has a tendency to panic. And he is under pressure here both because of his inadequate Latin, and the speed at which he works. For example, he does substantial rewrites of his play in the short space between the rehearsal and performance. So, aware of the need to press on and panicking because of his thin Latin, he has produced a line which has amused audiences ever since, and has his hero thank the moon for her '*sunny beams*'.

But the confusion goes deeper than the occasional verbal howler for he sometimes fails to grasp both large and small features of the Latin text before him. He misses, for example, the extreme youthfulness of the lovers. Details in their story in Ovid suggest Pyramus and Thisbe are not much more than children. By day, for example, both can be found playing in their gardens. It is while doing so that they discover they can communicate with each other through the fissure in the wall; at first they talk *through* the wall in 'tiny whispers' (*Murmure . . . minimo* 70), and then childishly talk *to* the wall, first chiding it as 'jealous' (*Invide* 73), then repenting to thank it for its kindness (*Nec sumus ingrati* 76; 'nor are we ungrateful'). When he first introduces the play, however, Quince tells Nick Bottom and the others that Thisbe is a 'lady' (1.2.42) and Pyramus 'a proper man' (80), a 'gentlemanlike man' (81), and raises no objection when Bottom suggests playing Pyramus in a beard (83ff.). His mistaking the ages of Ovid's lovers is compounded in his play when it is performed where Pyramus has become a 'knight' (5.1.266) and Thisbe a 'dame' (282).

On a lesser scale, there is Thisbe's 'mask'. When Flute objects to playing Thisbe on the grounds that he has a beard coming, Quince immediately responds 'You shall play it in a mask' (1.2.45). Editors explain this as a reference to the Elizabethan custom of ladies, wearing masks,[16] but, in the Latin text before Quince, Thisbe has her face covered. When she slips out of her father's house into the darkness to keep her fatal assignation, she has 'her face concealed' (*adoperta . . . vultum* IV.94). However, she does so not with a mask but a veil. She is wearing an *amictus*; deriving from *amicere* ('to throw round or wrap about'), this is an item of clothing she has draped about herself which could be a cloak or a veil. What shows it is a veil is the epithet used with it (*tenuis*—'thin', 'fine') and the fact that it is in the plural form—*tenues amictus* (104). Before leaving home, such was her anxiety not to be recognized, Thisbe had thrown several thin, fine veils over her head to cover her face; presumably, as she made her way to meet Pyramus, she held these on with one or both hands, which is why being light, they are the article of her clothing that falls to the ground when she flees in panic at the sight of the lioness. (If they needed it, sixteenth-century readers would have found confirmation of Thisbe as a veiled figure in Raphael Regius' philological notes which were alongside the text in the standard edition of the *Metamorphoses* of the day, where *amictus* is rendered *velum* ('a veil').)[17] Peter Quince's Latin has let him down again; he has picked up the fact that Thisbe has her face covered, not grasped the meaning of *tenues amictus*, and simply made up his own explanation. Moreover, having done so, with the problem of Francis Flute's stubble in mind, he has extended the use of Thisbe's 'mask' from the second half of the story where there is reference to the girl having her face covered to the earlier garden scene where there is none.

Finally, his thin Latin and dictionary-dependence account for the muddle in his thinking as to what exactly 'Pyramus and Thisbe' is. He initially introduces it as 'our interlude' (1.2.5) and then when he announces the full title, despite its content, he refers to it as a 'Comedy'. The word 'interlude' for a play was being used less and less at this time, and while other plays of a tragic nature included the word 'comedy' in their title, they contained comic elements and episodes. It might sound outlandish to say it of a play that caused such hilarity over the years but there is not a vestige of comedy in Peter Quince's treatment of his subject; he intends the story to be taken for what it is, 'tragicall'. He himself unwittingly lays it open to laughter at times with an unthinking and crass insensitivity to the nuances of language as when his heroine kisses the Wall's 'stones' (188) or 'hole' (199). But consciously he devotes his energies to making sure his play is not laughed at; in rehearsal there is the effort to make sure reference is to the 'odours' and not the 'odious savours' of Thisbe's breath (3.1.79–81), and his irritated but ultimately vain attempt to avoid the schoolboy joke of his lovers meeting at 'Ninny's tomb' (5.1.200). As with his absurd attribution of 'sunny beams' to the moon, it is again his use of Cooper that accounts for the serious-minded Quince terming his play an 'interlude' and referring to it as a 'Comedy'. In the *Metamorphoses*, when Ovid first introduces the story of Pyramus and Thisbe, he refers to it as *vulgaris fabula non est* (IV.53; 'a fable not commonly known'). And when Quince turned to *fabula* in Cooper, he found it defined not only as a 'tale' but also as an '*interlude, or comedie*' [my italics]. One can only conclude that as he went about turning the story into a play, the blatantly contradictory title, 'The most lamentable comedy and most cruel death of Pyramus and Thisbe' (1.2.11–12), and the reference to an 'interlude', are his befuddled, unthinking attempts to somehow be true to what he has found in the Latin.

Besides his actors intermittently sabotaging his script (the prime example is surely Bottom's thorough confusion of the senses in 'I see a voice; now will I to the chink, / To spy and I can hear my Thisbe's face' 5.1.190–1),[18] other elements that defy Quince's efforts to produce a 'straight' play are his solutions of 'two hard things' (3.1.45). Representing 'Moonshine' (57) as a man with a thornbush, a lantern, and a dog, and 'Wall' (63) as a man with loam and plaster holding his fingers apart for a 'cranny', is well-intentioned but patently risible. It is so amateurish that the only place one could imagine such things is in a school play where the audience, in the absence of means and facilities, would perforce be called on to exercise such imaginative licence. And if the other leader of the company, Nick Bottom, is also a 'grammarian', both he and Quince could be recalling similar experiences from their own schooldays. There was and had long been a thriving tradition of staging plays in grammar schools in both Latin and English.[19]

Thus, to what he found or thought he found in his play's Latin source, Quince has added a touch of romance—with the unfortunately muddled recall of famous lovers such as 'Limander' and 'Shafalus' (5.1.193 and 196). He also sought to give a flourish with a florid description of the appearance of his lovers, blithely ignorant of the indecorum of items such as 'eyes green as leeks' (322); and equally indecorous is his taste for melodramatic tragic apostrophe, 'O grim-looked night! O night with hue so black!' (168), 'O wherefore, Nature, didst thou lions frame' (280). Add the eccentricities of a cast which, in between occasionally mispronouncing the words he had written, was, with Quince's own misguided support, scrupulously devoted to destroying any vestige of dramatic illusion and, for all Quince's earnest intention for it to be taken seriously, 'Pyramus and Thisbe' brings tears to the eyes of its audience for reasons other than those he intended.

This examination of the shadowy, self-effacing figure of Peter Quince reveals a playwright who like his creator, William Shakespeare, has 'small Latine'.[20] In view of the fact that 'latten' is a kind of brass, the story of Shakespeare asking Ben Jonson to 'translate' the 'Latten Spoones' he bought for a christening present for one of Jonson's children[21] suggests the dramatist's limited Latin was something of a joke between himself and his friends. What better way of sending himself up than by a caricature as a workaday playwright who is not only occasionally unsure of his English but so uncertain of his Latin that he blunders into howlers like the 'sunny beams' of the moon and the 'Comedy' of 'Pyramus and Thisbe' because in his dependence on his Latin dictionary common sense has gone out the window. But in Quince, he is caricaturing himself and exaggerating his faults. He could clearly read Latin, and did so on special occasions; writing *The Rape of Lucrece* for the Earl of Southampton, for instance, he not only used the *Fasti* for which there was no current English translation, but also consulted the Latin notes and commentary on the text by Paul Marsus in the standard edition of Ovid's poem.[22] On the other hand, his habitual and lifelong use of translations suggests reading Latin involved some effort. William Beeston, whose father belonged to

The Lord Chamberlain's Men, is reported as commenting on the matter that 'He understood Latin pretty well'—not 'very well' or 'well' but *moderately well*.[23]

If it were limited to a matter of 'small Latine', the resemblance between Quince and his creator would be of only passing interest but Quince is also an actor/playwright who takes roles in his own work in the way that Shakespeare did. In Heminges and Condell's *Comedies, Histories, and Tragedies* (1623), perhaps understandably the dramatist heads the list of 'the Principall Actors in all these Plays', but he is also listed among 'The principall Comoedians' who performed *Every Man In His Humour* in 1598, and among 'The principall Tragoedians' in *Sejanus* in 1603.[24] It may well have been his talent as an actor that initially led to his being recruited by the players; Aubrey relates hearing that as an actor in the 'Play-house', he 'did act exceedingly well'.[25] The only hint from a contemporary, however, of his range as an actor comes from John Davies of Hereford who in 1610 wrote of his playing 'Kingly parts'.[26] In 1709, Rowe claimed as the result of extensive enquiry, he played 'the Ghost in his own *Hamlet*' and later from the disorderly notes of Oldys, the story emerged that he played Adam in *As You Like It*.[27] What evidence there is points to a character actor who had an air of *gravitas* and who specialized in playing old men. Significantly, initially Quince intends playing 'Thisbe's father' (1.2.59). In the event he takes an important but limited part, acting as 'Prologue', setting the scene for what follows just as 'The Chorus' does in *Henry V*, another role anecdotally associated with Shakespeare. There are occasions when one hears the authoritative tones of a director's voice in Shakespeare, none more so than in Hamlet's advice to the players (3.2.1–45). Such moments strengthen the probability that the dramatist limited his involvement as an actor—normally parts with which he has been associated are less than 100 lines—to attend to his more important role of 'dramatist-director of his own productions';[28] and this again takes us back to Peter Quince.

Like Shakespeare, Quince also has a reputation as both playwright and poet—'I will get Peter Quince to write a ballad of this dream' (4.1.212–13)—and a remarkably ready facility for writing. As we have seen, he quickly rewrites substantial parts of the play in the short space between the rehearsal and performance, eliminating some characters and adding others. This was the quality of Shakespeare's writing picked out as most remarkable by Heminges and Condell in the First Folio: 'his mind and heart went together, and what he thought he uttered with that easiness that we have scarce received from him a blot in his papers'.[29] Quince, too, has a relaxed disposition and equable temperament of the kind associated with Shakespeare who was 'generous . . . in minde and moode'.[30] He rewrites quickly without complaint and is even prepared to discuss with leading members of the company which metre additional material is to be in. Finally, Quince is fond of Ovid; this shows not only in his choice of subject but also in his fondness for 'mellifluous and honey-tongued' Ovidian imagery, some of which he cannot handle properly. Shakespeare's *Venus and Adonis* had cast a spell on the young poets of the early nineties but, as the decade wore on, lush Ovidian poetry gave way to harsher satiric poetic fashions. Through Quince, his creator is himself mocking his earlier poetry, as he is his earlier drama with his tortured parody of tragic apostrophe.

And for all their appearance of amateurishness, there are moments when Quince and company appear very professional in attitude. Quince himself fulfils the offices of book-keeper and stage-keeper, retaining the master copy of the play, penning and distributing the parts complete with cues to be conned by individual actors, directing the performance, ensuring performers are ready on cue, and acting as prompter. As he additionally draws up a 'list of properties' (1.2.98) and decides on what will be the 'tiring house' for a company performing in an unfamiliar location (3.1.4), discusses forms of dialogue with his leading man, and takes a role in his own play, one is reminded of the energy Shakespeare displayed in the playhouse, and of the mockery of him as early as 1592 as a 'Johannes Factotum'.[31] Other details suggesting a professional aura are Snug being 'slow of study', an expression still used in the theatre today for tardiness in learning a part, and Bully Bottom's advice to his fellow actors to get 'good strings to your beards, new ribbons to your pumps' (4.2.33–4), and 'eat no onion nor garlic, for we are to utter sweet breath' (4.2.40–1), advice of more than usual value, given they were going to be performing in close proximity to their genteel audience.[32]

There is also the way they follow their play with a 'Bergomask dance' (5.1.352). Bergamo, a region in Italy, was famed for its rusticity and clownishness in the sixteenth century, and a 'Bergomasco', the name for a native of this region, another name for a bumpkin.[33] The 'Bergomask dance' performed by two of the 'hempen homespuns', and this is the sole use of the term in English (*OED*), was clearly a rustic, clownish dance. And at the time *A Midsummer Night's Dream* was written, professional performances in the playhouse also concluded with clownish dances. Enormously popular, and called 'jigs', these were dances usually for three or four performers who sang dialogue as they danced, periodically leaving the stage and then rejoining the action as a plot unfolded which normally centred on adultery.[34] A short, musical, scripted drama, the jig with its bawdy content and 'uncleanly handlings, gropings, and kissings'[35] delighted the groundlings and scandalized Puritans. One is not suggesting that the tradesmen's clownish 'Bergomask dance' was a jig; there is no record of its having dialogue nor would it be reasonable to hold up the action of *A Midsummer Night's Dream* while a plot unfolded. But coming where it did, immediately after their 'performance' in the place the jig normally occupied, and with Will Kemp, the great comedian and 'the most celebrated jig-maker of the age',[36] on stage playing Bottom (see below), the 'Bergomask dance' would have aroused certain expectations in the audience. It seems therefore reasonable to infer that Kemp who was famed for his dancing, with a fellow actor in the female role, did a low comedic dance which would have been in keeping with Shakespeare's 'marriage-play', perhaps a clownish parody of a courtship, wedding, and the married life that followed. This would have provided a low-life contrast to the stately matrimonial events with their fairy accompaniment that close *A Midsummer Night's Dream*. One of Shakespeare's concerns, as we shall later note, was to offset the unreality of the delicacy of his play's dramatic illusion, and the Bergomask dance, doubtless a close relative of the jig, would have helped in that cause.

Kemp is also a reminder that it is not only the resident playwright of the Lord Chamberlain's Men who is being caricatured in the burlesque. We have evidence of only two roles Kemp played, Peter (in *Romeo and Juliet*), and Dogberry;[37] but while we do not have categorical evidence that he played Bottom, there is some impressive, unremarked internal evidence. Like Richard Tarlton, whose heir he claimed to be, Kemp was ugly; in the dedication of his account of his famous morris dance from London to Norwich, *Kemps nine daies wonder*, he confesses to Anne Fitton he has 'an ill face'.[38] As we shall see, there are indications that this became a running joke in his famous jigs; and it was taken up by Shakespeare. Hence when Kemp as Dogberry, during the interview with Conrad and Borachio, starts to boast of qualities he conspicuously lacks, he begins by claiming 'I am a wise fellow . . .' (*Much Ado* 4.2.77–8), and then goes on to make a surprising and unexpected claim that is rather out of character for Dogberry, 'and which is more, *as pretty a piece of flesh as any is in Messina*' (79–80 [my italics]). At this point, one can imagine the effect of a pause and the kind of pulled face or gurney for which Kemp was famous. And exactly the same effect, plus the repetition of the same two qualities to which Dogberry laid claim, is obtained by the drugged Titania's lavish compliment to Bottom, 'Thou art as wise as thou art beautiful' (3.1.142), when under the influence of 'Love-in-Idleness', she is seeing everything upside down. Once again Kemp is centre stage, his 'ill face' puckered and screwed up, and once again Shakespeare is exploiting one of his clown's most obvious assets. And when Dogberry reflects philosophically not that 'Comparisons are odious' but that 'Comparisons are odorous' (3.5.15), the dramatist is inverting the joke in his earlier comedy when Bottom misreads Quince's script, 'Thisbe, the flowers of *odious* savours sweet', at which the aggrieved author moans 'Odorous! odorous!' (77–8).

There is also the amusing play on two soubriquets of which the widely travelled Kemp was fond. On 'The first daies journey' of *Kemps nine daies wonder*, he uses the first when ebulliently introducing himself, 'my selfe, thats I, otherwise called *Cavaliero* Kemp. . .' [my italics]. His fondness for the second is apparent in *Singing Simpkin* which appeared in Stationers' Register in 1595 as 'a ballad called Kemp's new jig betwixt a soldier and a miser and Sim the clown'.[39] At Kemp's appearance as Sim, the married woman with whom he is having an affair, asks, 'How is't *Monsieur* Simkin, why are you so sad?' (9 [my italics]).[40] Both soubriquets had long attached themselves to Kemp; when *An Almond For*

A Parrat (1589–90), a pamphlet sometimes attributed to Nashe and part of the Martin Marprelate controversy, was dedicated to him, its writer who apparently knew him, addresses it to 'that most comicall and conceited *cavaliere Monsieur du Kempe*' [my italics].[41] Kemp was a burly, round figure and it is ironic that when both soubriquets are used in *A Midsummer Night's Dream* in the scene in Titania's bower, they are attached not to Kemp-as-Bottom but to two beautiful, sylph-like fairies:

> *Bottom.* Give me your neaf, *Monsieur* Mustardseed. Pray you, leave your courtesy, good *monsieur*.
> *Mustardseed.* What's your will?
> *Bottom.* Nothing, good *monsieur*, but to help *Cavalery* Peaseblossom to scratch . . . (4.1.19–23; my italics)[42]

The joke here is akin to that in *Singing Simpkin* where Kemp who would have been at least thirty-five by the time he played the clown Sim, is referred to as a '*young sweet fac'd* fellow' (45 [my italics]). Finally, everything about Kemp, including his spectacular morris dances, tells us that he was an attention-grabber. And his wishing to dominate the stage and be the perpetual centre of attention is hilariously sent up when Kemp-as-Bottom wants to play all the play's parts; he has already proposed crashing the gender and generic barriers by playing both the lovers ('Thisne, Thisne!'—'Ah Pyramus my lover dear . . .' 1.2.48–9) and the Lion ('I will roar, that I will do any man's heart good . . .' 66–7) before Quince lays down the law, 'You can play no part but Pyramus' (79). Internal evidence thus points to Bottom as the most substantial role Shakespeare created for Will Kemp, the brilliant clown, and one which gave him the opportunity to take centre stage with one of 'his much loved simpletons'.[43] But at the same time, as he does in his own case, as Shakespeare exaggerates and mocks Will Kemp's faults, there is nothing but good humour. And Kemp is also offered a generous peace offering. A 'ballad' or 'ballet' was also another name for a jig[44] and when Bottom awakens from his dream and immediately resolves 'I will get Peter Quince to write a *ballad* of this dream' [my italics], Shakespeare and Kemp were much in harmony.[45]

Finally, there is one last point to be made about Peter Quince. This playwright who is concerned to the exclusion of everything else with his play and its performance, turns aside for small talk on only one occasion, for a quip on premature baldness. This was one of the few personal topics that surface in the work of Shakespeare, a writer who normally tells us very little about himself.[46] And what Quince says on this occasion, 'Some of your French crowns have no hair at all' (1.2.90), is a reference to the 'French disease', syphilis. If one accepts Katherine Duncan Jones's suggestion that Shakespeare himself suffered from syphilis as a legacy of his life-style in London, the comment has ironic and hidden application.[47] After the appearance of the chancre in the first stage of the disease, premature loss of hair took place in the second which could happen up to three years after being infected; the third dreadful stage which could involve madness, blindness or failure of any of the vital organs took hold at any time between three and forty years following infection. There is no proof he had the disease but he had spent most of his adult life living away from his wife and family with a bohemian set. Manningham recorded the story of 'Richard III and William the Conqueror' on 13 March 1602, when both the principals involved, Burbage and Shakespeare, were very much on the scene;[48] as a member of the Inns of Court with an interest in the playhouse and players, whether this particular story was factual or not, Manningham would have known the life-style of those involved. And if Shakespeare, like Burbage, was prepared to bed the playhouse 'groupies' of his day, he was living a life that brings the promiscuous, infected 'Dark Lady' of the *Sonnets* into view (see particularly 144) and women of the sort to give their sexual partners disease. Moreover, a progressive, ultimately terminal sexual disease as a cause of the death of a man who had made his will and seems to have scrupulously prepared for his end is far more persuasive than the 'Rhenish wine' theory. The idea that he is actually joking about having it is, of course, unthinkable. But through the mouth of his dramatic *alter ego*, he may be commenting incidentally and in a sidelong way on a matter of personal moment.

The traditional approach to the burlesque has concentrated on identifying which minor Elizabethan literary fry have been set in the literary stocks.[49] J. Thomson for his inglorious poetic assault on Pyramus and Thisbe in *A Handfull of Pleasant Delites* is very much to the fore; one or two details from the anonymous poem on the myth in *A Gorgeous Gallery* are also picked up; and from Golding's version where the translator inevitably fills his lines up with pleonastic 'do's' and 'did's', and has his lovers thank the 'courteous' wall.[50] To these can be added the early translators for the weird Latin syntax to which they had been led by Thomas Phaer who himself is mocked for one eccentric detail with Bottom's 'hopping' heart.[51] But the whole business has proved a gigantic red herring. As well as diverting attention away from the burlesque as the culmination of the extensive and systematic subversion of the myth of Pyramus and Thisbe that threads the *Dream*,[52] it has entirely obscured the fact that the one writer who above all is being mocked is William Shakespeare. And like his Orlando, through the *persona* of Peter Quince, the playwright is largely and characteristically intent on 'chiding no breather in the world but myself' (*As You Like It* 3.2.274).

While it is the source of much genial, warm humour in the play, the dramatist's taking a place amongst the 'rude mechanicals' and portraying himself as a tradesman also inevitably evokes at some level the low esteem in which other people and he himself held players and their profession. It was not unknown for those connected with the playhouse to be referred to as 'tradesmen' during the 1590s, and such references could be scornful. In *The Second Part of The Return from Parnassus*, when Philomusus and Studioso, two Cambridge graduates, having tried most jobs and being at the end of their tether, decide as a last resort to become players, Philomusus asks reflectively, 'and must the basest trade yeeld us reliefe?'[53] There are shades here of a profession located on the wrong side of the river amid bloodsports, brothels and the dregs of London. And Shakespeare, a playwright who aspired to gentility, while living a life bound up with players and the playhouse, occasionally voiced a similarly low estimate of a profession in which 'I have gone here and there / And made myself a motley to the view' (Sonnet 110, 1–2) and which in the opinion of others 'doth staine pure gentle bloud'.[54]

As he worked on *A Midsummer Night's Dream*, his 'first great comic masterpiece',[55] increasingly confident of his powers, Shakespeare repeatedly and teasingly sowed doubts about the credibility of the play's poised and delicate dramatic illusion. Nowhere is this more evident than in the lines that lead up to Theseus's warning against the dangers of the imagination ('The lunatic, the lover, and the poet'), when, discussing the lovers' adventures in the forest, he declares:

> I never may believe
> These antique fables, nor these fairy toys (5.1.2–3)

He is not only proclaiming disbelief in the fairy world but in the world of ancient legend of which he and Hippolyta are a part. The audience is being reminded by the play's voice of cold reason that what they are seeing is an illusion, a 'dream', a 'trick' of the imagination, an 'airy nothing' to which 'the poet's pen' has given 'A local habitation and a name'. Wake up, they are being told, through the deconstructing voice of the play's representative of good order and rule, and you will see that this is all just make-believe, fiction, and that these people before you are only 'players' ('antics').

What this article has attempted to show is that this teasing ambivalence also extends to what might in some ways be considered the most realistic strand of the plot, the tradesmen. They are involved in proceedings for the most practical of reasons, money—their leaders coveting sixpence a day for life, and they seem to connect the play up to the everyday world. But here, too, Shakespeare playfully and teasingly dispels the illusion of drama by showing behind the parts of these 'hempen homespuns' are the Lord Chamberlain's Men. Peeping through the roles of the 'rude mechanicals', like Snug's face through the Lion's mask, are the faces of members of the foremost playhouse company of the age as they go about creating another, make-believe dramatic world, and recognizable among them are Will Kemp and, more intriguingly, William Shakespeare.

NOTES

This article develops and enlarges upon one of the features of 'Golding's Ovid, Shakespeare's "Small Latine", and the Real Object of Mockery in "Pyramus and Thisbe"', *Shakespeare Survey* 42 (1990), pp. 53–64. It has been read in draft form by Gordon Braden, Andrew Gurr and Niall Rudd to whom I am grateful for their comments and encouragement.

1. Reference is to *A Midsummer Night's Dream*, ed. H.F. Brooks (London and New York, 1979); reference to other works of the dramatist are to *The Complete Oxford Shakespeare*, ed. S. Wells and G. Taylor (Oxford, 1987).

2. The 53 added lines consist of the prologue introducing the characters who take part (5.1.126–50), Wall's speech (153–63), that part of Pyramus's opening speech where 'Wall' responds to his request (172–9), Wall's lines at his exit (202–3), Lion's speech to 'You Ladies' (214–22) which the company had asked to be inserted, and Moonshine's introductory lines (235–6).

3. M. H. Curtis, 'Education and Apprenticeship', *Shakespeare Survey* 17 (Cambridge, 1964), p. 62.

4. Curtis, 'Education', pp. 61ff.

5. By the 1563 'Statute of Artificers'; for the terms and conditions of apprenticeship which was of a minimum of seven years' duration and did not end until the apprentice was twenty-four years old, see O. Jocelyn Dunlop, *English Apprenticeship and Child Labour* (London, 1912), *passim*.

6. Reference is to a standard sixteenth-century text of the *Metamorphoses* containing the notes of Regius, Micyllus and Petrus Lavinius, *Metamorphoseon Publii Ovidii Nasonis* (Venice, 1545). [Translations are my own.] I approach Quince's play as Jonathan Bate does, as a flawed attempt at *'translatio'* which has the tang of the schoolroom; see *Shakespeare and Ovid* (Oxford, 1993), pp. 131–3.

7. See, for example, the footnote to 3.1.77 in R.A. Foakes's edition of *A Midsummer Night's Dream* (Cambridge, 1984).

8. Reference is to John Brinsley's account of the teaching of Latin syntax in *Ludus Literarius or The Grammar Schoole* (1627), ed. E.T. Campagnac (London, 1917), pp. 158ff. Brinsley's account is translated from Georgius Macropedius's *Methodus de conscribendis Epistolis* which was published in London in 1595. For the widespread influence and use of the work of Macropedius (1487–1558) in the grammar school, see T.W. Baldwin, *William Shakspere's Small Latine & Lesse Greeke*, 2 vols. (Urbana, Illinois, 1944), vol. 2, pp. 256–67 and *passim*.

9. 'Certayne Notes of Instruction' (1575), *Elizabethan Critical Essays*, ed. G.G. Smith, 2 vols. (Oxford, 1904), vol. I, p. 53.

10. Although there are other precepts involved in 'Rhetoricall order' (see Brinsley, *Ludus Literarius*, pp. 159ff.), in the discussion that follows, reference is confined to the distinctive first precept.

11. There are features of Spenser's poetry that also seem similar to Latin syntax but there is no reason to believe that Spenser is relevant here whereas evidence of the early Elizabethan translators' involvement in *A Midsummer Night's Dream* is explicit in Nick Bottom's long-recognized parody of Studley—'The raging rocks, / And shivering shocks . . .' (1.2.27–34).

12. For convenience, illustrations are confined to Phaer. For a consideration of Phaer's influence on the syntax of the other translators, see my *Shakespeare's Ovid and Arthur Golding* (forthcoming). Reference to Phaer is to *The Aeneid of Thomas Phaer and Thomas Twynne: A Critical Edition*, ed. S. Lally (New York and London, 1987).

13. Chaucer refers in *The Legend of Thisbe* to 'a wyld lyonesse' (805), and in their translations of Ovid's poem, Golding to 'a Lionesse' (4.120), and Sandys to 'a Lyonesse'. Reference is to *The Works of Geoffrey Chaucer*, ed. F. N. Robinson, 2nd edition (Boston, 1957); *The xv Bookes of P. Ovidius Naso, entytuled Metamorphosis* (1567), ed. W. H. D. Rouse (London, 1904; repr. 1961); and *Ovid's Metamorphoses Englished* (Oxford, 1632), ed. S. Orgel (London and New York, 1976).

14. In one of the dictionaries specially designed for use in schools, Richard Huloet's *Abcedarium Anglico Latinum* (London, 1552; revised edition 1572), for example, one finds *rima* defined as '*Chincke*, clyft, *crany*' [my italics]; and the first Latin-English dictionary for schools, *Promptorium Parvulorum* (London, 1449; five times reprinted) suggests that 'cranny' had long been the traditional translation of *rima* in English schools. The use of 'chink' was also well established; see, for example, Peter Levins's *Manipulus Vocabulorum* (London, 1570). (Both 'chink' and 'cranny' have needlessly been identified as debts to Arthur Golding's translation of the *Metamorphoses* (1567); for details of these and other mistaken debts to Golding, see Taylor, 'Golding's Ovid, Shakespeare's "Small Latine", and the Real Object of Mockery in "Pyramus and Thisbe"'.)

15. Reference is to Thomas Cooper's *Thesaurus Linguae Romanae & Britannicae* (London, 1565).

16. They did so either to conceal identity or to avoid unfashionable tanned faces. Masks were oval in shape with holes for the eyes and covered either the upper or the whole face. They were made of silk or velvet, usually lined, of various colours, and sometimes held in position by an attached button which was gripped by the teeth. (See C. W. and P. Cunnington, *Handbook of English Costume in the Sixteenth Century* (London, 1954), pp. 188–9.)

17. Accordingly, Regius also identifies the garment Pyramus finds when he arrives, *vestem* (107) as a veil (*velum*). (The Loeb translator also presents Thisbe leaving her father's house as a veiled figure, rendering *adoperta . . . vultum* (94) as 'her face well veiled'; reference is to *Metamorphoses*, ed. F. J. Miller (London, 1916; 2nd edition, repr. 1960).

18. Cf. Bottom's even more thorough confusion of the senses in his celebrated Pauline parody: 'The eye of man hath not heard, the ear of man hath not seen, man's hand is not able to taste, his tongue to conceive, nor his heart to report, what my dream was' (4.1.209–12). (See also my 'John Hart and Bottom "goes but to see a noise"' (forthcoming)).

19. 'While school plays were usually in Latin, English ones were not uncommon, even before Elizabeth's reign' (William Nelson, 'The Teaching of English in Tudor Grammar Schools', *Studies in Philology*, 49 (1952), 138–9).

20. The discussion of Shakespeare that follows is based on information supplied for the most part by the dramatist himself or his contemporaries. There is minimal use of later anecdotes.

21. The story is in a manuscript by Sir Nicholas L'Estrange dated 1629–55; it is cited by S. Schoenbaum, *William Shakespeare: A Documentary Life* (Oxford, 1975), p. 206.

22. See T. W. Baldwin, *On The Literary Genetics of Shakspere's Poems and Sonnets* (Urbana, Illinois, 1950), pp. 97–9.

23. Cited by Schoenbaum, *Documentary Life*, p. 88; *OED* records the use of 'pretty well' as meaning 'moderately or tolerably well' in the sixteenth and seventeenth centuries.

24. See Schoenbaum, *Documentary Life*, pp. 147 and 150.

25. Cited by T. W. Baldwin, *The Organization and Personnel of the Shakespearean Company* (Princeton, 1927), p. 264.

26. 'To our English Terence Mr. Will. Shakespeare', Epigram 159 in *The Scourge of Folly*; cited by Schoenbaum, *Documentary Life*, p. 148.

27. See Schoenbaum, *Documentary Life*, p. 149.

28. Baldwin, *Shakespearean Company*, p. 265.

29. John Heminges and Henry Condell, 'To the Great Variety of Readers' in the First Folio, reprinted in the *Complete Oxford Shakespeare* among the 'Commendatory Poems and Prefaces (1599–1640)', p. xxxix.

30. Davies of Hereford, *Microcosmus*; cited by Schoenbaum, *Documentary Life*, p. 205.

31. For Robert Greene's famous sideswipe at Shakespeare in *A Groatsworth of witte*, see Schoenbaum, *Documentary Life*, p. 115.

32. The reference to 'pumps' may be testimony to Bottom's conviction that their play is 'a sweet comedy' (4.2.42); for the point about breath, I am indebted to Andrew Gurr in private correspondence.

33. See, for example, *Antonio and Mellida: The First Part* (1602), ed. G. K. Hunter (London, 1965), p. 5.

34. The jig reached unprecedented heights of popularity in the latter half of the 1590s and in the succeeding decade before it declined post-1612. For the jig, see primarily C. R. Baskervill, *The Elizabethan Jig and Related Song Drama* (Chicago, 1929); useful information is also supplied by D. Wiles, *Shakespeare's Clown: Actor and Text in the Elizabethan Playhouse* (Cambridge, 1987), pp. 43ff., and P. Thomson, *Shakespeare's Professional Career* (Cambridge, 1992), pp. 133ff.

35. Wiles, *Shakespeare's Clown*, p. 45.

36. Wiles, *Shakespeare's Clown*, p. 45.

37. Kemp is named in the Q2 copy of *Romeo and Juliet*, and in the 1600 Quarto of *Much Ado About Nothing*. Apart from his two known roles, there has also been a great deal of speculation about Kemp's possible roles; see, for example, Baldwin, *The Organization and Personnel of the Shakespearean Company*, pp. 241–4; H. D. Gray, 'The Roles of William Kemp', *Modern Language Review*, xxv (1930), 261–73; and Wiles's book, while being an invaluable collection of all the known facts about Kemp, also has a speculative strand—see, for example, pp. 116–35.

38. Dedicating his pamphlet to Anne Fitton, Kemp writes '(having but an ill face before) I shall appear to the world without a face, if your fayre hand wipe not away their [i.e. his detractors'] foule colours'. Reference is to *Kemps nine daies wonder* (London, 1600).

39. Wiles, *Shakespeare's Clown*, p. 51.

40. Reference is to the text of the jig reprinted by Baskervill, *Elizabethan Jig*, pp. 444–9.

41. *The Works of Thomas Nashe*, ed. R. B. McKerrow in 4 vols. (London, 1905), vol. 3, p. 341.

42. For 'Cavalery' as a version of 'cavaliero', see the notes on this scene of Brook, and of P. Holland (ed.), *A Midsummer Night's Dream* (Oxford, 1994). (The name 'Bottom' taken from the weaver's ball of thread (*OED*) may also be a good-natured dig at Kemp's physical shape.)

43. Thomson, *Professional Career*, p. 134.

44. This was because 'ballads' (often 'ballets' in the sixteenth century (*OED*)) often incorporated singing and also a dance to interpret the words of the song, and naturally evolved into the jig. One chapter in Baskervill's *Elizabethan Jig* bears the title, 'The Simple Ballad as jig', pp. 164–218.

45. There is not space here to present all the internal evidence; for a fuller examination of Kemp in the role, see my 'Will Kemp as Bottom' (forthcoming).

46. It has become traditional, for instance, to interpret the opening of Sonnet 73 as a reference to the poet's baldness:

That time of year thou mayst in me behold
When yellow leaves, or none, or few do hang
Upon those boughs which shake against the cold.

In the recent Arden edition of the *Sonnets*, the editor, Katherine Duncan-Jones, reads the lines as 'a visual analogy between an almost-leafless tree and the almost-hairless head' of Shakespeare (*Shakespeare's Sonnets* (London, 1997), p. 256).

47. *Ungentle Shakespeare: Scenes from his Life* (London, 2001), pp. 224–6.

48. For the entry in Manningham's diary, see Schoenbaum, *Documentary Life*, p. 152.

49. Kenneth Muir set out the targets in his ground-breaking article, 'Pyramus and Thisbe: A Study in Shakespeare's Method', *Shakespeare Quarterly*, 5 (1954). Over the years, these have reduced in number with the elimination of Moffet by Katherine Duncan-Jones, 'Pyramus and Thisbe: Shakespeare's Debt to Moffet Cancelled', *Review of English Studies*, n.s. 32 (1981), 296–301, and Chaucer by the present writer, 'Chaucer's Non-Involvement in Pyramus and Thisbe', *Notes and Queries*, n. s. 36 (1989), 317–20.

50. I have changed my position on the pleonastic use of the verb 'to do' since publishing 'Golding's Ovid, Shakespeare's "Small Latine", and the Real Object of Mockery in "Pyramus and Thisbe"'.

51. See my 'Thomas Phaer and Bottom's "hopping" Heart', *Notes and Queries*, n.s. 34 (1987), 207–8.

52. See my 'Ovid's Myths and the Unsmooth Course of Love in *A Midsummer Night's Dream*' in *Shakespeare and the Classics*, ed. C. Martindale and A. B. Taylor, scheduled for publication by Cambridge University Press in 2004.

53. *The Three Parnassus Plays* (1598–1601), ed. J. B. Leishman (London, 1949), 1846.

54. John Davies of Hereford, *Microcosmus*, cited by Schoenbaum *Documentary Life*, p. 205.

55. C. L. Barber, *Shakespeare's Festive Comedy: A Study of Dramatic Form and its Relation to Social Custom* (Princeton, 1959), p. 11.

BIBLIOGRAPHY

❧

Baxter, John. "Growing to a Point: Mimesis in *A Midsummer Night's Dream*." *English Studies in Canada*, vol. 22, no. 1 (March 1996): 17–33.

Belsey, Catherine. "Peter Quince's Ballad: Shakespeare, Psychoanalysis, History." *GRAAT*, vol. 13 (1995): 105–21.

Bevington, David. "'But We Are Spirits of Another Sort': The Dark Side of Love and Magic in *A Midsummer Night's Dream*." *Medieval and Renaissance Studies*. Edited by Siegfried Wenzel. Chapel Hill: University of North Carolina Press (1978): 80–92.

Blits, Jan H. *The Soul of Athens: Shakespeare's A Midsummer Night's Dream*. Lanham, Maryland: Lexington Books, 2003.

Brown, John Russell. *Shakespeare and His Comedies*. London: Metheun, 1957.

Buccola, Regina. *Fairies, Fractious Women, and the Old Faith: Fairy Lore in Early Modern British Drama and Culture*. Selinsgrove, Pa.: Susquehanna UP, 2006

Calderwood, James L. "*A Midsummer Night's Dream*: Anamorphism and Theseus' Dream." *Shakespeare Quarterly*, vol. 42, no. 4 (Winter 1991): 409–40.

———. "*A Midsummer Night's Dream*: The Illusion of Drama." *Shakespearean Metadrama*. Minneapolis: University of Minnesota Press (1971): 120–48.

Carroll, William C. "*A Midsummer Night's Dream*: Monsters and Marriage." *The Metamorphoses of Shakespearean Comedy*. Princeton, N.J.: Princeton University Press (1985): 141–77.

Casey, Janet Galligani. "'Hounds and Echo in Conjunction': Musical Structure in *A Midsummer Night's Dream*." *Studies in Humanities*, vol. 21, no. 1 (June 1994): 31–44.

Conlan, J.P. "The Fey Beauty of *A Midsummer Night's Dream*: A Shakespearean Comedy in its Courtly Context." *Shakespeare Studies*, vol. 32 (2004): 118–72.

Dent, R.W. "Imagination in *A Midsummer Night's Dream*." *Shakespeare Quarterly* 15 (1964): 115–29.

Hassel, R. Chris, Jr. "Faith in *A Midsummer Night's Dream*." *Faith and Folly in Shakespeare's Romantic Comedies*. Athens: The University of Georgia Press (1980): 52–76.

Holland, Norman. "Hermia's Dream." *The Dream and the Text: Essays on Literature and Language*. Edited by Carol Schreier Rupprecht and Norman Holland. Albany: State University of New York Press (1993): 178–99.

Holloway, Julia Bolton. "Apuleius and *Midsummer Night's Dream*: Bottom's Metamorphoses." *Tales Within Tales: Apuleius through Time*. New York: AMS (2000): 123–37.

Hutton, Virgil. "*A Midsummer Night's Dream*: Tragedy in Comic Disguise." *Studies in English Literature, 1500–1900*, vol. 25, no. 2 (Spring 1985): 289–305.

Joughin, John J. "Bottom's Secret . . . " *Spiritual Shakespeares*. London: Routledge (2005): 130–56.

Kehler, Dorothea, ed. *A Midsummer Night's Dream: Critical Essays*. New York: Garland, 1998.

Lewis, Alan. "Reading Shakespeare's Cupid." *Criticism*, vol. 27, no. 2 (2005): 117–213.

Longo, Joseph A. "Myth in *A Midsummer Night's Dream*." From *Cahiers Élisabéthains*, no. 10 (October 1980): 17–27.

Lynch, Kathryn L. "Baring Bottom: Shakespeare and the Chaucerian Dream Vision." *Reading Dreams: The Interpretation of Dreams from Chaucer to Shakespeare*. Edited by Peter Brown. Oxford, England: Oxford University Press (1999): 99–124.

McGuire, Philip C. "Hippolyta's Silence and the Poet's Pen." *A Midsummer Night's Dream*. Edited by Richard Dutton. New York: St. Martin's Press (1996): 139–60.

Nuttall, A.D. "*A Midsummer Night's Dream*: Comedy as Apotrope of Myth." *Shakespeare Survey* 53 (2000): 49–59.

Olsen, Paul A. "*A Midsummer Night's Dream* and the Meaning of Court Marriage." *ELH* 24 (1957): 95–119.

Ormerod, David. "*A Midsummer Night's Dream*: The Monster in the Laboratory." *Shakespeare Survey* 11 (1978): 39–52.

Parker, Patricia. "(Peter) Quince: Love Potions, Carpenter's Coigns and Athenian Weddings." *Shakespeare Survey* 56 (2003): 39–54.

Pask, Kevin. "Engrossing Imagination: A Midsummer Night's Dream." *Where Are We Now in Shakespearean Studies? III*. Aldershot, England: Ashgate (2003): 172–92.

Paster, Gail Kern and Howard Skiles, eds. *A Midsummer Night's Dream: Texts and Contexts*. Boston, Mass.: Bedford (1999).

Rudd, Niall. "Pyramus and Thisbe in Shakespeare and Ovid." *Shakespeare's Ovid: The Metamorphoses in the Plays and Poems*. Edited by A.B. Taylor. Cambridge: Cambridge University Press (2000): 113–25.

Smith, Hallett. "*A Midsummer Night's Dream* and *The Tempest.*" *Shakespeare's Romances: A Study of Some Ways of the Imagination.* San Marino, Calif.: The Huntington Library (1972): 121–44.

Starnes, D. T. "Shakespeare and Apuleius." *PMLA* 60 (1945): 1,021–50.

Staton, Walter F., Jr. "Ovidian Elements in *A Midsummer Night's Dream.*" *Huntington Library Quarterly*, vol. 26 (1962): 165–78.

Stavig, Mark. *The Forms of Things Unknown: Renaissance Metaphor in Romeo and Juliet and A Midsummer Night's Dream.* Pittsburgh, Pa.: Duquesne UP, 1995.

Stewart, Garrett. "Shakespearean Dreamplay." *English Literary Renaissance* 11 (1981): 44–69.

Taylor, A. B. "Ovid's Myths and the Unsmooth Course of Love in *A Midsummer Night's Dream.*" *Shakespeare and the Classics.* Cambridge, England: Cambridge University Press (2004): 49–65.

Thomsen, Kerry Lynne. "Melting Vows: *A Midsummer Night's Dream* and Ovid's *Heroycall Epistles.*" *English Language Notes*, vol. 40, no. 4 (June 2003): 25–33.

Uman, Deborah. "Translation, Transformation and Ravishment in *A Midsummer Night's Dream.*" *Allegorica* 22 (2001): 68–91.

Warner, Marina. "Painted Devils and Aery Nothings: Metamorphoses and Magic Art." *Shakespeare and the Mediterranean.* Edited by Tom Clayton, Susan Brock and Vincente Forès. Newark, Del.: University of Delaware Press (2004): 308–31.

Wiles, David. "The Carnivalesque in *A Midsummer Night's Dream.*" *Shakespeare and Carnival: After Bakhtin.* Basingstoke, Hampshire: Macmillan Press; New York: St. Martin's Press (1998): 61–82.

Wyrick, Deborah Baker. "The Ass Motif in *The Comedy of Errors* and *A Midsummer Night's Dream.*" *Shakespeare Quarterly* 33 (1982): 432–48.

Young, David. *Something of Great Constancy: The Art of "A Midsummer Night's Dream."* New Haven: Yale University Press, 1966.

ACKNOWLEDGMENTS
❧

Twentieth Century

Barber, C.L. "May Games and Metamorphoses on A Midsummer Night." *Shakespeare's Festive Comedy: A Study of Dramatic Form and its Relations to Social Custom*. Princeton, N.J.: Princeton University Press (1959): 119–62. © 1959 by Princeton University Press, 1987 renewed PUP. Reprinted by permission.

Goddard, Harold. *"A Midsummer Night's Dream." The Meaning of Shakespeare*. Chicago: The University of Chicago Press (1951): 74–80. © 1951 by The University of Chicago Press. Reprinted by permission.

Nevo, Ruth. "Fancy's Images." *Comic Transformations in Shakespeare*. London and New York: Methuen & Co. Ltd. (1980): 96–114. © 1980 by Ruth Nevo. Reprinted by permission.

Frye, Northrop. "The Bottomless Dream." *Northrop Frye on Shakespeare*. New Haven: Yale University Press (1986). © 1986 by Northrop Frye. Reprinted by permission.

Van Doren, Mark. *"A Midsummer Night's Dream." Shakespeare* (1939): New York: Holt (1939) © 1939 by Mark Van Doren. Reprinted by permission.

Wiles, David. "The Carnivalesque in *A Midsummer Night's Dream*." *Shakespeare and Carnival: After Bakhtin*. Edited by Ronald Knowles. London: Macmillan Press Ltd.; 61–82. © 1998 by Macmillan Press Ltd. Reprinted by permission.

Twenty-first Century

Taylor, A.B. "'When Everything Seems Double': Peter Quince, the Other Playwright in *A Midsummer Night's Dream*." *Shakespeare Survey*, vol. 56 (2003): 55–66. Cambridge, UK and New York: Cambridge University Press. © 2003 by Cambridge University Press. Reprinted by permission.

INDEX

❧

Characters in literary works are indexed by first name (if any), followed by the name of the work in parentheses